CW01262203

The Third Indochina War

The Third Indochina War – comprising the Vietnam–Kampuchea War from 1978 to 1990 and the brief Sino-Vietnamese War in February 1979 – has received far less scholarly attention than the earlier two Indochina Wars. Ang Cheng Guan utilises a wide range of archival and secondary material, including Vietnamese, Cambodian, Chinese, Soviet, American, British, Australian, and Association of Southeast Asian Nations (ASEAN) sources, to provide a comprehensive new analysis of the conflict. By carefully reconstructing its chronology, Ang traces the life cycle of the war from its origins, through the conduct of military engagements, to its eventual resolution. He focuses on multiple actors simultaneously, highlighting the interconnected perspectives of the war's major protagonists: Vietnam, Cambodia, and China. In demonstrating the roles of the USSR, the US, and ASEAN in both prolonging and ending the conflict, he situates the Third Indochina War fully in its Asian, global, and Cold War contexts.

ANG CHENG GUAN is Professor of the International History of Southeast Asia. He specialises in the international history of contemporary Asia, with a focus on Southeast Asia.

The Third Indochina War

An International History

ANG CHENG GUAN
Nanyang Technological University

CAMBRIDGE
UNIVERSITY PRESS

CAMBRIDGE
UNIVERSITY PRESS

Shaftesbury Road, Cambridge CB2 8EA, United Kingdom

One Liberty Plaza, 20th Floor, New York, NY 10006, USA

477 Williamstown Road, Port Melbourne, VIC 3207, Australia

314–321, 3rd Floor, Plot 3, Splendor Forum, Jasola District Centre, New Delhi – 110025, India

103 Penang Road, #05–06/07, Visioncrest Commercial, Singapore 238467

Cambridge University Press is part of Cambridge University Press & Assessment, a department of the University of Cambridge.

We share the University's mission to contribute to society through the pursuit of education, learning and research at the highest international levels of excellence.

www.cambridge.org
Information on this title: www.cambridge.org/9781009560092

DOI: 10.1017/9781009560078

© Ang Cheng Guan 2025

This publication is in copyright. Subject to statutory exception and to the provisions of relevant collective licensing agreements, no reproduction of any part may take place without the written permission of Cambridge University Press & Assessment.

When citing this work, please include a reference to the DOI 10.1017/9781009560078

First published 2025

A catalogue record for this publication is available from the British Library

A Cataloging-in-Publication data record for this book is available from the Library of Congress

ISBN 978-1-009-56009-2 Hardback
ISBN 978-1-009-56005-4 Paperback

Cambridge University Press & Assessment has no responsibility for the persistence or accuracy of URLs for external or third-party internet websites referred to in this publication and does not guarantee that any content on such websites is, or will remain, accurate or appropriate.

Contents

Acknowledgements	page vi
List of Abbreviations	vii
Introduction	1
1 Vietnam–Cambodia–China Relations (1950s–1975)	18
2 From the Fall of Saigon to the Invasion of Cambodia (April 1975–December 1978)	42
3 The Sino-Vietnamese War (February 1979)	69
4 Regional Responses to the Vietnamese Invasion	90
5 The Long-Drawn Endgame	110
Epilogue	142
List of Characters/Dramatis Personae	175
Bibliography	190
Index	205

Acknowledgements

I wish to acknowledge my debt to the many scholars who have written about the Third Indochina War upon whose works I have drawn. I wish to thank Chong Yee Ming, Huang Zihao, Joachim Lai, Vu Minh Hoang, Tran Thi Bich, Ha Hoang Hop, and Terence Chia for their help. I also wish to express my appreciation to Lucy Rhymer at Cambridge University Press for her support, Rose Martin, Dan Harding, Natasha Whelan, Sunantha Ramamoorthy as well as the anonymous reviewers for their constructive comments and suggestions. Any mistakes and shortcomings in this book are my own.

This book is perhaps the culmination of my long-time interest in both contemporary and international history, particularly that of Southeast Asia, and also the Indochina Wars, which began under the tutelage of the late Professor Ralph Smith. His pioneering multi-volume international history of the Vietnam War inspired this book. This book is dedicated to his memory.

Abbreviations

ANS	Armée Nationale Sihanoukiste
ASEAN	Association of Southeast Asian Nations
CCP	Cambodian People's Party
CGDK	Coalition Government of Democratic Kampuchea
COMECON	Council for Mutual Economic Assistance
COSVN	Central Office for South Vietnam
CPK	Communist Party of Kampuchea
CPP	Cambodian People's Party
DK	Democratic Kampuchea
FCO	Foreign and Commonwealth Office
FUNCINPEC	National United Front for an Independent, Neutral, Peaceful and Cooperative Cambodia
GRUNK	The Royal Government of the National Union of Kampuchea
ICC	International Criminal Court
ICP	Indochinese Communist Party
JIM	Jakarta Informal Meeting
KPNLF	Khmer People's National Liberation Front
KPRP	Kampuchean (Khmer) People's Revolutionary Party
KUFNS	Kampuchean United Front for National Salvation
MFA	Ministry of Foreign Affairs
MIA	missing in action
NSC	National Security Council
PAVN	People's Army of Vietnam
PLA	People's Liberation Army
PRC	People's Republic of China
PRK	People's Republic of Kampuchea
RCAF	Royal Cambodian Armed Forces
SNC	Supreme National Council

SOC	State of Cambodia
UN	United Nations
UNTAC	United Nations Transitional Authority in Cambodia
USSR	Union of Soviet Socialist Republics
VCP	Vietnamese Communist Party

Introduction

I

On 31 May 2019, Singapore's Prime Minister Lee Hsien Loong sent a condolence letter to his Thai counterpart, Prayut Chan-o-cha, on the passing of former Thai Prime Minister and Privy Council President General Prem Tinsulanonda, who passed away on 26 May 2019 aged 98. The condolence letter was also posted on the prime minister's Facebook page. It would have been one of those innocuous diplomatic letters which friendly countries occasionally send, except that in this case, it caused a brief diplomatic incident between Cambodia as well as Vietnam and Singapore. Both Cambodia and Vietnam took issue with Lee's account of General Prem's contribution to the region during his tenure as prime minister from 1980 to 1988, which coincided with the Third Indochina War.

The disputed paragraph in the condolence letter is as follows. According to Prime Minister Lee:

General Prem's leadership has benefited the region. His time as Prime Minister coincided with the five countries of ASEAN [Association of Southeast Asian Nations] coming together decisively to resolutely oppose Vietnam's invasion of Cambodia and the Cambodian government that replaced the Khmer Rouge. Thailand was on the frontline, facing Vietnamese forces across its border with Cambodia. General Prem was resolute in not accepting this fait accompli. Supported by his able Foreign Minister, Air Chief Marshal Siddhi Savetsila, General Prem worked with ASEAN partners to support the resistance forces of the Coalition Government of Democratic Kampuchea from Thai territory, and to oppose the Vietnamese occupation in international forums. This effective collective resistance prevented a military invasion and regime change from being legitimized, and protected the security of other Southeast Asian countries. Eventually the invasion forces withdrew, a peace settlement was signed, and internationally supervised elections were held to elect a new Cambodian government. This decisively shaped the subsequent course of Southeast Asia. It paved the way for Vietnam, Cambodia and Laos to join ASEAN, as partners in promoting the region's peace and development.[1]

It should also be noted that Prime Minister Lee in his speech at the opening of the 18th edition of the Shangri-La Dialogue, also on 31 May 2019, of which the first part of his speech was a survey of the international history of Southeast Asia, also referred to the Vietnamese invasion of Cambodia as a milestone.[2]

When General Tea Banh (deputy prime minister and minister of national defence of Cambodia) arrived in Singapore for the Shangri-La Dialogue, he asked Singapore's Defence Minister Ng Eng Hen to inform Lee to 'make correction on his remark' as it was 'not true and not reflective of the history … It is not true at all because he said that Vietnamese troops invaded Cambodia. We cannot accept what he said. We have already clarified that Vietnamese volunteer troops came to liberate our people.'[3]

Leap Chanthavy, a political analyst based in Phnom Penh, berated Lee for 'being disrespectful to the Khmer Rouge victims and those who sacrificed their lives in deposing the genocidal regime of Khmer Rouge' and 'denying legitimacy of the new Cambodian government that saved lives of the remaining four million Cambodians with support from the Vietnamese forces'. She reminded readers that 'Singapore has never denounced auto-genocide conducted by the Pol Pot regime … even recognized the rogue state and killing machines, provided military assistance, and mobilized international community to deny the legitimacy of Heng Samrin's regime to deny humanitarian assistance to survivors of the Khmer Rouge'.[4] Youk Chhang (executive director,

---

[1] Condolence Letter on the Passing of Former Thai PM and Privy Council President General Prem Tinsulanonda, Prime Minister's Office, 31 May 2019, www.pmo.gov.sg/Newsroom/Condolence-Letter-on-the-Passing-of-Former-Thai-PM-General-Prem-Tinsulanonda, accessed on 5 April 2022. Siddhi Savetsila was foreign minister of Thailand from 1980 to 1990 and passed away in 2015.

[2] PM Lee Hsien Loong at the IISS Shangri-La Dialogue 2019, www.pmo.gov.sg/Newsroom/PM-Lee-Hsien-Loong-at-the-IISS-Shangri-La-Dialogue-2019, accessed on 5 April 2022.

[3] 'Minister, lawmaker lash out at Singaporean prime minister over Vietnamese invasion', *Khmer Times*, 4 June 2019, www.khmertimeskh.com/610795/minister-lawmaker-lash-out-at-singaporean-prime-minister-over-vietnamese-invasion/, accessed on 5 April 2022.

[4] 'Lee Hsien Loong disrespectful of Khmer Rouge victims', *The Independent*, 3 June 2019, https://theindependent.sg/political-analyst-accuses-pm-lee-of-being-disrespectful-to-khmer-rouge-victims/, accessed on 5 April, 2022.

Introduction 3

Documentation Centre of Cambodia and a survivor of the Khmer Rouge's killing fields) remarked that Lee's words 'showed there was a need to establish an Asean peace and human rights education programme for the region – starting with Singapore'.[5] On 6 June 2019, Cambodia's Prime Minister Hun Sen in his Facebook post wrote that he 'deeply regretted Lee's remarks' and accused Lee of supporting the Khmer Rouge genocide. Hun Sen said that Lee's statement 'is an insult to the sacrifice of the Vietnamese military volunteers who helped to liberate Cambodia from the genocidal regime' and also 'reveals to the Singaporean people and the world that [the] leader of Singapore has contributed to the massacre of Cambodian people'. He ended by asking whether Lee considered the trial of the Khmer Rouge leaders to be legitimate.[6]

The Vietnamese too were upset by Lee's condolence letter. The spokeswoman of Vietnam's Ministry of Foreign Affairs said that Vietnam regrets that the statement 'did not reflect history reflect history objectively, causing negative public opinions' and revealed that her ministry had 'discussed' the matter with her Singapore counterpart. She also said that 'Vietnam's contribution and sacrifice in helping [the] Cambodian people end Khmer Rouge's genocide is true and widely recognized'.[7]

Although both Cambodia and Vietnam disagreed with Lee's interpretation of the history, Lee's statement created much more furore in Cambodia than in Vietnam. It clearly touched a raw nerve in Cambodia. As Kimkong Heng noted, Cambodians 'have been divided, so divided over their differing interpretations of their country's historical events. Some historical facts such as the Liberation Day on 7 January has been over-politicised. Two conflicting narratives prevail and dominate the social and political discourses in the Kingdom.' Those who were critical or against the Hun Sen government generally

---

[5] 'Hun Many "surprised" by Singapore's leader's remarks', *Phnom Penh Post*, 4 June 2019.
[6] 'Hun Sen accuses Singapore PM Lee Hsien Loong of "supporting genocide" as war of words over Cambodia's Khmer Rouge-era escalates', *South China Morning Post*, 6 June 2019. I also wish to thank Vu Minh Hoang for sharing Hun Sen's Facebook post.
[7] 'Vietnam opposes Lee Hsien Loong's remarks on Cambodia "invasion"', 4 June 2019, https://e.vnexpress.net/news/news/vietnam-opposes-lee-hsien-loong-s-remarks-on-cambodia-invasion-3933809.html, accessed on 7 April 2022.

held the view that 7 January 'marked the invasion and occupation of Cambodia by Vietnam'.[8]

Sophar Ear (an Cambodian-American political scientist at Occidental College in the US and who survived the Khmer Rouge regime) said that Lee's statement was 'factually correct ... but of course, Phnom Penh wants to rewrite history and have everyone who opposed the Vietnamese-backed regime of the 1980s apologise, because anyone against them was pro-Khmer Rouge'.[9] Theara Thun noted that 'Hun Sen's long years in power' has allowed him 'to reconstruct a collective historical narrative that draws a direct and continuous connection between the People's Republic of Kampuchea (PRK) formed after Vietnam's removal of the Khmer Rouge in 1979, and his current regime'. One way of doing so is through the annual Liberation Day commemoration – by promoting the notion of Vietnam's 'liberation' of Cambodia, along with the role played by his Cambodian People's Party (CCP). Thun highlighted that the term 'Liberation' for the Vietnamese invasion of Cambodia in December 1979 remains 'controversial' both in Cambodia and abroad, although in his view many of those who opposed Hun Sen, including royalist supporters, 'have gradually abandoned their criticisms of the Liberation Day celebration due to his narrative and consolidation of power'.[10]

Kimkong Heng, on the other hand, speculated that given the 'current political development', the 'two divergent narratives over this contentious day are here to stay, whether one likes it or not, [and] will further divide the Cambodian people for years to come'. He called for Cambodians, particularly the politicians, to move beyond the 'contrasting narratives' and 'find common ground to maintain peace and stability and bring prosperity to Cambodia and its people'.[11]

---

[8] 'Conflicting historical narratives are divisive', *Khmer Times*, 6 June 2019. At the point of writing this commentary, Heng was a PhD candidate at the University of Queensland and a research fellow at the Cambodian Institute for Cooperation and Peace. See also, Kimkong Heng, 'January 7 in Cambodia: one date, two narratives', *The Diplomat*, 16 January 2019.
[9] 'Hun Sen accuses Singapore PM Lee Hsien Loong of "supporting genocide" as war of words over Cambodia's Khmer Rouge-era escalates', *South China Morning Post*, 6 June 2019.
[10] Theara Thun, '"Invasion" or "Liberation"? Contested Commemoration in Cambodia and within ASEAN', *TRaNS*, Volume 9, 2021, p. 219.
[11] 'Conflicting historical narratives are divisive', *Khmer Times*, 6 June 2019.

Introduction 5

On 7 June 2019, the Singapore Foreign Ministry said in a statement that 'Singapore highly values its relations with Cambodia and Vietnam' and that 'notwithstanding our differences in the past, we have always treated each other with respect and friendship' and that they have taken 'the path of cooperation, dialogue and friendship'.[12] The three countries agreed to move on from the controversy and focus on the future. Hun Manet (the current prime minister since August 2023), the oldest son of Hun Sen who was then groomed to succeed his father, paid an introductory visit to Singapore on 11–13 June 2019. It was reported that Hun Manet and the Singapore leaders 'reaffirmed the longstanding ties' between the two countries and their 'wide-ranging and substantive cooperation which has benefited both countries and the region'.[13] Prime Minister Lee Hsien Loong met Hun Sen on 23 June in Bangkok for the 34th ASEAN Summit, their first meeting since 31 May 2019. In his Facebook post after the meeting, Lee remarked that it was 'good to meet directly to understand each other's positions'.[14] Thus, this brought an end to what Tan Bah Bah claimed would have been 'a routine walk in the park' but which became 'unplanned and unnecessary diversions into a mini minefield'.[15]

II

We now shift our focus to another facet of the politics of historical memory, commemoration, and forgetting with regard to the Third Indochina War.

---

[12] 'S'pore committed to good ties with Vietnam and Cambodia: MFA', *The Straits Times*, 8 June 2019.
[13] Introductory Visit of Royal Cambodian Armed Forces Deputy Commander-in Chief and Commander of Army Lieutenant-General Hun Manet, 11 to 13 June 2019, www.mfa.gov.sg/Newsroom/Press-Statements-Transcripts-and-Photos/2019/06/20190611_RCAF-DCIC-Hun-Manet, accessed on 7 April 2022. See also, Prashanth Parameswaran, 'Hun Manet introductory visit highlights Singapore-Cambodian relations', *The Diplomat*, 17 June 2019.
[14] 'PM Lee on Vietnam-Cambodia controversy: helpful to meet directly to understand where we stand', *Mothership*, 24 June 2019, https://mothership.sg/2019/06/pm-lee-cambodia-comments/, accessed on 7 April 2022.
[15] 'Cambodia: paying the high price of regional neglect?', *The Independent*, 9 June 2019, https://theindependent.sg/cambodia-paying-the-high-price-of-regional-neglect/, accessed on 7 April 2022.

The *New York Times* article of 9 April 1989 noted that

many Vietnamese view the decade-long involvement in Cambodia with some pride for the salvation of a close neighbour from the degradation and genocide of the Khmer Rouge Government of Pol Pot, whom Vietnamese troops ousted from power when they invaded [on] 25 December 1978. The Vietnamese also take pride in the assistance that enabled Hanoi's chosen government in Phnom Penh to rebuild a semblance of normal life from the detritus of 'Year Zero'.

But there was a darker side as well. The article further noted that there had been some disaffection among those who returned from the war front 'to face a not always appreciative citizenry' and the difficulty of finding a job in an economy where the unemployment rate was as high as 30 per cent, a consequence of Vietnam's long presence in Cambodia, prioritising security concerns above everything else.[16]

For those who survived the Khmer Rouge regime, they have now changed their initial view of the Vietnamese as 'liberators' to 'occupiers' of their country. The Cambodians to the dismay of the Vietnamese did not show gratitude while 'hostility towards the Vietnamese remains ubiquitous'. According to Carlyle Thayer, 'Cambodia was an unpopular war for Vietnam', unlike the earlier wars against the French and Americans. Veterans of the Cambodia war feel that they have been 'forgotten'. Kevin Doyle described it as 'Vietnam's forgotten Cambodian war'.[17]

The Chinese too were silent about their role in the Third Indochina War. On 17 February 1979, about 300,000 Chinese troops attacked Vietnam in response to Vietnam's invasion in Cambodia two months earlier. Zhang Jie (researcher at the Chinese Academy of Social Sciences) explained that the anniversary 'is a bit sensitive' and 'Chinese officials still begin from the perspective of maintaining the big picture of relations with Vietnam'. It could also be because, as Collin Koh (senior fellow at the S. Rajaratnam School of International Studies) pointed out, the People's Liberation Army (PLA) performed poorly in the war. According to Derek Grossman (senior analyst, RAND Corporation),

---

[16] 'Vietnam's Vietnam: scars of Cambodia', *New York Times*, 8 April 1989.
[17] 'Vietnam's forgotten Cambodian war', BBC, 14 September 2014, www.bbc.com/news/world-asia-29106034, accessed on 10 April 2022. See also, 'What happened to Vietnam's forgotten veterans?', *Southeast Asia Globe*, 25 December 2018.

Beijing's 'reticence on the anniversary had mixed results for China, and affected regional conversations with Asian neighbours about past and present conflicts'.[18]

The anniversary is sensitive for the Vietnamese side as well. As mentioned earlier, there is no consensus in the interpretation of 'Liberation Day' or 'Victory Day' in Cambodia and this remains one of the unresolved issues in their bilateral relations.[19] Until today, there has also not been any official commemoration of the 1979 Sino-Vietnamese War. According to Duong Danh Dy (first secretary of the Vietnamese Embassy in China in 1979), 'Vietnam's reticence to discuss the war was motivated by the greater cause of fostering amity' between the two neighbours. Nguyen Ngoc Truong, a former Vietnamese diplomat, noted that no senior Vietnamese official made a statement about the anniversary of the Sino-Vietnamese War and explained that 2019 was 'the first time the Vietnamese media had been allowed to write about the anniversary so publicly, due in large part to public sentiment about the war'.[20] It is perhaps more than just wanting to preserve amity, as Tuong Vu pointed out – the war

still divides Hanoi's leadership today. One faction puts the blame on Le Duan ... known for being anti-China, while the other faction believes the

---

[18] '40 years on, Chinese veterans defy official silence to remember the Vietnam border war', *South China Morning Post*, 19 February 2019. See also, 'Chinese regime prohibits Sino-Vietnam veteran memorial', *The Epoch Times*, 14 February 2009.

[19] See Kimkong Heng, 'Cambodia-Vietnam Relations: Key Issues and the Way Forward', *Perspective*, Number 36, 12 April 2022. See also, 'Vietnam tense as China war is marked', *BBC News*, 16 February 2009; 'Vietnam muted ahead of border war anniversary', *Voice of America*, 12 February 2014.

[20] '40 years on, Chinese veterans defy official silence to remember the Vietnam border war', *South China Morning Post*, 19 February 2019. See also, Nguyen Ming Quang, 'The bitter legacy of the 1979 China-Vietnam War', *The Diplomat*, 23 February 2017 and Martin Grossheim, 'How the Vietnamese began to remember a Forgotten War', Wilson Center, 7 September 2021, www.wilsoncenter.org/blog-post/how-vietnamese-began-remember-forgotten-war?fbclid=IwAR1WY6_b6nKqBXA-Cwc2p1df5Q5MR5orjG9jt72gxIcj9L_ggOrb0g2QsYc, accessed on 12 April 2022, as well as Martin Grossheim, 'Remembering a Forgotten War: The Vietnamese State, War Veterans and the Commemoration of the Sino-Vietnamese War (1979–89)', *Journal of Southeast Asian Studies*, Volume 53, Number 3, 2022, pp. 459–487. In Vietnam, over the years, low-profile anniversaries have been organized each year in local cemeteries in the northern border provinces where the fighting took place. There were also small-scale demonstrations in Hanoi.

party was wrong all along for having trusted China too much. Allowing any discussion of the war threatens that rift and the survival of the party and would expose the mistakes of party leadership. Teaching children about this war might over time create public pressure that forces the party to move away from China and closer to the US, which it does not want to.[21]

In sum, as Christelle Nguyen observed, both the Chinese and Vietnamese governments have 'deliberately tried to bury memories of their 1979 war'.[22] Not everyone in Vietnam and China agree that silence is the best approach. As Qingfei Yin and Kosal Path noted:

development of the official and Chinese and Vietnamese memories of the war largely mirrored each other ... how China and Vietnam remember, forget and re-remember the Sino-Vietnamese War reflects not only the fluctuations in Sino-Vietnamese relations but also the changing relationships between the state and society in the two countries as they undergo rapid transformations. The Chinese and Vietnamese governments both continue to try to create highly selective memories of the war.[23]

Turning to Cambodia, in his eagerness to appease his Chinese benefactor, in Hun Sen's account of the history of the war, he had excluded China from his narrative, maintaining silence about Chinese support for the Khmer Rouge.[24] As noted earlier, Hun Sen has been rewriting the history of the Third Indochina War since he ousted his co-premier Norodom Ranariddh in July 1997 (and along with that eradicated the Khmer Rouge military threat). Six months after the coup, the Cambodian People's Party (CPP) President Chea Sim called on the Cambodian people to consider 7 January (Liberation Day) as the second birthday of the country – the day the Cambodian people

---

[21] Travis Vincent, 'Why won't Vietnam teach the history of the Sino-Vietnamese War?', *The Diplomat*, 9 February 2022.
[22] Christelle Nguyen, 'How the Sino-Vietnamese War was purposefully forgotten', *The Diplomat*, 17 February 2023.
[23] See Qingfei Yin and Kosal Path, 'Remembering and Forgetting the Last War: Discursive Memory of the Sino-Vietnamese War in China and Vietnam', *TRaNS*, Volume 9, Number 1, May 2021, pp. 11–29.
[24] 'Xi's fake history lesson for Hun Sen', *Foreign Policy*, 10 March 2020, https://foreignpolicy.com/2020/03/10/xi-jinping-fake-history-lesson-hun-sen-china-cambodia-khmer-rouge/, accessed on 10 April 2022. See also, 'China says it won't' apologise for supporting the Khmer Rouge', *New York Times*, 7 November 2000; Alex Willemyns, 'Cambodia and China: rewriting (and repeating) history', *The Diplomat*, 15 January 2018.

regained their rights and freedom, peace, and hope for the future.[25] In Hun Sen's interpretation, Vietnamese soldiers had sacrificed their lives for 'the survival of the Cambodian people and the country'.[26] In 2019, the Hun Sen government marked twenty years of peace in Cambodia with days of celebration starting from 29 December dating back to 1998 instead of 1991. From 2020, Paris Peace Agreement Day on 23 October each year, which celebrates the signing of the Paris Peace Agreements in 1991 that marked the end of the Third Indochina War, was removed from the list of public holidays in Cambodia. According to Hun Sen, the Paris Peace Agreement was 'no longer relevant' (more of this in the Epilogue).[27] Two-thirds of Cambodians are under the age of thirty and were born after the Paris Peace Agreements were signed, and therefore have no direct knowledge of the Third Indochina War.[28] Their knowledge is mostly derived from the Hun Sen who believed that 'only the victor can claim a righteous cause and write history'.[29]

As for ASEAN, there is general agreement that the resolution of the decade-long Cambodian issue was 'the greatest diplomatic success' since its inception in August 1967. That is, however, the assessment from the perspective of the ASEAN-5 members. Since the expansion

[25] Theara Thun, '"Invasion" or "Liberation"? Contested Commemoration in Cambodia and within ASEAN', *TRaNS*, Volume 9, 2021, p. 219.
[26] 'Vietnam the only country that helped Cambodia during its darkest hours: PM Hun Sen', *Thanh Nien*, 8 January 2012; 'Vietnam did not invade, but revived Cambodia: Hun Sen', *Thanh Nien*, 24 June 2013.
[27] 'Hun Sen says Paris Peace Agreement no longer relevant, critics disagree', *VOA Cambodia*, 22 October 2019, www.voacambodia.com/a/hun-sen-says-paris-peace-agreement-no-long-relevant-critics-disagree/5134511.html, accessed on 12 April 2022. See also, Luke Hunt, 'The truth about war and peace in Cambodia', *The Diplomat*, 5 January 2019; Courtney Weatherbee and William M. Wise, 'Why the Paris Peace Agreements deserve a place in Cambodia's national calendar', *The Diplomat*, 31 January 2022; Pou Sothirak, 'The significance of the Paris Peace Agreements', *Khmer Times*, 22 October 2023.
[28] 'They don't know about war': the legacy of forgotten horrors', *New York Times*, 16 March 2022. See also, Federick J. Ngo, 'Revision for Rights? Nation-Building through Post-war Cambodian Social Studies Textbooks, 1979–2009', in James H. Williams (ed.), *(Re)Constructing Memory: School Textbooks and the Imagination of the Nation* (Rotterdam: Sense Publisher, 2014), chapter 8.
[29] Hun Sen quoted in Theara Thun, '"Invasion" or "Liberation"? Contested Commemoration in Cambodia and within ASEAN', *TRaNS*, Volume 9, 2021, p. 219.

of ASEAN to ten in 1999, it has become harder, if not impossible, to celebrate this achievement as a group given the contrasting interpretations of the Cambodian issue as this account illustrated. In his foreword in the publication 'Cambodia: Progress and Challenges since 1991' commemorating the twentieth anniversary of the Paris Peace Agreement on Cambodia, Prince Sirivudh highlighted how the book 'focused on the future prospects of Cambodia, looking ahead and putting acrimony behind'.[30]

As Theara Thun reminded us, 'history written by the winner may not be history but instead pure propaganda. Although leaders of Cambodia, Vietnam and Singapore may have agreed to disagree over the issue, they should leave the debate on the meanings of the historic event to historians who are capable of grounding their argument in sources and critiques rather than specific political agendas'.[31]

Thus, the purpose of this book is precisely to elucidate this 'verbal war after the war' in 2019 recounted in the opening of this chapter that necessitates a new history of the Third Indochina War. Instead of forcing the present to fit the past as so many of those countries involved still do, we need to revisit the war and situate it in its truly international context.

III

This book is thus an attempt to present a dispassionate account of the Third Indochina War. It hopes to explain the deep and precipitating causes of the war which led to the Vietnamese invasion of Cambodia in December 1979, the evolution of the war from 1979 to the Paris Peace Agreement signed in 1991, the United Nations Transitional Authority in Cambodia (UNTAC) phase from February 1992 to September 1993, the events leading to the July 1997 coup that ousted the First Prime Minister Prince Ranariddh, to Cambodia's admission into ASEAN in April 1999. While most accounts of the Third Indochina War end with the Paris Peace Agreement signed on 23 October 1991 – the date which formally marks the end of the

---

[30] Pou Sothirak, Geoff Wade, and Mark Hong (eds), *Cambodia: Progress and Challenges since 1991* (Singapore: ISEAS, 2012). The three co-editors are a Cambodian, an Australian, and a Singaporean.
[31] Theara Thun, '"Invasion" or "Liberation"? Contested Commemoration in Cambodia and within ASEAN', *TRaNS*, Volume 9, 2021, p. 233.

war – this author is of the view that bringing the narrative to 1999 is much more meaningful and offers a fuller and more satisfactory history of the conflict. As Diep Sophal (Cambodian historian, Institute of Military History) noted: 'The Paris Peace Agreements ... did not actually end the civil war in Cambodia ... war (with the Khmer Rouge) only ended on December 29 1998.'[32]

The book is modelled on the late Ralph Smith's much-lauded *An International History of the Vietnam War*, also referred to as the Second Indochina War, which preceded the subject of this book.[33] *An International History of the Vietnam War* is an example of Smith's scrupulous and impeccable attention to both evidence and chronology, two aspects which I hope my book will also exude. I further hope that this narrative will be impartial, for in the words of Smith, 'the principal task of the historian is to try to understand why things happen as they did'.[34] As Isaiah Berlin noted, to explain is to understand but to understand does not mean to justify.[35]

Although on the surface the origins of the Third Indochina War involved the relationship between Cambodia and Vietnam, it was in fact a multinational conflict, or quickly morphed into one. Thus, the war can only be fully understood in the broader context of events in the region and beyond. One of the most challenging problems in writing international history is to strike the right balance between the analysis of situations in terms of everything happening at one time (within the chosen perspective) and the pursuit of a narrative of the sequence of events in one place or institution over a period. International history gives precedence to the former.

This book adopts an essentially chronological approach following the life-cycle of the conflict by first locating the origins of both wars,

---

[32] 'Banh marks anniversary of PM's "struggle"', *Phnom Penh Post*, 20 June 2019.
[33] R. B. Smith, *An International History of the Vietnam War* (London: Macmillan). Three volumes were published before Professor Smith abandoned the project. Volume 1 cover the years 1955–1961 (published in 1983), volume 2 covers the period 1961–1965 (published in 1985), and volume 3 covers the years 1965–1966 (published in 1991).
[34] R. B. Smith, *An International History of the Vietnam War, Volume 3: The Making of a Limited War, 1965–66* (London: Macmillan, 1991), p. 16.
[35] Ved Mehta, *Fly and the Fly-Bottle* (London: Weidenfeld and Nicolson, 1963), p. 103. See also, Isaiah Berlin, 'Historical Inevitability', in Henry Hardy (ed.), *Isaiah Berlin: Liberty* (Oxford: Oxford University Press, 2002), pp. 94, 131.

both the deep and precipitating causes, from the interconnected perspectives of the three main protagonists: Vietnam, Cambodia, and China. Following that, it describes the conduct of both wars and their eventual resolution. This is where, apart from the three main protagonists, the Soviet Union, the US (and its European allies), and ASEAN come into the picture. Although these countries were not directly involved in the fighting, they played a significant role in both prolonging the war and bringing about its end. In short, we need to consider the decision-making on all sides of the conflict.

Marshalling old and new Vietnamese, Cambodian, Chinese, Soviet, American, and ASEAN, as well as British and Australian, archival sources, this reconstruction of the war thus takes an international history perspective focusing on the simultaneous decision-making of all sides directly or indirectly involved in the conflict which, in the words of Odd Arne Westad, 'created shockwaves within the international system of states'.[36] What is commonly known as the 'Third Indochina War'[37] comprises two related wars: the Vietnam–Kampuchea War from 1978 to 1990 and the brief Sino-Vietnamese War in February 1979. Although the latter military confrontation was brief, China and Vietnam were technically at war until the resolution of the Cambodian conflict in 1990.

IV

The literature of the Third Indochina War has been dominated by journalists and political scientists, particularly international relations specialist with an interest in Asia and/or Indochina writing during the duration of the conflict. Like all contemporary accounts, they are very much dependent on open sources and media reports with very limited access to archival sources, if at all. They should also be read with a critical mind as media reporting is not always 'politically, socially

---

[36] Odd Arne Westad and Sophie Quinn-Judge (eds), *The Third Indochina War: Conflict between China, Vietnam and Cambodia, 1972–79* (London: Routledge, 2006), p. 1.
[37] The 'First' was the Vietnamese war against the French, which culminated at the Battle of Dien Bien Phu and ended with the signing of the Geneva Agreements both in 1954. The 'Second' (more popularly known as the Vietnam War) was the Vietnamese war against the Americans, which ended in April 1975.

or culturally neutral'.[38] Interest and writings on the war dwindled in the early 1990s. Also, compared to the abundance of writing (which continues to proliferate) on the better-known Second Indochina War (more commonly known as the Vietnam War), the literature on the Third Indochina War is sparse in comparison, and its increment hardly moves the dial.[39] Unlike the 'First' and 'Second' Indochina wars, which lasted just as long, 'the post-1975 period in general and the Third Indochina War in particular continue to be, as Edwin Martini noted, relegated to footnotes and epilogues'.[40] Although Martini made this observation in 2009, the state of the field has not changed much today.

Faced with limited archival sources, few historians have focused on this topic. While there have been numerous articles, book chapters, and books which deal with various aspects and phases of the Third Indochina War, there is still no single-authored book which attempts to reconstruct the war from start to end in a coherent manner. In 2013, I wrote a book, *Singapore, ASEAN and the Cambodian Conflict 1978–1991*, which was an account of the war from principally the Singapore (and to an extent the ASEAN-5) perspective, based on Singapore archival sources. In this book, I attempt to cover a broader canvas. It is not by any means a definitive account. While we know more now than what we did then during the Cold War years, sources remain limited. There will never be a time when the internal archives of the Southeast Asian countries as well as China will be opened. I hope this book will at least be an all-inclusive, impartial, and dispassionate account which future historians can build on. As what Ralph Smith wrote in the context of the Vietnam War, our concern here is not who

---

[38] See Gea D. M. Wijers, 'Framing Cambodian Affairs: French and American Scholarship, Media and Geopolitics', in Albert Tzeng, William L. Richter, and Ekaterina Koldunova (eds), *Framing Asian Studies: Geopolitics and Institutions* (Singapore: ISEAS, 2018), p. 121; Geoffrey C. Gunn and Jefferson Lee, *Cambodia Watching Down Under* (Institute of Asian Studies, Chulalongkorn University, IAS Monograph, Number 047, 1991).

[39] The most recent book published is Kosal Path, *Vietnam's Strategic Thinking during the Third Indochina War* (Wisconsin: University of Wisconsin Press, 2020). Also, Hoang Ming Vu's 2020 Cornell PhD thesis, *The Third Indochina War and the Making of Present-Day Southeast Asia*, https://ecommons.cornell.edu/handle/1813/103452, accessed on 14 April 2022. Kosal Path is a political scientist. Hoang is a historian by training.

[40] Ed Martini in his review of Mark Bradley's book 'Vietnam at War', *Journal of Vietnamese Studies*, Volume 5, Number 1, Winter 2009, pp. 218–221. Martini posed his observation as a question.

is right or who is wrong but 'with the unfolding of the conflict itself, and the interactions of decisions by the opposing sides'.[41]

In writing this book, I have drawn on a voluminous number of writings spanning the 1960s to the present. I am indebted to numerous scholars and researchers, too long to list but which are evident from the notes and Bibliography. It is perhaps helpful to provide a brief survey of the English-language historiography of the 'Third Indochina War' here. Under Pol Pot, Cambodia was a very closed society. Our knowledge of the Khmer Rouge – their origin and roots, ideology, policies and practices, and relations with Vietnam came notably from the scholarship of Ben Kiernan, Steven Heder, Michael Vickery, and David Chandler; about the root problems in Sino-Vietnamese relations culminating in the February 1979 war from noted Vietnam historian William Duiker, Chang Pao-min, King C. Chen, Eugene K. Lawson, Robert S. Ross, Anne Gilks, and Steven J. Hood. These studies, mostly by political scientists (David Chandler and William Duiker being the exceptions), were mainly published in the 1980s and were based mainly on contemporary information and open sources. Three accounts of the conflict which I found most helpful are Grant Evans (a socio-anthropologist) and Kelvin Rowley (a sociologist) in 1984 – *Red Brotherhood at War: Indochina Since the Fall of Saigon* – which was described as the first major study of Indochina since the end of the Vietnam War in 1975; and Nayan Chanda's (then the chief of the Washington Bureau of the *Far Eastern Economic Review*) *Brother Enemy: The War after the War* in 1986. The third is by political scientist Stephen J. Morris on political culture and the causes of the Vietnamese invasion of Cambodia.

There was another long lull after that before the publication in 2006 of *The Third Indochina War: Conflict between China, Vietnam and Cambodia, 1972–1979*, edited by Odd Arne Westad and Sophie Quinn-Judge, which essentially focuses on developments in the 1970s leading to the conflict. As the editors noted, few scholars have revisited the war since the Russians and Chinese archives were opened in the early 1990s.[42] The book is very informative but does not really

---

[41] R. B. Smith, *An International History of the Vietnam War, Volume 3: The Making of a Limited War, 1965–66* (London: Macmillan, 1991), p. 16.

[42] Odd Arne Westad and Sophie Quinn-Judge (eds), *The Third Indochina War: Conflict between China, Vietnam and Cambodia, 1972–79* (London: Routledge, 2006).

Introduction 15

get to grips with the two key questions: why did Vietnam launch its invasion of Cambodia (then known as Kampuchea) on 25 December 1978; and why did China attack Vietnam on 17 February 1979 and withdraw a month later? These questions were somewhat more directly addressed in a much earlier book, also entitled *The Third Indochina War*, edited by David Elliot. Published in 1981, in the wake of the war, the book was the product of a panel at the annual meeting of the Association for Asian Studies in late March 1979 and a follow-up conference of the contributors (except for one) on 2 April 1979. The aim of the book was to 'analyse the origins and development of the Third Indochinese Conflict and the problems posed by the complex issues involved'.[43] Though dated, it too remains a very informative book.

Bringing this very brief overview of the state of the field to a close are three recent books published in 2014, 2015, and 2020 respectively: *Brothers in Arms: Chinese Aid to the Khmer Rouge 1975–1979* by Andrew Mertha; *Deng Xiaoping's Long War: The Military Conflict between China and Vietnam 1979–1991* by Xiaoming Zhang (which is useful to read alongside Edward C. O'Dowd's *Chinese Military Strategy in the Third Indochina War: The Last Maoist War* (2007)); and the most recent, Kosal Path's *Vietnam's Strategic Thinking during the Third Indochina War*, which has a chapter on Vietnam's decision to invade Cambodia in which he argues that the geopolitics (the alliance between Democratic Kampuchea and China backed by the US) was a more significant reason for the war then the border conflict and the historical animosity between Democratic Kampuchea and Vietnam.[44] All these books extend our knowledge of an aspect of the

---

[43] For details of the origins and objective of this book, see David W. P. Elliot, *The Third Indochina Conflict* (London: Routledge, 2019), preface. The book was first published by Westview Press in 1981 and reissued in 2019 by Routledge.

[44] Andrew Mertha, *Brothers in Arms: Chinese Aid to the Khmer Rouge, 1975–1979* (Ithaca, NY: Cornell University Press, 2014); Xiaoming Zhang, *Deng Xiaoping's Long War: The Military Conflict between China and Vietnam, 1979–1991* (Chapel Hill: University of North Carolina Press, 2015); Edward C. O'Dowd, *Chinese Military Strategy in the Third Indochina War: The Last Maoist war* (London: Routledge, 2007); Kosal Path, *Vietnam's Strategic Thinking during the Third Indochina War* (Madison: University of Wisconsin Press, 2020), chapter 2. Chapter 3 takes the story from the Chinese invasion in February 1979 to 'punish' the Vietnamese, which led to a 'two-front war'.

war but they do not cover the Third Indochina War as a whole. One rare and recent study which deserves to be mentioned is Hoang Minh Vu's 2020 PhD thesis, *The Third Indochina War and the Making of Present-Day Southeast Asia, 1975–1995*, which this author hopes that Hoang will eventually recast into a monograph to reach a wider reading public. Hoang concurs with Kosal Path, arguing that the conflict was not inevitable and that it grew out of mutual misunderstandings, in his words 'overlapping misperceptions', and that ASEAN prioritise non-interference over human rights. He also argues that Hanoi found it difficult to extricate from Cambodia and did not intentionally stay in the country for a decade.[45]

V

This book consists of seven chapters, inclusive of the Introduction and the Epilogue. Chapters 1 and 2 focus on both the deep and precipitating issues and events that led to the war in December 1978, which was quickly followed by that of February 1979. Chapter 1 deals with the deep causes, the period from the 1950s to 1975, while Chapter 2 examines the precipitating causes of the conflict, from 1975 to 1979. Chapter 3 recounts the events leading to the Sino-Vietnamese War in February 1979 and its immediate aftermath. Chapter 4 covers the 1980s and concentrates on the regional, namely ASEAN, response to the Vietnamese invasion and the Sino-Vietnamese War. Chapter 5 continues the narrative, expanding beyond the regional to the global up until the signing of the Paris Peace Agreements on 23 October 1991. This period lasting a decade can be characterised by a 'talk–fight' strategy. The Epilogue brings the account of the conflict to its end. It describes the brief UNTAC period (1992–1993), culminating with the May 1993 general elections in Cambodia. The story ends with the July 1998 general election and Cambodia joining ASEAN in April 1999. It is the belief of this author that bringing the narrative to 1998–1999 provides better closure and a more complete account than the dominant representation of the conflict being over with the signing of the Paris Peace Agreement in October 1991. Indeed, 1998 marks

[45] Hoang Minh Vu, *The Third Indochina War and the Making of Present-Day Southeast Asia, 1975–1995*, unpublished PhD thesis, Cornell University, December 2020.

the beginning of a new phase in both Cambodian and regional politics in the post-Cold War era.[46]

Historians may never agree on every strand of this narrative. As Queen Elizabeth II said (although in a different context), 'some recollections may vary'. But as the late Ralph Smith, remembered for his pioneering work *An International History of the Vietnam War*, wrote, 'the principal task of the historian must be to try to understand why things happen as they did'; I hope I have achieved that in the narrative you are about to read.

[46] See Ang Cheng Guan, *Southeast Asia after the Cold War: A Contemporary History* (Singapore: NUS Press, 2019).

1 Vietnam–Cambodia–China Relations (1950s–1975)

I

In the attempt to produce a satisfactory account of the origins of the Third Indochina War, there is no need to go as far back as premodern Cambodian history to describe the already well-documented 'age-old resentments and suspicions'[1] that the Cambodians generally hold against the Vietnamese (and indeed, towards the Thais as well). Our narrative proper therefore begins during the period when many of the main protagonists in the Third Indochina War were already active in the arena of conflict. Over the years, many have passed on, such as Sihanouk, who at the time of the 1954 Geneva Conference was thirty-two years old. Sihanouk, widely regarded as the 'Father of (Cambodia's) independence',[2] died in 2012; and Pol Pot (aka Saloth Sar), who was the general secretary of the Communist Party of Kampuchea (CPK) from 1963 to 1981 and the prime minister of Democratic Kampuchea until the Vietnamese invasion in 1978, died in 1998. Others are still alive, such as Hun Sen, who was once a member of the CPK and who at twenty-seven years old was the foreign minister in the then Vietnamese-installed government of the PRK established in January 1979. He was the prime minister of Cambodia, a position he held from 1993 to 2023 (the first four years as the second prime minister). Sihanouk, Pol Pot, and Hun Sen, three of the most prominent actors during the period under study, were all wary of the Vietnamese in their own ways.

Despite the history of resentments and suspicions, both Cambodia's and Vietnam's struggles for independence were intricately connected.

---

[1] Phrase borrowed from Odd Arne Westad and Sophie Quinn-Judge (ed.), *The Third Indochina War: Conflict between China, Vietnam and Cambodia, 1972–79* (London: Routledge, 2006).
[2] Roger M. Smith, 'Prince Norodom Sihanouk of Cambodia', *Asian Survey*, Volume 7, Number 6, June 1967, p. 353.

According to a French report of November 1947, the Khmer Issarak and Viet Minh had agreed on a plan to collaborate to fight against the French – Vietnamese and Khmer units could either choose an Issarak or a Viet Minh commander. The Viet Minh would send instructors to train Khmer Issarak. Both sides could also operate in each other's territory according to agreed limits.[3] In Cambodia, in April 1950, the inaugural Congress of the Khmer Resistance was convened under the leadership of Son Ngoc Minh (Achar Mean). Other key personalities included Tou Samouth and Sieu Heng, all close to the Vietnamese communists. The United Issarak Front was established initially with only forty ethnic Cambodian members from the Indochinese Communist Party (ICP), although hundreds were being trained in communist political schools set up by the Vietnamese.[4] As Shawn McHale noted, despite the collaboration, 'Vietnamese–Khmer relations from 1945 to 1954 were marked by distrust and even violence ... the norm was a fragile coexistence'.[5] According to McHale, 'as the super space of French Indochina crumbled, Cambodia and Vietnam were refashioned by dominant ethnic elites into new, ethnically defined nation-states'. The 'extensive ethnic violence' (rarely mentioned in the secondary literature) 'followed by France's 1949 award of Cochinchina to the new state of Vietnam, reshaped Khmer–Vietnamese relations and contributed to Khmer Rouge antipathy to the Vietnamese'. In his analysis, the Khmer Rouge attacks on Vietnam from 1975, and their desire to reclaim the Mekong Delta and 'to purge Cambodia proper of Vietnamese', were a continuation of the earlier conflicts.[6]

In May 1951, the Second Congress of the ICP (Vietnam, Cambodia, and Laos) decided to split the clandestine party into three separate parties, but Vietnam would continue to direct the overall resistance struggle. Following that decision, the Kampuchean (Khmer) People's

---

[3] For details, see Shawn McHale, 'Ethnicity, Violence, and Khmer-Vietnamese Relations: The Significance of the Lower Mekong Delta, 1757–1954', *The Journal of Asian Studies*, Volume 72, Number 2, May 2013, pp. 367–390.
[4] David P. Chandler, *A History of Cambodia* (Boulder: Westview Press, 1992), p. 181.
[5] Shawn McHale, 'Ethnicity, Violence, and Khmer–Vietnamese Relations: The Significance of the Lower Mekong Delta, 1757–1954', *The Journal of Asian Studies*, Volume 72, Number 2, May 2013, p. 373.
[6] Shawn McHale, 'Ethnicity, Violence, and Khmer–Vietnamese Relations: The Significance of the Lower Mekong Delta, 1757–1954', *The Journal of Asian Studies*, Volume 72, Number 2, May 2013, pp. 385–386.

Revolutionary Party (KPRP) was established in June 1951.[7] Like McHale, David Chandler also noted that 'the interplay between nationalism and internationalism inside the Cambodian Communist movement ... has plagued the party since the early 1950s'.[8] It is worth noting that the KPRP is recognised as the precursor of the CPP, the party which is currently ruling Cambodia under Hun Sen. The KPRP was also the precursor of the CPK led by Pol Pot, which was dissolved in 1981, a consequence of the Vietnamese invasion of Cambodia in December 1978. More of this later. French intelligence reported in 1953 that the KPRP had recruited and trained many guerrilla fighters, particularly in eastern Cambodia bordering Vietnam. Mostly trained by the Vietnamese, many of the anti-colonial Cambodian guerrilla forces were also 'led and staffed by Vietnamese'. As a political force, the KPRP, however, could not compete with Sihanouk, who in 1952 led a 'royal crusade' and towards the end of 1953 succeeded in arm-twisting the French to grant Cambodia independence.[9]

The 1954 Geneva Conference is one of the most important turning points in the Cold War in Southeast Asia. Much has been written about the conference which, in the words of Chen Jian and Shen Zhihua, 'ended the First Indochina War, while at the same time, prepared conditions for the unfolding of the process leading to the Second Indochina War'.[10] What concerns us here is it how the decisions reached at Geneva in 1954 affected Cambodia. The Geneva Agreements 'drastically changed relations between the Khmer and Vietnamese communists'.[11] Wilfred Burchett rightly noted that 'when historians put their fingers on the major impediment to the Cambodian revolution, they must point to the consequences of the 1954 Geneva Conference on Indochina'.[12]

---

[7] See Takashi Shiraishi and Motoo Furuta (eds), *Indochina in the 1940s and 1950s* (Ithaca, NY: SEAP, Cornell University, 1992), chapter 5.

[8] David P. Chandler, *A History of Cambodia* (Boulder: Westview Press, 1992), p. 182; Martin Stuart-Fox, *A History of Laos* (Cambridge: Cambridge University Press, 1997), pp. 80–81.

[9] David Chandler, *Facing the Cambodian Past: Selected Essays 1971–1994* (St Leonards, Australia: Allen & Unwin, 1996), p. 219.

[10] 'The Geneva Conference of 1954', *Cold War International History Project Bulletin*, Number 16, Fall 2007/Winter 2008, p. 7.

[11] Dmitry Mosyakov, 'The Khmer Rouge and the Vietnamese Communists: A History of Their Relations as Told in the Soviet Archives', https://gsp.yale.edu/node/297.

[12] Wilfred Burchett, *The China Cambodia Vietnam Triangle* (Chicago: Vanguard Books, 1981), p. 27.

The conference affirmed the independence of Cambodia and Sihanouk as the leader. The Vietnamese communists led by Pham Van Dong at the conference were unable to persuade the others that the KPRP should to be represented. The Khmer Issarak were not even given any territory in Cambodia to regroup (like the Pathet Lao in Laos). Without any sanctuary in Cambodia, a few thousand Khmer Issarak retreated into North Vietnam. Many were imprisoned or killed by the Sihanouk regime.[13]

Pham Van Dong did what he could but the Vietnamese communists themselves were weak and Hanoi was dependent on Chinese and Soviet support, which on this issue was not forthcoming. Moscow, represented by Soviet Foreign Minister Molotov, did not support the representation of both the Khmer Issarak and Pathet Lao at Geneva. Beijing, represented by Foreign Minister Zhou Enlai, was prepared to recognise the legitimacy of the Sihanouk-led government if Sihanouk did not allow any American bases to be established in his country. Sihanouk himself believed that neutrality was the best policy for Cambodia, which pleased the Chinese (and eventually the North Vietnamese communists as well). Indeed, until his ouster on 18 March 1970 by Lon Nol, who steered Cambodia towards the US, Sihanouk increasingly demonstrated his 'genuine independence of the West' and his 'friendship towards China'.[14]

The Geneva Agreements further required the Vietnamese communists to withdraw their forces from Cambodia. The last Khmer-Vietminh units left Cambodia in October 1954.[15] In December 1955, Le Duan, who was then based in South Vietnam, put forward a fourteen-point action plan that called for a more aggressive and militant approach to complement the political struggle in the South, which was rejected by the Hanoi leadership. The Hanoi leadership assessed that they were not ready to accelerate the military struggle in the South. Beijing and Moscow were also not in favour of any action that could lead to a

---

[13] Ben Kiernan, 'Wild Chickens, Farm Chickens, and Cormorants: Kampuchea's Eastern Zone under Pol Pot', in David P. Chandler and Ben Kiernan (eds), *Revolution and Its Aftermath in Kampuchea: Eight Essays* (New Haven: Yale University Southeast Asia Studies, Monograph Series No. 25, 1983), pp. 153–154.
[14] R. B. Smith, *An International History of the Vietnam War, Volume 1: Revolution and Containment 1955–1961* (London: Macmillan, 1983), p. 117.
[15] Philip Short, *Pol Pot: Anatomy of a Nightmare* (New York: Henry Holt and Company, 2004), p. 104.

new military confrontation. Had Le Duan's proposal (which had been endorsed by the Nam Bo Regional Committee) been accepted, there would have been a step up in Vietnamese support of activities there, as recommended in the fourteen-point proposal, as Cambodia was deemed to be of strategic importance to the Vietnamese communist reunification plan. According to the US State Department, while there had been numerous reports since 1956 of Vietnamese communist cells in Cambodia, there was no indication of any serious intensification of communist activities there.[16] Hanoi's policy up to the point when the Khmer Rouge took control of Cambodia on 17 April 1975 (ahead of the Vietnamese communist reunification of North and South Vietnam on 30 April 1975) was consistently to prioritise its own independence struggle before that of Cambodia, and that they would assist the Khmer Rouge after reunification. Hanoi chose Sihanouk, who had real power over the Cambodian communists, believing that the latter were too small to be effective, and wanted 'all Cambodian dissidents to pursue a united front route (managed covertly by the Vietnamese Communist Party (VCP) which would include Cambodians) and make primary use of ethnic Vietnamese living in Cambodia'.[17] The years after Geneva were 'the nadir of the Cambodian communist movement'.[18] Cambodia 'lived in the shadow of the Vietnam War'.[19]

II

This is where we introduce Pol Pot. Saloth Sar (his name before the change to 'Pol Pot' in 1976) was 25 (or 26) years of age at the time of the Geneva Conference. He had returned to Cambodia from Paris in 1953.

---

[16] Memorandum from the Deputy Assistant Secretary of State for Far Eastern Affairs (Rice) to the Deputy Under Secretary of State for Political Affairs (Johnson), 10 April 1963, *Foreign Relations of the United States (FRUS), Southeast Asia, 1961–1963, Volume 23*, pp. 231–233.

[17] *Vietnam–Cambodia Conflict, Report Prepared at the Request of the Subcommittee of Asian and Pacific Affairs Committee of International Relations by the Congressional Research Service, Library of Congress* (Washington, DC: US Government Printing Office, 1978), p. 5.

[18] Anne Ruth Hansen and Judy Ledgerwood (eds), *At the Edge of the Forest: Essays on Cambodia, History and Narrative in Honor of David Chandler* (Ithaca, NY: Southeast Asia Program, Cornell University, 2008), p. 11.

[19] Qiang Zhai, 'China and the Cambodian Conflict, 1970–1975', *Searching for the Truth*, Second Quarterly Issue, Special English Edition, July 2003, p. 15.

Back in Cambodia, he was inducted into the ICP and mentored by Tou Samouth, one of the two founding members of the KPRP, eventually establishing himself as Tou's secretary and principal aide. During this period, Saloth Sar also became friends with several other fellow travellers, notably Ieng Sary, Khieu Ponnary (whom he subsequently married), Sok Thuok (Vorn Vet), and Nuon Chea. Sar was able to witness the heavy-handedness of the Vietnamese, their control of the KPRP, and their 'constant use of Cambodians to carry out menial tasks'.[20] As David Chandler noted, the KPRP had to be 'reconstituted in the context of Hanoi's informal alliance with Sihanouk', which meant that the KPRP 'was to be brought back to life, encouraged to expand, but kept silent and forbidden to engage in armed struggle'.[21] The Khmer Rouge had two choices, in the words of Chandler, 'between guidance from Vietnam on the one hand and independence, confrontation, and the possibility of obliteration on the other'.[22]

One group of Khmer Rouge, notably associated with Tou Samouth, was inclined to cooperate with the Vietnamese, whereas another, notably Pol Pot, leaned towards decoupling from the Vietnamese. Those closely associated with Pol Pot (some have coined the term the 'Paris wing' for this group) apparently had a visceral hatred for the Vietnamese. One of the most 'pronounced features' of Polpotism was its 'anti-Vietnamese character'.[23] For example, Pol Pot's view of the 1954 Geneva Conference was that it was 'a deliberate Vietnamese "sell-out" of Kampuchea',[24] when, as briefly described earlier, it was much more complicated. The Vietnamese communists at Geneva also did not achieve what they wanted.

Stephen Heder's fieldwork research, however, showed that it is a 'myth that there was an "internationalist" or "pro-Vietnamese" stream within the Cambodian communist movement ... it was not

---

[20] Philip Short, *Pol Pot: Anatomy of a Nightmare* (New York: Henry Holt and Company, 2004), pp. 96–97, 100.
[21] David P. Chandler, *Brother Number One: A Political Biography of Pol Pot* (Boulder: Westview Press, 1992), p. 61.
[22] David P. Chandler, *Brother Number One: A Political Biography of Pol Pot* (Boulder: Westview Press, 1992), p. 61.
[23] See Matthew Galway, *The Emergence of Global Maoism: China's Red Evangelism and the Cambodian Communist Movement* (Ithaca, NY: Cornell University Press, 2022), pp. 184–187, p. 184.
[24] Wilfred Burchett, *The China Cambodia Vietnam Triangle* (Chicago: Vanguard Books, 1981), p. 72.

about whether to oppose Vietnamese hegemony over Cambodia, but about how to do so'.[25] Indeed, until mid-1978, those who disagreed with Pol Pot's policies 'remained deeply committed to opposing any Vietnamese invasion or attempt to assert political influence over Cambodia'. In the latter half of 1978, those who disagreed with Pol Pot 'remained divided among themselves over how much Vietnamese help should be accepted in the fight against Pol Pot and on what terms'. Heder concluded that, 'despite whatever political debts' Pol Pot's opponents 'may feel the Cambodian people and they themselves genuinely owe the Vietnamese, historical anti-Vietnamese sentiments remain not that far from the surface'.[26] To Pol Pot and his group, Hanoi was a 'regional representative of hegemonic, bureaucratic communism'.[27] The Vietnamese in turn looked upon the Khmer Rouge as 'Maoist primitives'.[28]

The Khmer Rouge perspective of Vietnam as having always wanted to annex and swallow Cambodia, as well as exterminate the Cambodian race, is another example of Pol Pot's extreme views. As the *Black Book* (issued by the Khmer Rouge in September 1978) pointed out, one of the means by which the Vietnamese hoped to achieve their goal was through the strategy of an 'Indochina Federation'.[29] There were two schools of opinion within the Vietnamese communist movement on the issue of its relations with Cambodia and Laos. One was for a unified Indochina communist party with Vietnam assuming the role of a 'big brother'. The other advocated a looser form of unity between the three Indochinese countries whereby assistance could be given to one another as and when the need arose. This was the arrangement that the Chinese favoured, whereas Le Duan and his closest associates were for a unified communist movement led by Vietnam. In the minds

---

[25] Stephen Heder, 'Reflections on Cambodian Political History: Backgrounder to Recent Developments', Strategic and Defence Studies Centre, Canberra, Working Paper No. 239, September 1991, p. 12.
[26] Stephen Heder, 'Reflections on Cambodian Political History: Backgrounder to Recent Developments', Strategic and Defence Studies Centre, Canberra, Working Paper No. 239, September 1991, p. 12.
[27] William S. Turley and Jeffrey Race, 'The Third Indochina War', *Foreign Policy*, Number 38, Spring 1980, p. 96.
[28] William S. Turley and Jeffrey Race, 'The Third Indochina War', *Foreign Policy*, Number 38, Spring 1980, p. 96.
[29] This is the theme of the *Livre Noir/Black Book*. Also see 'KR Intelligence on Cambodia: Edited Excerpts...', *Phnom Penh Post*, 22 May–4 June 1998, p. 5.

of Le Duan and those close to him, it was the Chinese who had forced them to accede to the French demand that the problems of Cambodia and Laos be separated from that of Vietnam in 1954.[30]

Most Vietnam specialists have concluded that the idea of an Indochina Federation was abandoned in the late 1930s. There is no doubt that in its behaviour, Vietnam continued to display a neocolonialist attitude towards Cambodia (and Laos).[31] This would explain the Cambodian perception of Vietnam as well as the view of ASEAN that Vietnam's invasion of Cambodia in 1978 was part of Hanoi's plan to re-establish the Indochina Federation. It is perhaps worth considering David Elliot's remark that

> to say that many of the major episodes in the complex chain of causality that led to Vietnam's invasion of Kampuchea originated outside Vietnam's borders does not necessarily exculpate Hanoi from responsibility for its actions. But to accept the common view of Vietnam as an expansionist garrison state is to misread the motives underlying its actions – whatever the consequences of those actions may have been.[32]

We return to this in Chapter 2.

At the 2nd Party Congress of the KPRP at the end of September 1960, convened under orders from Hanoi, there were disagreements between Saloth Sar and his group, who championed a more militant struggle against imperialism and Sihanouk on the one hand, and the senior leaders of the party (led by Tou Samouth), who continued to advocate political struggle within the framework of Sihanouk's regime (as advocated by the Vietnamese) on the other.[33] The latter view prevailed despite Sihanouk's repressive actions against the left. These measures led thousands of Khmer Issarak forces to retreat

---

[30] See *Vietnamese Foreign Ministry White Book on Relations with China*, BBC/SWB/FE/6238/6 October 1979, and BBC/SWB/FE/6242/11 October 1979.

[31] For a Soviet perspective, see Dmitry Mosyakov, *The Khmer Rouge and the Vietnamese Communists: A History of Their Relations as Told in the Soviet Archives*, https://gsp.yale.edu/sites/default/files/gs15_-_the_khmer_rouge_and_the_vietnamese_communists_a_history_of_their_relations_as_told_in_the_soviet_archives.pdf, p. 56.

[32] David W. P. Elliott, 'Vietnam in Asia: Strategy and Diplomacy in a New Context', *International Journal*, Volume 38, Number 2, Spring 1983, p. 290.

[33] See Ben Kiernan, *How Pol Pot Came to Power* (London: Version, 1985), pp. 189–193, 367; David P. Chandler, *The Tragedy of Cambodian History: Politics, War and Revolution since 1945* (New Haven: Yale University Press, 1991), pp. 112–115, 205, n. 33.

into North Vietnam, where they remained to await Hanoi's consent to resume armed struggle. This group became known as the pro-Hanoi faction of the Khmer Rouge. Opposing this group was Saloth Sar, who, as we have noted, opposed Vietnamese domination of their movement. On 20 July or thereabouts, Tou Samouth died under questionable circumstances (which we do not need to go into here). As a result, Saloth Sar became the acting secretary-general of the party and was subsequently confirmed as secretary-general at the 3rd Congress of the KPRP on 20–21 February 1963. In the words of Ralph Smith: 'Therein lay the origins of the bitter conflict which emerged twenty years later for control of Democratic Kampuchea.'[34]

The presence of two Khmer Rouge factions – one 'friendly' and the other 'hostile' towards the Vietnamese – also explains the subsequent disagreement over the date of the formation of the KPRP. The current CPP, led by Hun Sen, traces its origins to the 1st Party Congress held in June 1951. It acknowledges the 2nd Congress in 1960 (mentioned earlier) and the 3rd Congress in 1979, rejecting the 1963 (when Pol Pot was confirmed as secretary-general), 1975, and 1978 congresses convened by Pol Pot. The CPK led by Pol Pot, on the other hand, traces its origins to 30 September 1960 (the 2nd Party Congress) when he was elected to the Central Committee of the KPRP while disclaiming the legitimacy of the 1951 Congress as it was deemed to be directed by the Vietnamese.[35]

We now know that after becoming secretary-general of the KPRP, in 1965 and 1966, Saloth Sar made trips to North Vietnam and China for consultations. The visits also gave the Vietnamese as well as the Chinese an opportunity to get to know Tou Samouth's successor.

---

[34] R. B. Smith, *An International History of the Vietnam War, Volume 1: Revolution and Containment 1955–1961* (London: Macmillan, 1983), p. 82.
[35] See K. Viviane Frings, 'Rewriting Cambodian History to "Adapt" It to a New Political Context: The Kampuchean People's Revolutionary Party's Historiography (1979–1991)', *Modern Asian Studies*, Volume 31, Number 4, 1997, pp. 807–846; David P. Chandler, 'Revising the Past in Democratic Kampuchea: When Was the Birthday of the Party?', *Pacific Affairs*, Volume 56, Number 2, Summer 1983, pp. 288–300; R. B. Smith, *An International History of the Vietnam War, Volume 1: Revolution and Containment 1955–1961* (London: Macmillan, 1983), pp. 235–238; Ben Kiernan and Chanthou Boua (eds), *Peasants and Politics in Kampuchea 1952–1981* (London: Zed Press, 1982), pp. 252–253.

To his chagrin, the Vietnamese rejected his proposal for an 'armed struggle against Sihanouk and a freestanding Cambodian revolution'.[36] We do not fully know what transpired in China but apparently Sar received better treatment there, or at least he felt the Chinese were more understanding and supportive of him, although Sihanouk's 'regular anti-American, pro-Chinese stance probably meant that the Khmer Rouge got only nominal attention from Beijing at the time'.[37] As Philip Short noted: 'Rhetoric aside, the Chinese were, at heart, no more anxious than Vietnam to see armed struggle develop in Cambodia – and for exactly the same reasons: Sihanouk's cooperation was vital to the pursuance of the war in the South.'[38] Nevertheless, the visit to China, at least from Sar's perspective, marked the 'start of a *de facto* alliance' – 'If we want to keep our distance from Vietnam, we will have to rely on China', said Saloth Sar after the visit.[39] What could have led Sar to this conclusion was his meeting with Kang Sheng (who was in charge of the Chinese Communist Party relations with the international communist fraternity), who took a liking to Sar and adopted him as a protégé and promoted him as the 'true voice of the Cambodian revolution'. We do not have enough information of Kang Sheng's meddling into what was considered the Foreign Ministry's turf, except that Deng Yingchao reportedly told a visiting Thai delegation in the early 1980s that it was Kang Sheng who was responsible for Beijing's support of Pol Pot. Kang Sheng was a staunch supporter of the Cultural Revolution and the Gang of Four who opposed the pragmatic approach of Zhou Enlai and the Chinese Foreign Ministry. Kang Sheng died in December 1975. In contrast, Pol Pot did not have any ties with Moscow.[40] In 1969, Le Duan, at the behest of the Soviet

[36] Anne Ruth Hansen and Judy Ledgerwood (eds), *At the Edge of the Forest: Essays on Cambodia, History and Narrative in Honor of David Chandler* (Ithaca, NY: Southeast Asia Program, Cornell University, 2008), pp. 12–13.
[37] Sophie Richardson, *China, Cambodia, and the Five Principles of Peaceful Coexistence* (New York: Columbia University Press, 2010), p. 54.
[38] Philip Short, *Pol Pot: Anatomy of a Nightmare* (New York: Henry Holt and Company, 2004), p. 160. See also, Sophie Richardson, *China, Cambodia, and the Five Principles of Peaceful Coexistence* (New York: Columbia University Press, 2010), pp. 52–55; Ben Kiernan and Chanthou Boua (eds), *Peasants and Politics in Kampuchea 1952–1981* (London: Zed Press, 1982), pp. 254–255.
[39] Quoted in Philip Short, *Pol Pot: Anatomy of a Nightmare* (New York: Henry Holt and Company, 2004), p. 161.
[40] John Byron and Robert Pack, *The Claws of the Dragon* (New York: Simon & Schuster, 1992), pp. 356–357.

ambassador in Hanoi, tried unsuccessfully to persuade him to establish relations with the Communist Party of the Soviet Union.[41]

From the report of a 29 June 1968 conversation between Zhou Enlai and Pham Hung (who headed the Central Office for South Vietnam (COSVN)), we learned that Beijing was concerned about the problematic relationship of the Vietnamese communists and Khmer Rouge. He advised the Vietnamese to work on improving the relationship and to help the Khmer Rouge 'understand the overall context and be aware of the greater task of defeating the US ... In short, make them understand the international approach and understand that one cannot fight many enemies at the same time.' Zhou revealed that he had instructed Chinese embassy staff in Phnom Penh not to fraternise with the Khmer Rouge because 'the problem will be too complicated'. According to Zhou, 'the Cambodian comrades wish to develop armed struggle. Sihanouk will oppress them, and you (the Vietnamese) can no longer go through Cambodia. And if Sihanouk oppresses the Cambodian communists, China can no longer provide Cambodia will weapons.'[42] Beijing was, however, aware that Sihanouk, in Zhou Enlai's words, was 'double dealing' and in 1969 veering towards the right.[43]

Despite the US bombing of eastern Cambodia (with Sihanouk's acquiescence) and the restoration of US–Cambodia diplomatic relations on 11 June 1969, Hanoi still refused to countenance an armed struggle in Cambodia. Sihanouk shrewdly balanced his reconciliation with the US by recognising the Provisional Revolutionary Government of South Vietnam established on 8 June 1969 by the Hanoi-directed National Liberation Front. The Hanoi leadership maintained that Sihanouk was a valuable pawn against the US and rejected the idea

---

[41] See *Black Paper: Facts and Evidences of the Acts of Aggression and Annexation of Vietnam against Kampuchea* (Department of Press and Information of the Ministry of Democratic Kampuchea, September 1978), or *Black Paper* for short, p. 33.

[42] Zhou Enlai and Pham Hung, Beijing, 19 June 1968, in Odd Arne Westad et al. (eds) *77 Conversations between Chinese and Foreign Leaders of the Wars in IndoChina, 1964–1977*, Working Paper Number 22, Cold War International History Project, May 1998, Washington, DC.

[43] Zhou Enlai, Kang Sheng, Pham Van Dong, Hoang Van Thai, Pham Hung, and Others in the COSVN Delegation, Beijing, 20 and 21 April 1969, in Odd Arne Westad et al. (eds) *77 Conversations between Chinese and Foreign Leaders of the Wars in IndoChina, 1964–1977*, Working Paper Number 22, Cold War International History Project, May 1998, Washington, DC.

of overthrowing him. Relations between the Khmer Rouge and its Vietnamese counterpart, which had not been smooth under Pol Pot's tenure, worsened drastically in 1969. As the *Black Paper* put it, 'Friendship' and 'Solidarity' were only empty words. Relations remained tense till 18 March 1970 when Sihanouk was ousted.[44]

III

The ouster of Sihanouk by Lon Nol on 18 March 1970 is the seminal event in Cold War Cambodian history. As described earlier, Sihanouk was the reason why both the Vietnamese and Chinese restrained the Khmer Rouge from launching an armed struggle of their own. The ouster of Sihanouk altered the game plan. The ouster of Sihanouk by the pro-American and anti-Vietnamese Lon Nol adversely affected the ability of the Vietnamese communist to conduct the war.[45] Pol Pot by coincidence was in Beijing (after his unpleasant trip to Hanoi) when the coup took place. As Steve Heder noted, after telling Saloth Sar and Nuon Chea for more than two years that their policies were incorrect, their attitude towards the Khmer Rouge militancy changed '180 degrees'.[46] The Cambodian communists were further energised after an initially reluctant Sihanouk was successfully persuaded by the Chinese to establish a united front with the Khmer Rouge on 23 March 1970 – the Royal Government of the National Union of Kampuchea (GRUNK) was the government-in-exile based in Beijing. Immediately, the Khmer Rouge received the international recognition it failed to get during the 1954 Geneva Conference. Riding on the immense popularity of the deposed Sihanouk, the Khmer Rouge ranks increased exponentially although not everyone who joined necessarily shared Pol Pot's views and vision.

It was never going to be an easy relationship. But as Sophie Richardson noted, 'Sihanouk feared the KR's [Khmer Rouge]

---

[44] *Black Paper: Facts and Evidences of the Acts of Aggression and Annexation of Vietnam against Kampuchea* (Department of Press and Information of the Ministry of Democratic Kampuchea, September 1978), or *Black Paper* for short, pp. 27, 34.

[45] For Hanoi and Beijing's reaction to the coup, see Ang Cheng Guan, *Ending the Vietnam War: The Vietnamese Communists' Perspective* (London: Routledge, 2004), pp. 45–48.

[46] Steve Heder, *Cambodian Communism and the Vietnamese Model, Volume 1: Imitation and Independence 1930–1975* (Bangkok: White Lotus Press, 2004), p. 157.

radicalism and growing military strength; the KR feared his indisputable popularity among Cambodians' but 'without the kind of infrastructure only the KR maintained inside Cambodia, it was unlikely Sihanouk would ever be able to retain control of the country; without Sihanouk's international profile, it would be difficult for the KR to garner much assistance'.[47] Zhou Enlai did what he could to mediate between Pol Pot and Sihanouk even while he was in hospital dying of cancer, but to no avail. According to Nayan Chanda, Zhou was concerned about the future of Cambodia if the Khmer Rouge triumphed over Sihanouk.[48] Within China in the 1970s, there was an intensifying tussle between the radicals (such as Kang Sheng mentioned earlier) and moderates (such as Zhou who had been ill since 1972 and died in January 1976), which the radicals eventually won, albeit briefly.

Another set of difficulties involved Sihanouk/Khmer Rouge–Vietnamese communist relations. We now know that in the immediate aftermath of the March coup, Beijing as well as Hanoi briefly tried to strike a deal with Lon Nol. When that failed, both the Chinese and the Vietnamese threw their full support behind Sihanouk. Beijing sponsored the Indochinese Summit Conference (24–25 April), which brought together Sihanouk, Pham Van Dong, Nguyen Huu Tho, and Souphanouvong (of Laos) in Guangzhou. On 30 April 1970, Hanoi informed COSVN that 'Indochina has become a single battlefield'[49] – 'ironically because the VWP [Vietnamese Workers' Party] suddenly gave the Cambodians literally overwhelmingly support, that triggered Cambodian fears of VWP hopes to revive the old ICP project of a militarily and politically unified Indochina'.[50]

According to Chinese sources, Zhou Enlai made a special trip to Guangzhou to help reconcile the differences between Sihanouk

---

[47] Sophie Richardson, *China, Cambodia, and the Five Principles of Peaceful Coexistence* (New York: Columbia University Press, 2010), pp. 68, 76.
[48] Cited in Sophie Richardson, *China, Cambodia, and the Five Principles of Peaceful Coexistence* (New York: Columbia University Press, 2010), pp. 77–78.
[49] For details of the military developments in Cambodia, see Ang Cheng Guan, *Ending the Vietnamese War: The Vietnamese Communists' Perspective* (London: Routledge, 2004), pp. 50–53.
[50] Steve Heder, *Cambodian Communism and the Vietnamese Model, Volume 1: Imitation and Independence 1930–1975* (Bangkok: White Lotus Press, 2004), p. 159.

and Pham Van Dong to produce a joint declaration at the end of the conference.[51] Sihanouk was very concerned about letting the Vietnamese communists operate unfettered in Cambodia and had to be assured that Hanoi would respect Cambodia's territorial integrity. According to the *Black Paper*, Pol Pot too was uncomfortable with the large influx of Vietnamese troops as well as Cambodians who had been living in northern Vietnam since the 1950s entering or returning into Cambodia. The Vietnamese apparently continuously pressured the Khmer Rouge to accept the idea of mixed commands of Vietnamese cadres operating in Cambodian villages, communes, and districts. Pol Pot objected to the Vietnamese-proposed Joint Resistance Command headquarters, and in a November 1970 meeting the Vietnamese allegedly attempted to assassinate him and those who opposed the idea.

The relationship between the two sides further deteriorated in 1971.[52] Vietnamese accounts acknowledged that their differences and problems with the Khmer Rouge were obvious for all to see even though 'the Pol Pot-Ieng Sary clique' were reliant on the Vietnamese communists, and thus did not openly oppose them. But as the differences grew more acute, the Khmer Rouge allegedly confiscated Vietnamese ammunition and kidnapped and even killed Vietnamese cadres.[53] Indeed, at a July 1971 meeting, the Khmer Rouge leadership decided to break with the Vietnamese communists and went as far as declaring them the principal enemy of the Cambodian revolution. A purge of Cambodians seen or perceived to be pro-Hanoi was carried out and such purges intensified in 1972. According to Tran Van Tra, because the top priority was the war against the Americans, the Hanoi leadership tried to downplay their problems with the Khmer Rouge.[54]

---

[51] See Qiang Zhai, *China and the Vietnam Wars, 1950–1975* (Chapel Hill: University of North Carolina Press, 2000), pp. 190–191, n. 66.
[52] *Black Paper: Facts and Evidences of the Acts of Aggression and Annexation of Vietnam against Kampuchea* (Department of Press and Information of the Ministry of Democratic Kampuchea, September 1978), pp. 58–59.
[53] *Lich Su Quan Doi Nhan Dan, Tap II* (Hanoi: Nha Xuat Ban Quan Doi Nhan Dan, 1988), p. 385.
[54] Thomas Engelbert and Christopher E. Goscha, *Falling out of Touch: A Study on Vietnamese Communist Policy towards an Emerging Cambodian Communist Movement, 1930–1975* (Victoria: Monash Asia Institute, 1995), pp. 99–100, nn. 162–166.

Military cooperation between the Vietnamese communists and Khmer Rouge ended in mid-1972 or thereabouts, around the time Hanoi was seriously trying to reach a settlement with the US. One of the issues being negotiated between Henry Kissinger and Le Duc Tho at their secret Paris talks was the presence of Vietnamese communist forces in Cambodia (and Laos). Pol Pot refused to have anything to do with the ongoing North Vietnam–US negotiations in Paris and Hanoi was unable to persuade him to cooperate. At a 26 January 1973 meeting, Le Duan informed Ieng Sary of Hanoi's decision to sign the Paris Peace Agreement (which was signed on 27 January 1973) and told him that the Khmer Rouge should coordinate with the Vietnamese. Pol Pot rejected the idea outright. With the signing of the Paris Peace Agreement, Cambodia would not receive any more assistance from the Vietnamese communists. Pham Van Dong and Vo Nguyen Giap advised Sihanouk 'not to throw oil on the fire of the war which was about to be extinct in Indochina'.[55]

Tran Van Tra recalled, in an interview with Thomas Engelbert in 1989, that when the Vietnamese communists withdrew from Cambodia, the Khmer Rouge took the opportunity to attack them. The attacks increased as more Vietnamese communist forces were withdrawn. This occurred all over Cambodia except for the north-eastern part, which Tra described as the 'strategic lifeblood of the southern resistance', where the Vietnamese remained in control.[56] Le Duc Tho, in a March 1980 interview, explained that in the assessment of the Khmer Rouge leadership, 'a ceasefire at that time was not to their advantage', because with the signing of the Paris Agreement 'the US defeat was obvious'. The agreement thus 'paved the way and created favourable conditions, both military and political, for the victory of the Kampuchean revolution'. They therefore wanted 'to fight to the end in order to seize total power in Kampuchea, rather than to have a ceasefire and then to

---

[55] Julio Jeldres, 'Cambodia Relations with Vietnam: Historical Mistrust and Vulnerability', *Journal of Greater Mekong Studies*, Volume 2, Number 1, February 2020, p. 68.

[56] Thomas Engelbert and Christopher E. Goscha, *Falling Out of Touch: A Study on Vietnamese Communist Party Policy towards an Emerging Cambodian Communist Movement, 1930–1975* (Clayton: Monash Asia Institute, 1995), pp. 101–108; Truong Nhu Tang, *Journal of a VietCong* (London: Jonathan Cape, 1986), pp. 101, 219.

negotiate a political settlement'.[57] Sihanouk too 'wanted to prolong the fighting'.[58]

It is perhaps worth noting that Zhou Enlai was of the view that Cambodia should not, in his words to Henry Kissinger in February 1973, 'become completely red now' as that would result in 'even greater problems'. Zhou asked Kissinger to persuade Lon Nol to allow Sihanouk to return to Phnom Penh as head of state. Washington, Sophie Richardson noted, did not heed Zhou's strategy until four days before the fall of Phnom Penh on 17 April 1975.[59] Washington's inability or unwillingness to move its client Lon Nol to reach a settlement with Sihanouk was a 'perpetual irritant in Sino-American relations' in 1973–1974.[60] Zhou Enlai was concerned that the fighting in Cambodia made it 'more difficult for Peking to acquiesce in the public manifestation of the rapprochement with Washington, it delays US military disengagement from Indochina, and it most certainly complicated relations with China's Indochina allies'.[61] Beijing, however, had only limited influence over the Khmer Rouge and, as one National Security Council (NSC) paper put it, 'most of their Cambodian eggs remain in the Sihanouk basket'. Sihanouk had been variously described as 'mercurial', 'irrepressible', 'intemperate', and not easy to control or influence. Kissinger had observed that in his conversation with Zhou on Cambodia, the latter at times betrayed a degree of exasperation with Sihanouk. We still do not have the

---

[57] Anthony Barnett, 'Interview with Le Duc Tho', in Anthony Barnett and John Pilger, *Aftermath: The Struggle of Cambodia and Vietnam*, NS Report 5, 1982, pp. 54–59.

[58] Zhou Enlai and Le Thanh Nghi, Beijing, 8–10 October 1973, in Odd Arne Westad et.al. (ed.), *77 Conversations between Chinese and Foreign Leaders of the Wars in IndoChina, 1964–1977*, Working Paper Number 22, Cold War International History Project, May 1998, Washington, DC.

[59] Sophie Richardson, *China, Cambodia, and the Five Principles of Peaceful Coexistence* (New York: Columbia University Press, 2010), p. 78.

[60] Priscilla Roberts (ed.), *Window on the Forbidden City: The Beijing Diaries of David Bruce 1973–1974* (University of Hong Kong, Centre of Asian Studies, 2001), p. 34.

[61] National Security Council (NSC) Memorandum to Henry A. Kissinger on Peking and the Cambodian Issue (Secret/Sensitive/No Foreign Dissem), 26 May 1973. US Ambassador to China, David Bruce, recorded in his diary that Zhou felt 'particular urgency' reaching a solution in Cambodia. See, Priscilla Roberts (ed.), *Window on the Forbidden City: The Beijing Diaries of David Bruce 1973–1974* (University of Hong Kong, Centre of Asian Studies, 2001), p. 72.

complete information, but evidently Zhou's support for Sihanouk, which was also the Chinese Foreign Ministry's position, was becoming untenable by July 1973. In November 1974, Deng Xiaoping (since rehabilitated), in a conversation with Henry Kissinger, gave the latter a clear impression that the Chinese leadership now preferred a 'red Cambodia' dominated by the Khmer Rouge rather than a return to the regime under Sihanouk. Both the Americans and the Chinese knew that Sihanouk would eventually end up a figurehead in a Khmer Rouge regime.[62]

In summary, while Hanoi and Beijing shared a common concern about the Khmer Rouge insistence on continuing to fight in Cambodia and would like to see the fighting stop, and both saw Sihanouk playing a role in post-war Cambodia, Hanoi wanted to see the victory of GRUNK led by Sihanouk over the US-backed Lon Nol regime, with the caveat that the Khmer Rouge (like the Pathet Lao) would be a junior partner of the Vietnamese communists and that the Khmer Rouge would have control over Sihanouk. Beijing, when Zhou Enlai was still in control of foreign policy, on the other hand, envisioned Sihanouk playing a leading role and not just acting as a figurehead in a post-war Cambodia. But as noted earlier, the Chinese position changed. Sihanouk would still have a role, only it would not be a leading one.

Sihanouk confided to Etienne Manac'h (French ambassador to China) in May 1973 that his relations with Hanoi was still 'superficially cordial' but 'in fact had become seriously strained and would most likely deteriorate further' as he believed that 'Hanoi had designs on Cambodia'.[63] According to Sihanouk, the Chinese had assured him that Hanoi would not be allowed to 'satellitise' Cambodia.[64] Beijing further wanted the US to continue to play a diplomatic role in Cambodia after the Vietnam War ended because they feared that

---

[62] See Wang Chenyi, 'The Chinese Communist Party's Relationship with the Khmer Rouge in the 1970s: An Ideological Victory and a Strategic Failure', Working Paper 88, Cold War International History Project, 13 December 2018.

[63] Julio Jeldres, 'Cambodia Relations with Vietnam: Historical Mistrust and Vulnerability', *Journal of Greater Mekong Studies*, Volume 2, Number 1, February 2020, p. 68.

[64] NSC Memorandum to Henry A. Kissinger on Peking and the Cambodian Issue (Secret/Sensitive/No Foreign Dissem), 26 May 1973.

a complete US withdrawal from Cambodia would lead to a vacuum which Moscow would exploit, hence they were vexed by Washington's lack of attention to the Cambodian problem.[65]

Pol Pot and the Khmer Rouge had always wanted to get out of Vietnam's shadow, finally achieved it by liberating Cambodia on 17 April 1975 ahead of the Vietnamese. The timing was deliberate on the part of the Khmer Rouge to make the point that they could achieve victory without Vietnamese assistance and in fact even quicker. Five days later, on 22 April, the Vietnamese Politburo finally gave the go-ahead to launch the attack on Saigon. Saigon fell on 30 April marking the end of the Second Indochina War. We do not know what the Hanoi leadership thought of the fall of Phnom Penh. They were probably too engrossed in their own war in the South to think about the implications of the liberation of Cambodia by the Khmer Rouge for Vietnam–Cambodia relations.

IV

We now turn our focus to Sino-Vietnamese relations before the fall of Saigon on 30 April 1975. Like in the case of Cambodia–Vietnam relations, there is no need to go far back into pre-modern Vietnamese and Chinese histories to explain the already well-documented difficulties and challenges in their relationship.

The People's Republic of China (PRC), which came into being in the autumn of 1949, was the first country in the world to establish diplomatic relations with North Vietnam on 18 January 1950 during the time when the Vietnamese were engaged in a war of resistance against the French, commonly referred to as the 'First Indochina War'. With considerable Chinese military support, the war ended with the French defeat at the Battle of Dien Bien Phu on 7 May 1954. The Vietnamese communists claimed that they had been pressured by Beijing (and Moscow) to end the war prematurely instead of continuing the fight to unify the country. North Vietnamese officials also claimed that, despite their negotiating advantage, they were forced

[65] NSC Memorandum to Henry A. Kissinger on Peking and the Cambodian Issue (Secret/Sensitive/No Foreign Dissem), 26 May 1973; Priscilla Roberts (ed.), *Window on the Forbidden City: The Beijing Diaries of David Bruce 1973–1974* (University of Hong Kong, Centre of Asian Studies, 2001), pp. 33–34, 445–446.

to concede more than necessary during the subsequent negotiations with the French.[66]

The Vietnamese view is disputed by the Chinese side and the Sinophile Hoang Van Hoan (North Vietnam's first ambassador to China), as well as American historian Pierre Asselin, who recently argued that Hanoi accepted the provisions of the Geneva Agreements not because of Chinese and/or Soviet pressure but because they concurred with the Chinese view that 'implementation [of the agreements] would bring peaceful reunification and promote the cause of socialism in Vietnam'.[67] According to the Chinese, the Vietnamese communists, having expended all their energy and resources to achieve the historic Dien Bien Phu victory, did not have the capacity to liberate the entire country at that time and were thus reasonably happy with their gains at the conference table.[68]

In the wake of their triumphant victory over the French at Dien Bien Phu, there were indeed some exuberant segments in the Vietnamese leadership who believed that they could unite the country. As Wang Bingnan (secretary-general of the Chinese delegation to the 1954 Geneva Conference) recalled, 'some people in the Vietminh hoped to unify the whole of Vietnam at one stroke'.[69] At the same time, there were other Vietnamese leaders, significantly Ho Chi Minh, who concurred with the Chinese, although they differed on the terms of the temporary settlement. Ho recognised the difficulties ahead and the likelihood of having to fight against not only the French but also the Americans and was thus prepared to settle for a temporary settlement.[70] Rumours of US intervention were then rife because of the ambiguous statements made by then Secretary of State John Foster Dulles and the many diplomatic consultations between Washington, London, and Paris.

---

[66] *Vietnamese Foreign Ministry White Book on Relations with China*, FE/6238/6 October, FE/6242/11 October 1979; *Beijing Review*, 23 November 1979, 30 November 1979, and 7 December 1979.

[67] See Pierre Asselin, 'Choosing Peace: Hanoi and the Geneva Agreement on Vietnam, 1954–1955', *Journal of Cold War Studies*, Volume 9, Number 2, Spring 2007, pp. 95–126.

[68] See *Beijing Review*, 23 November 1979, 30 November 1979, and 7 December 1979

[69] Zhai Qiang, 'China and the Geneva Conference of 1954', *The China Quarterly*, Number 129, March 1992, p. 112.

[70] See *Beijing Review*, 23 November 1979, 30 November 1979, and 7 December 1979.

The Vietnamese and the Chinese preferences also diverged over recognition of the resistance governments of the Pathet Lao and Khmer Issarak, both protégés of the Vietminh. At the first plenary session of the Geneva Conference on 9 May 1954, the communist bloc was united in demanding that both the Pathet Lao and Khmer Issarak must be recognised and represented. The non-communist governments objected, leading to a month-long stalemate. On 10 June, British Foreign Secretary Anthony Eden, one of the co-chairs of the conference, told the delegates that the differences were so wide that they must either make serious efforts to resolve them or accept failure. Three days later, Bedell Smith, the US assistant secretary of state, announced that he would be leaving Geneva at the end of the week. There were indications that the remaining ministers were also preparing to leave Geneva. A breakdown of the conference was imminent. On 16 June, in a restricted session between Chinese Premier Zhou Enlai and Anthony Eden, the Chinese broke ranks with the Vietminh when Zhou told the British foreign secretary that he could persuade the Vietminh to withdraw from Laos and Cambodia and that Beijing would recognise the royal governments of the two states on the condition that no American bases would be established there. According to James Cable, a member of the British delegation to the conference, 'after some polemics, Pham Van Dong (who was North Vietnam's Prime Minister and Head of the North Vietnamese delegation to the conference) seemed prepared, not very graciously, to acquiesce in Zhou's proposal'.[71]

Finally, the Chinese again pressured the Vietnamese to concede on the issue of the temporary demarcation of North and South Vietnam. Hoang Van Hoan recalled that he accompanied Zhou Enlai to consult with Ho Chi Minh in Liuzhou, a city near the Sino-Vietnamese border on 3–5 July 1954 concerning the temporary demarcation of North and South Vietnam and other issues. The Liuzhou meeting clearly showed Chinese pressure on the Vietnamese. Recent Vietnamese sources revealed that Ho and his top military commander, Vo Nguyen Giap, sought to gain the 13th parallel as the dividing line between North and South but were prepared to accept no less than the 16th parallel. Zhou said that he would try his best

---

[71] James Cable, *The Geneva Conference of 1954 on IndoChina* (London: Macmillan, 1986), p. 97.

to secure that, failing which he told an astonished Ho and Giap that they would have to settle for the 17th parallel. The 17th parallel was the demarcation line that John Foster Dulles had proposed to the French in late June. True enough, on 20 June, the Vietnamese side was forced to accept the 17th parallel.[72] At the Liuzhou meeting, Ho was also pressured to agree to the Chinese view that the Pathet Lao should only hold two provinces and the Khmer Issarak would be immediately demobilised. When the Geneva Agreements were eventually signed and the Chinese text was distributed describing how essential Chinese help had been in achieving the 'great victory', Pham Van Dong was incensed at China for having acquiesced to a division of the country. Privately, he felt that Zhou Enlai had double-crossed the Vietnamese revolution.[73]

Zhou Enlai never denied that he had put pressure on the Vietminh. The Chinese were able to negotiate directly with the French on fundamental points in reaching a solution to the Indochina question at the expense of the Vietnamese communists because Beijing was their sole military supplier and in control of the only aid supply route to Vietnam. When South Vietnam President Ngo Dinh Diem subsequently reneged on the Geneva Agreements in 1956, Zhou Enlai was apparently very upset although not surprised. He told Harrison Salisbury of the *New York Times* that 'never again' would he 'put pressure' on Hanoi to accept an international solution to the war modelled on the 1954 Geneva Conference. He himself had been 'personally responsible for urging the Vietnamese to go along with the agreement'.[74]

Notable among the Vietnamese who were angered by Chinese pressure at the 1954 Geneva Conference was Le Duan, who would eventually rise to become the first secretary of the VCP in 1960 until his death in 1986. This episode left a deep impression on him.[75]

---

[72] Priscilla Roberts (ed.), *Behind the Bamboo Curtain: China, Vietnam and the World beyond Asia* (Washington, DC: Woodrow Wilson Center Press, 2006), pp. 441–442.

[73] David Chanoff and Doan Van Toai, *Portrait of the Enemy: The Other Side of the War in Vietnam* (London: I. B. Tauris, 1987), p. 26.

[74] Harrison E. Salisbury, *To Peking and beyond: A Report on the New Asia* (New York: Quadrangle, 1973), pp. 225–226, cited in Zhai Qiang, 'China and the Geneva Conference of 1954', *The China Quarterly*, Number 129, March 1992, pp. 103–122.

[75] See Lien-Hang T. Nguyen, *Hanoi's War: An International History of the War for Peace in Vietnam* (Chapel Hill: University of North Carolina Press, 2012).

The Chinese tempered pressure with inducements and economic rewards. Having pressured the Vietnamese to concede to Chinese demands, in late November 1954, discussions on Chinese aid for North Vietnam's economic reconstruction began culminating in an agreement on a substantial aid package which was announced on 24 December 1954. According to the joint communiqué, Chinese aid would be given to rebuild the Hanoi–Nanguan railway, postal and telecommunication facilities, highway construction, civil air service, and water conservancy. Chinese experts would be sent to North Vietnam to give advice on technical matters. The monetary value of the aid package was not revealed, perhaps because China was having financial problems of its own and thus chose to emphasise their technical assistance rather than the monetary value of the aid package. The Chinese People's Relief Administration also donated 10,000 tons of rice and 5 million metres of cloth to the Vietnamese.[76] As Laura Calkins noted, by mid-1955, 'Sino-Vietnamese relations had reached a new plateau in cooperative consolidation which would help the Vietnamese to continue their struggle for unification'.[77] Between 1950 and mid-1978, the total value of China's military and economic aid (including grants and interest-free loans) to Vietnam amounted to more US$20 billion and exceeded that given by the Soviet Union. This is supposedly the 'largest in amount' and of the 'longest duration' among its foreign aid until 1978.[78]

Because of their dependence on Chinese economic and military assistance, Hanoi made it a point to seek Chinese views (but not always), and as far as possible, their concurrence as well. But despite this dependence, Hanoi resisted Chinese pressure to take their side during the Sino-Soviet split (the rift which began in 1956 and culminated in the severance of the relationship in 1969), sever relations with the Soviet Union, and move into the Chinese camp. Hanoi also refused to adhere to Chinese advice (and Moscow's as well)[79] to slow down

---

[76] Laura M. Calkins, *China and the First Vietnam War 1947–54* (London: Routledge, 2013), p. 127.
[77] See Laura M. Calkins, *China and the First Vietnam War 1947–54* (London: Routledge, 2013), pp. 126–130.
[78] Chinese sources from Xinhua and Renmin Ribao cited in B. E. Shinde, *Mao Zedong and the Communist Policies 1927–1978* (New Delhi: Sangam Books, 1993), pp. 95–96.
[79] Soviet assistance was not converted into proportionate political influence. See Ilya Gaiduk, *The Soviet Union and the Vietnam War* (Chicago: Ivan R. Dee, 1966).

the pace of the war with the US. The Vietnamese communists were fully in control of their own decision-making in both the conduct of the war as well as the appropriate timing to negotiate with the US. Ho Chi Minh's death in September 1969 eroded Hanoi's finely calibrated relations with Beijing and Moscow. Ho was also very familiar with China and had good personal relations with the Chinese leadership,[80] which was not the case with Le Duan.

Hanoi was unhappy with both Beijing and Moscow for pursuing détente with the US while the Vietnam War was ongoing. But it was especially unhappy with the Chinese for the Nixon visit in February 1972. As Le Duc Tho recalled, 'the 1972 Agreement between the United States and China marked the beginning of the open and comprehensive collusion between imperialism and the Peking rulers'.[81] According to Ilya Gaiduk, although Chinese influence remained strong in Vietnam through the duration of the Vietnam War, by 1973, because of the Sino-US rapprochement, it had diminished considerably. Moscow was the beneficiary of this development. North Vietnamese officials from 1973 onwards expressed their preference for Soviet views and guidance on important domestic and foreign policy issues.[82] It is worth noting that Hanoi did not comment or report on Nixon's visit to Moscow in July 1974.

In January 1974, Saigon and Beijing clashed over the Paracel Islands, which both sides claimed to belong to them. The Chinese took control of the islands and henceforth 'the disputed islands ... became a time-bomb in the Sino-Vietnamese relations until today'.[83] Beijing reiterated that it had 'indisputable' sovereignty over the Paracel, Spratly, and

[80] For details, see Ang Cheng Guan, *The Vietnam War from the Other Side: The Vietnamese Communists' Perspective* (London: RoutledgeCurzon, 2002) and *Ending the Vietnam War: The Vietnamese Communists' Perspective* (London: RoutledgeCurzon, 2004).

[81] Anthony Barnett, 'Interview with Le Duc Tho', in Anthony Barnett and John Pilger, *Aftermath: The Struggle of Cambodia and Vietnam*, NS Report 5, 1982, pp. 54–59.

[82] Ilya Gaiduk, *The Soviet Union and the Vietnam War* (Chicago: Ivan R. Dee, 1966), pp. 247–248; Stephen J. Morris, *The Soviet–Chinese–Vietnamese Triangle in the 1970s: The View from Moscow*, Working Paper 25, Cold War International History Project, April 1999, pp. 19–21.

[83] For an account of the naval battle, see Xiaobing Li, *The Dragon in the Jungle: The Chinese Army in the Vietnam War* (New York: Oxford University Press, 2020), pp. 216–219.

Pratas Islands as well as the Macclesfield Bank.[84] Hanoi, preoccupied by its war with Saigon, could only raise a lame protest in private. In March 1974, Hanoi closed the only Chinese-language newspaper and suspended the activities of the Sino-Vietnamese Friendship Association. The high profile accorded to Khieu Samphan's visit to Beijing in April 1974, where he met Mao Zedong, compared to the low-key publicity given to Pham Van Dong's visit in the same month clearly showed that Sino-Vietnamese relations were not well. By August, Zhou was too ill to oversee the bilateral relationship and Le Thanh Nghi's visits to Beijing in August and October 1974 failed to extract any significant economic and military assistance from China. The relations deteriorated so much that the Chinese indicated that they were ready to have direct and independent contact with the Provisional Revolutionary Government in South Vietnam, bypassing Hanoi. While never publicly declared, it was not a secret that Beijing preferred two separate Vietnams rather than a united Vietnam as the latter could potentially pose a threat to China's south-western border.[85]

---

[84] 'Statement of the Spokesman of the Ministry of External Affairs of the PRC', 11 January 1974, *BBC/SWB/FE/4459*, 14 January 1974.
[85] See Ang Cheng Guan, *Ending the Vietnam War: The Vietnamese Communists' Perspective* (London: RoutledgeCurzon, 2004), pp. 164–165.

2 From the Fall of Saigon to the Invasion of Cambodia (April 1975–December 1978)

I

April 1975 is a significant month, the highpoint of the communists in Indochina. On 17 April, the Khmer Rouge captured Phnom Penh, bringing an end to the fight between the communists and anti-communists (backed by the US particularly after the ouster of Sihanouk in March 1970). On 30 April, Saigon fell to the Vietnamese communists, marking the end of the Second Vietnam War. In December, the Pathet Lao (supported by the Vietnamese communists throughout the civil war in Laos) took full control of Laos. By the end of 1975, the whole of Indochina was communist. Unbeknown to those outside the communist camp, it was also a low point in Vietnam–Cambodia relations as well as Sino-Vietnamese relations, though not yet the nadir. This chapter describes and explain how the relationships further deteriorated from where we left off in Chapter 1, from April 1975 culminating in Vietnam's invasion of Cambodia at the end-1978.

Soon after the victories of both the Khmer Rouge in Cambodia and the Vietnamese communists in Vietnam, the Khmer Rouge and their Vietnamese counterparts in May 1975 began fighting over territory. In early May, Khmer Rouge forces launched 'small-scale but violent attacks' along their border with southern Vietnam. The Khmer Rouge accused the Vietnamese of refusing to vacate the sanctuaries in Cambodian territory that they established during the Vietnam War.[1] Both sides also briefly fought after the Khmer Rouge took over the Vietnamese Tho Chu (Poulo Panjang) and was subsequently expelled by the Vietnamese. Before that, the Khmer attacked the Vietnamese-controlled island of Phu Quoc. The dispute over their sea border was because the Khmer Rouge did not agree to the interpretation of the 1939

---

[1] See *Black Paper: Facts and Evidences of the Acts of Aggression and Annexation of Vietnam against Kampuchea* (Department of Press and Information of the Ministry of Democratic Kampuchea, September 1978), Chapter 6.

Brevie Line drawn up by France for administrative purpose during the colonial phase of their histories.[2] A June 1976 meeting in Phnom Penh failed to resolve their differences. According to the Vietnamese, agreement was in fact reached to settle the dispute and negotiations began, but they were prematurely terminated by the Khmer Rouge.[3] Pol Pot's visit to Hanoi (11–14 June 1975) and Le Duan's visit to Cambodia in late July 1975 did not lead to any improvement in bilateral relations. The border disputes persisted through 1977 and 1978. There is general agreement that while the 'border dispute is at once secondary and crucial' to the Vietnam–Cambodia war, it was not the cause of the conflict. As Stephen Heder explained, it is secondary because it is symptomatic of wider disagreements between the two sides and because 'only a small area is in dispute'. It is crucial because the Khmer Rouge 'uses it to gauge Vietnamese attitudes' and it is also a 'measurement of the regime's nationalist credentials'.[4] As Gabriel Kolko noted, the border dispute reflected 'Phnom Penh's provocative internal strategy, with its need for conjuring an external threat'.[5] The Khmer Rouge believed that the Vietnamese were illegally occupying Cambodian territory and the Vietnamese refusal to withdraw their forces from the disputed areas transformed the frontier into a 'military flashpoint'.[6] It is worth noting that border negotiations continue to this day.[7]

---

[2] For a discussion of the ownership of Phu Quoc or Koh Tral (to the Cambodians), see Jeff Mudrick, 'Cambodia's impossible dream: Koh Tral', *The Diplomat*, 17 June 2014.

[3] For details, see Wilfred Burchett, *The China Cambodia Vietnam Triangle* (London: Zed Press, 1981), pp. 144–147; Thu-huong Nguyen-vo, *Khmer-Viet Relations and the Third Indochina Conflict* (Jefferson: McFarland & Company, Inc., Publishers), pp. 78–80; Julio Jeldres, 'Cambodia Relations with Vietnam: Historical Mistrust and Vulnerability', *Journal of Greater Mekong Studies*, Volume 2, Number 1, February 2020, pp. 69–70; *Vietnam-Cambodia Conflict, Report Prepared at the Request of the Subcommittee of Asian and Pacific Affairs Committee of International Relations by the Congressional Research Service, Library of Congress* (Washington, DC: US Government Printing Office, 1978), pp. 8–9.

[4] Stephen Heder, 'Origins of the Conflict', *Southeast Asia Chronicle*, Number 64, September/October 1978, pp. 17–18.

[5] Gabriel Kolko, 'Avoiding Misconceptions about Indochina', *Journal of Contemporary Asia*, Volume 9, Number 1, 1979, p. 117.

[6] Stephen Heder, 'Origins of the Conflict', *Southeast Asia Chronicle*, Number 64, September/October 1978, pp. 17–18.

[7] 'VN, Kingdom agree major border line segments: PM', *Phnom Penh Post*, 22 May 2022.

The following episode recounted by Julio Jeldres best encapsulates the Khmer Rouge attitude towards the Vietnamese. Sihanouk attended Vietnam's first National Day on 2 September 1975, at the invitation of the Vietnamese. When in Hanoi, Prime Minister Pham Van Dong suggested to Sihanouk that the '"brothers and comrade in arms" from North Vietnam and representatives from the South, Laos and Cambodia should meet over a joint dinner'. Khieu Samphan intervened and said to Dong that they were happy to accept a 'bipartite dinner' between Hanoi, the host, and the Cambodian delegation. Khieu Samphan would later tell Sihanouk that 'we must never fall in the trap prepared by these Viets who wish to dominate and swallow up our Kampuchea by incorporating it in their Indochinese Federation. We must remain very vigilant. This projected quadripartite dinner was a dangerous trap! We must not fall into it.'[8]

According to the Vietnamese side, the Khmer Rouge ignored several requests from Hanoi to sign a friendship treaty (a friendship treaty between the Vietnamese and the Laotians was signed in July 1977[9]). The Khmer Rouge account, however, claimed that it was they who proposed a friendship and non-aggression treaty in June 1975 when Pol Pot led a top-ranking delegation to Hanoi. The Khmer Rouge further accused the Vietnamese of attempting to assassinate their top leadership, including Pol Pot.[10] This would explain the killings of thousands of Cambodians suspected of colluding with the Vietnamese – 'Khmer bodies with Vietnamese minds', most notably in the Eastern Zone.[11] All who opposed Pol Pot's policies on any issue were considered 'traitorous, part of a Vietnamese plot to dispose of the only group who

---

[8] Julio Jeldres, 'Cambodia Relations with Vietnam: Historical Mistrust and Vulnerability', *Journal of Greater Mekong Studies*, Volume 2, Number 1, February 2020, pp. 70–71.

[9] In the words of Norodom Sihanouk, 'the Laotian leadership is more Vietnamese than anything ... The Laotian civil service, public works, economy, are actually headed and staff by Vietnamese.' See Norodom Sihanouk, *War and Hope: The Case for Cambodia* (New York: Pantheon Books, 1980), pp. 99–100.

[10] *Black Paper: Facts and Evidences of the Acts of Aggression and Annexation of Vietnam against Kampuchea* (Department of Press and Information of the Ministry of Democratic Kampuchea, September 1978), pp. 75–76.

[11] Ben Kiernan, 'Wild Chickens, Farm Chickens, and Cormorants: Kampuchea's Eastern Zone under Pol Pot', in David P. Chandler and Ben Kiernan (eds), *Revolution and Its Aftermath in Kampuchea: Eight Essays* (Monograph Series No. 25, Yale University Southeast Asia Studies, 1983), p. 138.

could defeat Vietnamese designs to establish political control over Kampuchea. As a result, criticism was never evaluated and taken into consideration, it was simply labelled as treason and dealt with accordingly.'[12]

Only after Pol Pot, the arch anti-Vietnamese, had eliminated all those who opposed him and consolidated his position did he have the full authority to turn fully against Vietnam. In February 1977, Vietnamese deputy Foreign Minister Hoang Van Loi failed to persuade Cambodia to participate in another Indochina Summit. Relations continued to deteriorate to the point that the Khmer Communist Party Central Committee in June 1977 issued a resolution identifying 'Vietnam as our enemy number 1, our eternal enemy'.

It is here that we must introduce Hun Sen, then a 25-year-old regimental commander in region 21, Eastern Zone, who would become a major protagonist in our narrative to this day. On the night of 20 June 1977, Hun Sen (along with four comrades) defected to Vietnam. Hun Sen's June 'heroic' escape has since been mythologised in present-day Cambodia. As Kosal Path and Boraden Nhem noted, towards the second half of 1977, Pol Pot's purge of 'real and perceived "Vietnamese agents"' had reached the lower echelons of the Eastern Zone, where Hun Sen was 'a potential target'.[13] Hun Sen's defection coincided with Hanoi's plan to 'establish an anti-Pol Pot Cambodian revolution in southern Vietnam to take over Cambodia'. Having won the trust of the Vietnamese, Hun Sen (with their support) was able to organise the first army unit – Unit 125 comprising Cambodian refugees and Khmer Rouge defectors – of the new Cambodian revolution. Unit 125 was the early beginning of the Royal Cambodian Armed Forces (RCAF),

---

[12] Martin Stuart-Fox and Bunhaeng Ung, *The Murderous Revolution: Bunhaeng Ung's Life with Death in Pol Pot's Kampuchea* (Bangkok: The Tamarind Press, 1986), pp. 163–164.

[13] For details of the escape and subsequent developments in Vietnam, see Kosal Path and Boraden Nhem, 'Vietnam's Military and Political Challenges in Cambodia, and the Early Rise of Cambodia's Strongman, Hun Sen, 1977–79', TRaNS, www.cambridge.org/core/journals/trans-trans-regional-and-national-studies-of-southeast-asia/article/abs/vietnams-military-and-political-challenges-in-cambodia-and-the-early-rise-of-cambodias-strongman-hun-sen-197779/ C0B8E412FF295B7C38569FCE7F993A69 (published online on 26 July 2021), accessed on 22 August 2022; Harish C. Mehta and Julie B. Mehta, *Strongman: The Extraordinary Life of Hun Sen* (Singapore: Marshall Cavendish Editions, 2013), chapter 4.

and the veterans remain Prime Minister Hun Sen's most loyal generals today.[14] Hun Sen has always insisted that he is not a communist. He joined the Khmer Rouge not 'because of any allegiance to communism by any stretch of imagination but instead in response to the then-deposed, but beloved head of state, Prince Sihanouk'.[15] Indeed, he turned from an ardent supporter to become a 'fierce opponent' of the prince only after the Vietnamese invaded Cambodia.[16]

The rapid slide in the relationship was described by Vietnam's Deputy Foreign Minister Nguyen Co Thach to Wilfred Burchett – between 1970 and 1975, the Khmer Rouge considered Vietnam as its 'Number 1 friend' (although this author rather doubts this – see Chapter 1). After April 1975, China moved to first place and Vietnam dropped to seventh position. By April 1977, Vietnam had become 'enemy Number 1' and China remained its 'Number 1' friend.[17] Indeed, according to Sihanouk, Khieu Samphan told him that the Vietnamese had always been the 'enemy number one' and 'American imperialism only occupying second place as far as enemies of Kampuchea were concerned'.[18]

Because the border issues remained unresolved, except for the brief lull between mid-1975 and 1976, the fighting continued, and these grew from skirmishes to increasingly large-scale clashes, particularly from late September 1977. According to Bui Tin, the fighting became progressively more severe, especially after a massacre at Chau Doc on the night of 30 April 1977, which was also the second anniversary of the fall of Saigon.[19] In September 1977, the intensified border conflict

---

[14] Kosal Path and Boraden Nhem, 'Vietnam's Military and Political Challenges in Cambodia, and the Early Rise of Cambodia's Strongman, Hun Sen, 1977–79', TRaNS, www.cambridge.org/core/journals/trans-trans-regional-and-national-studies-of-southeast-asia/article/abs/vietnams-military-and-political-challenges-in-cambodia-and-the-early-rise-of-cambodias-strongman-hun-sen-197779/C0B8E412FF295B7C38569FCE7F993A69 (published online on 26 July 2021), accessed on 22 August 2022.

[15] Nem Sowath, *Civil War Termination and the Source of Total Peace in Cambodia* (Phnom Penh: Ponleu Khmer Printing House, 2012), pp. 306–307.

[16] Pov Sok, *Samdech Hun Sen: Supreme Founder and Father of Peace of Cambodia* (Phnom Penh: Ponleu Khmer Printing and Publishing House, 2021), p. 197.

[17] Wilfred Burchett, *The China Cambodia Vietnam Triangle* (London: Zed Press, 1981), pp. 148–149.

[18] Ben Kiernan and Chanthou Boua (eds), *Peasants and Politics in Kampuchea 1942–1981* (London: Zed Press, 1982), p. 265.

[19] Bui Tin, *Following Ho Chi Minh: Memoirs of a North Vietnamese Colonel* (London: Hurst and Company, 1995), p. 116.

coincided with Pol Pot's highly publicised and triumphant visit to China where he was warmly welcomed by Hua Guofeng, Mao's successor. At his meeting with Hua, Pol Pot said that he had successfully eliminated all 'Vietnamese agents'.[20]

His visit was preceded by a lengthy speech revealing the existence of the CPK and extolling its singular role in the revolutionary struggle.[21] Hanoi tried to get the Chinese to mediate without success. The warm welcome of Pol Pot and Chinese failure to mediate – it is not clear whether it was a case of unwilling or unable – created the impression, in the eyes of the Vietnamese, that Beijing supported the Khmer Rouge actions. According to Soviet sources, the presence of Chinese military personnel training and arming the Khmer Rouge, and building roads and military bases, including an Air Force base in Kampong Chhnang which made it possible for military planes to reach Ho Chi Minh City in half an hour, forced the Vietnamese 'to think about the real threat to its security rather than about an Indochinese federation'.[22] In addition, on 18 July 1977, a Treaty of Friendship and Cooperation was signed between Vietnam and Laos. Vietnam had thus consolidated its 'special relationship' with Laos with little opposition. In the view of Hanoi, if it were not for Beijing's conspicuous support for the Khmer Rouge, Phnom Penh would have followed the path of Vientiane. China was thus seen as the obstacle preventing the Vietnamese from realising their aspiration of an Indo-China Federation – a repeat of what happened in 1954.

---

[20] Kosal Path and Boraden Nhem, 'Vietnam's Military and Political Challenges in Cambodia, and the Early Rise of Cambodia's Strongman, Hun Sen, 1977–79', TRaNS, www.cambridge.org/core/journals/trans-trans-regional-and-national-studies-of-southeast-asia/article/abs/vietnams-military-and-political-challenges-in-cambodia-and-the-early-rise-of-cambodias-strongman-hun-sen-197779/C0B8E412FF295B7C38569FCE7F993A69 (published online on 26 July 2021), accessed on 22 August 2022.

[21] For the intensity of the border fighting, see Bui Tin, *Following Ho Chi Minh: Memoirs of a North Vietnamese Colonel* (London: Hurst and Company, 1995), p. 116.

[22] Dmitry Mosyakov, 'The Khmer Rouge and the Vietnamese Communists: A History of Their Relations as Told in the Soviet Archives', p. 68, www.isn.ethz.ch/isn/Digital-Library/Publications/Detail/?lng=en&id=46645. There was an agreement signed on 17 July 1976 for Chinese troops to build the biggest airport in Southeast Asia at Kampong Chnang. See Bui Tin, *Following Ho Chi Minh: Memoirs of a North Vietnamese Colonel* (London: Hurst and Company, 1995), pp. 120–121.

On 30 September 1977, there was a Politburo meeting in Ho Chi Minh City chaired by Le Duan to evaluate the situation. The Politburo came up with two options: (1) facilitate a victory of the 'healthy' (meaning pro-Vietnam) forces inside Cambodia; (2) pressure Pol Pot to negotiate in a worsening situation. The opening move to achieve either option was to shift Vietnam's border war strategy from defensive to offensive.[23] The Vietnamese made one further (and futile) attempt to get the Chinese to intercede with the Khmer Rouge when Le Duan met with the Chinese leadership in Beijing in November. The November meeting also showed up the strains in Sino-Vietnamese relations.[24]

On 25 December 1977, to the surprise of the Khmer Rouge, Vietnamese forces invaded eastern Cambodia and briefly occupied the territory (in retaliation for the Khmer Rouge attack on Tay Ninh province in September) before withdrawing,[25] much to the dismay of Hun Sen.[26] The fighting along the Cambodia–South Vietnam border has been described as 'the most serious so far'[27] when the Vietnamese attacked deep into various parts of the Eastern Zone of Cambodia and withdrew soon after.[28] Pol Pot used the Vietnamese withdrawal (on its own volition) to claim it as 'the greatest victory in Khmer history'.[29]

It was clearly an exercise of intimidation by the Vietnamese and a warning to the Khmer Rouge. Not to be cowed, Phnom Penh also

---

[23] Dmitry Mosyakov, 'The Khmer Rouge and the Vietnamese Communists: A History of Their Relations as Told in the Soviet Archives', p. 69, www.isn.ethz.ch/isn/Digital-Library/Publications/Detail/?lng=en&id=46645.

[24] Nayan Chanda, *Brother Enemy: The War after the War: A History of Indochina since the Fall of Saigon* (New York: Colliers Books, 1986), pp. 201–203; 'Le Duan of Vietnam meets with Peking's leader', *New York Times*, 22 November 1977.

[25] See Elizabeth Becker, *When the War Was Over: Cambodia and the Khmer Rouge Revolution* (New York: Public Affairs, 1986), pp. 310–311.

[26] Harish C. Mehta and Julie B. Mehta, *Strongman: The Extraordinary Life of Hun Sen* (Singapore: Marshall Cavendish Editions, 2013), p. 114.

[27] David P. Chandler, *Brother Number One: A Political Biography of Pol Pot* (Boulder: Westview Press, 1992), p. 250.

[28] For details, see *Black Paper: Facts and Evidences of the Acts of Aggression and Annexation of Vietnam against Kampuchea* (Department of Press and Information of the Ministry of Democratic Kampuchea, September 1978), pp. 77–78; Wilfred Burchett, *The China Cambodia Vietnam Triangle* (London: Zed Press, 1981), pp. 149–155; Philip Short, *Pol Pot: Anatomy of a Nightmare* (New York: Henry Holt and Company, 2004), pp. 373–378.

[29] See Wilfred Burchett, *The China Cambodia Vietnam Triangle* (London: Zed Press, 1981), p. 151.

surprised the Vietnamese by breaking off diplomatic relations on 31 December 1977. The tensions and dispute between the two fraternal communist countries, which had been kept away from the limelight, finally became public for the first time. It would be another year before the Vietnamese leadership invaded Kampuchea and took control of Phnom Penh and the country. Sihanouk's analysis of the Vietnamese 'blitzkrieg' is worth highlighting here. While, on the surface, it appeared to be a failure, the Vietnamese gained 150,000 Khmer refugees which helped to 'furnish the Kampuchean United Front for National Salvation (KUFNS) formed in early December 1978 in Kratie province, near the Vietnam–Cambodia border to overthrow the Pol Pot regime'. Pol Pot's 'overweening pride' proclaiming the 'Victory of 6 January 1978' led to 'serious misjudgments of the enemy'.[30]

Why didn't the Vietnamese People's Army go all the way in December 1977, instead stopping twenty-four miles from Phnom Penh and then withdrawing and waiting for another twelve months? One reason was that in 1977–1978, there were some quarters in the party who held the view that 'the contradictions between the US and China would prevent the formation of an anti-Soviet and anti-Vietnamese alliance' and as such the anti-Maoists led by Deng Xiaoping in China would eventually choose the Soviet Union (and Vietnam) over the US.[31] These people would need to be convinced or neutralised. Thus, we must now turn to consider the state of Vietnam as well as Cambodia's relations with China, the Soviet Union, and the US until the end of 1977 before focusing on the critical year 1978.

II

Recall from Chapter 1 that Sino-Vietnamese relations, which had never been warm despite all the professions of both countries being as close as 'lips and teeth', turned complicated in July 1971 (coincidentally around the time when relations between the Khmer Rouge and

---

[30] Norodom Sihanouk, *War and Hope: The Case for Cambodia* (New York: Pantheon Books, 1980), chapter 12, pp. 69–71.

[31] Gareth Porter's interviews with Central Committee member of the VCP, Tran Phuong, 20 January 1981 and with Nguyen Co Thach, 16 November 1978 cited in Gareth Porter, 'Hanoi's Strategic Perspective and the Sino-Vietnamese Conflict', *Pacific Affairs*, Volume 57, Number 1, Spring 1984, pp. 7–25, nn. 67 and 68.

the Vietnamese communists were turning bad) with the announcement of President Nixon's forthcoming visit (to take place before May 1972) to Beijing.

Compared to the Vietnamese leadership's visits to China in 1974 (described in Chapter 1), as well as Le Duan's September 1975 visit, Pol Pot's visit to Beijing in June 1975 was better received by the Chinese and Mao lavished much praise on Pol Pot and the success of the Khmer Rouge. Pol Pot, on his part, projected himself as an ideological disciple of Mao. In a conversation with Pol Pot on 21 June 1975, Mao Zedong told him: 'We approve of what you do ... You are basically correct. I am not sure if you have any shortcoming. There are bound to be some and you rectify by yourself'.[32] We now know much more about Sino-Cambodian/Kampuchean relations due to the recent research of Sophie Richardson and Andrew Mertha.[33] In her book, Richardson showed that Beijing 'was neither ignoring Phnom Penh nor restraining its malignant policies' and that Beijing was not only aware of the Khmer Rouge leadership's 'proclivities toward extreme brutality, but it also in some cases facilitated them'. From her interviews with Chinese diplomats, the reason for the Chinese failure to intervene was 'a complex mix of beliefs consistent with the Five Principles (of peaceful coexistence)'.[34] Mertha, on the other hand, showed that the Chinese were not always able to influence Khmer Rouge policy decisions even if they wanted to. His study shows 'an emerging pattern in which Chinese proposals were adopted if they served DK (Democratic Kampuchea) interests but were politely but firmly brushed aside by the Cambodians if they did not'. But most importantly, there is general agreement among scholars that Chinese military aid and assistance to the Khmer Rouge was substantial and wide ranging and that 'no foreign country was more important to DK than China, particularly

---

[32] 21 June 1975 Conversation Record of Chairman Mao Zedong's Meeting with Pol Pot, Secretary of the Central Committee of the Communist Party of Kampuchea, https://digitalarchive.wilsoncenter.org/document/122052.
[33] Sophie Richardson, *China, Cambodia, and the Five Principles of Peaceful Coexistence* (New York: Columbia University Press, 2010); Andrew Mertha, *Brothers in Arms: Chinese Aid to the Khmer Rouge, 1975–1979* (Ithaca, NY: Cornell University Press, 2014). See also, John D. Ciociari, 'China and the Pol Pot regime', *Cold War History*, Volume 14, Number 2, 2014, pp. 215–235.
[34] Sophie Richardson, *China, Cambodia, and the Five Principles of Peaceful Coexistence* (New York: Columbia University Press, 2010), pp. 91–92.

The Fall of Saigon to Invasion of Cambodia (1975-1978) 51

when it came to military assistance'.[35] The Chinese feared losing influence in the region after the Vietnam War, and the deterioration in Sino-Vietnamese relations coupled with Hanoi's closeness to the Soviet Union meant that 'Beijing was willing to give DK whatever it wanted, as long as it guaranteed China a foothold in Indochina'.[36] As Qiang Zhai also noted, 'realising the determination and strength of the Khmer Rouge, Chinese leaders had apparently taken the position that if they wanted to maintain their influence over the Vietnamese and the Russians in Cambodia, they must back Pol Pot'.[37] Asked how Kampuchea, with 5-6 million people, dared to take on a battle-hardened Vietnam with a population of over fifty million, Nguyen Co Thach countered, 'why would Israel with a population of 3 million dare to invade Egypt with its population of 35 million? Because the Khmer Rouge are assured they have 800 million Chinese behind them, as Israel has the might of the United States to rely on'.[38] Mertha sums it up well when he wrote, 'without Chinese support, the DK regime would almost certainly have collapsed'.[39]

There is quite a sizeable body of writings on Sino-Vietnamese relations.[40] Besides the issues highlighted in Chapter 1, Hanoi and Beijing had disputes over their land and sea boundaries. Beijing was also unhappy with what it saw as Hanoi's anti-China propaganda and the treatment of Chinese residing in Vietnam.[41] Hanoi was unhappy with the reduction of Chinese economic assistance to Vietnam, particularly post-1975, and was unconvinced that it was due to the 'interference and

---

[35] Andrew Mertha, *Brothers in Arms: Chinese Aid to the Khmer Rouge, 1975-1979* (Ithaca, NY: Cornell University Press, 2014), p. 79.
[36] Andrew Mertha, *Brothers in Arms: Chinese Aid to the Khmer Rouge, 1975-1979* (Ithaca, NY: Cornell University Press, 2014), p. 78.
[37] Qiang Zhai, *China and the Vietnam Wars, 1950-1975* (Chapel Hill: University of North Carolina Press, 2000), pp. 212-213.
[38] Wilfred Burchett, *The China Cambodia Vietnam Triangle* (London: Zed Press, 1981), p. 149. Burchett interviewed Nguyen Co Thach in October 1978.
[39] Andrew Mertha, *Brothers in Arms: Chinese Aid to the Khmer Rouge, 1975-1979* (Ithaca, NY: Cornell University Press, 2014), p. 15. See also, Roger Faligot, *Chinese Spies from Chairman Mao to Xi Jinping* (Melbourne: Scribe Press, 2019), pp. 103-104.
[40] See Bibliography.
[41] All the issues were spelled out in 'Memorandum Outlining Vice-Premier Li Xiannian's Talk with Premier Pham Van Dong on 10 June 1977', *United Nations General Assembly and Security Council, A/34/189, S/13255, 18 April 1979*.

sabotage by the antiparty "gang of four" and the natural calamities' which had affected the Chinese economy (as explained by the Chinese side),[42] especially so when, during Pol Pot's June 1975 visit, he was promised more than $1 billion in economic and military assistance. The Vietnamese 'ever-growing' aid requests were indeed enormous.[43] Hanoi interpreted the drastic cuts in Chinese aid as 'Beijing's attempt to weaken Vietnam and limit its role in the region', which was not an unreasonable assumption given the common knowledge that China's would have preferred two separate Vietnams rather than the unified Vietnam achieved in April 1975.

If Pol Pot was the arch anti-Vietnamese, Deng Xiaoping (who returned to power in mid-1977) had developed a 'hatred toward the Vietnamese for their ingratitude'[44] while Le Duan 'detested China's "big brother" attitude toward Vietnam'.[45] It is perhaps worth noting that Pol Pot detested Vietnam's 'big brother attitude' while the Vietnamese accused the Pol Pot regime as being ungrateful.[46] At the 4th Party Congress of the Vietnamese Worker's Party in December 1976, the party leadership was purged of almost all the ostensibly pro-China group, the most prominent being Hoang Van Hoan, an old associate of Ho Chi Minh and Vietnam's first ambassador to China.[47] In February 1977, Beijing informed the Vietnamese that China was unable to provide any new economic aid (although Chinese financial

---

[42] 'Memorandum Outlining Vice-Premier Li Xiannian's Talk with Premier Pham Van Dong on 10 June 1977', *United Nations General Assembly and Security Council, A/34/189, S/13255, 18 April 1979*.

[43] Shu Guang Zhang, *Beijing's Economic Statecraft during the Cold War, 1949–1991* (Washington, DC: Woodrow Wilson Center Press, 2014), pp. 258–259.

[44] Kosal Path, *Sino-Vietnamese Relations, 1950–1978: From Cooperation to Conflict*, unpublished PhD thesis, University of Southern California, December 2008, p. 237.

[45] Kosal Path, *Vietnam's Strategic Thinking during the Third Indochina War* (Madison: University of Wisconsin Press, 2020), p. 25.

[46] Bernard K. Gordon, 'The Third Indochina Conflict', *Foreign Affairs*, Fall 1986, p. 69. Gordon recalled Nguyen Co Thach describing 'strongly and emotionally' to him the ingratitude of the Khmer Rouge during his visit to Hanoi in 1980. Other Vietnamese leaders had also described the Khmer Rouge as an 'ungrateful upstart'.

[47] See Ralph Smith, 'Vietnam's Fourth Party Congress', *The World Today*, Volume 33, Number 5, May 1977, pp. 195–202; Haong Van Hoan, *A Drop in the Ocean* (Beijing: Foreign Languages Press, 1988), pp. 353–360. Hoan would eventually defect to China in July 1979 where he lived until his death in 1991.

and technical aid to Cambodia was unaffected). It was Beijing's way of showing displeasure with the conduct and outcome of the 4th Party Congress. China's '"punitive" aid cut and trade policy toward Vietnam' inevitably caused Vietnam to turn even more towards the Soviet Union for aid.[48] Sino-Vietnamese relations took a dive and did not recovered until the 1990s.

Having said that, until early 1978, Hanoi remained unwilling to openly side with the Soviet Union in the Sino-Soviet ideological dispute and continued to strike a balance between Moscow and Beijing, at least on the surface. Vietnamese archival documents from the Ministry of Defence, Ministry of Foreign Trade, and Ministry of Foreign Affairs (seen by Kosal Path) revealed that there was an ongoing internal debate at the highest level of the Vietnamese leadership. For a short period, 'Hanoi's economics minded leaders succeeded in convincing the Party line, as opposed to the military leaders' argument for a formal military alliance with the Soviet Union against China, to maintain "restraint" and to recognize the continued relevance and importance of China's remaining substantial aid to Vietnam's post-1975 national reconstruction and alleviation of its poverty'.[49]

The Vietnamese communists had their share of disagreements with the Soviets,[50] beginning with the 1954 Geneva Conference. They continued to procrastinate over joining the Russian-led Council for Mutual Economic Assistance (COMECON) despite Soviet 'measured pressure'. Kosal Path's research into the Vietnamese archive shows that top Vietnamese diplomats attributed Moscow's suspension of industrial projects for Vietnam and rejection of Vietnam's emergency aid request for food and fuel in 1977 to Hanoi's official refusal to join

---

[48] Kosal Path, *Sino-Vietnamese Relations, 1950–1978: From Cooperation to Conflict*, unpublished PhD thesis, University of Southern California, December 2008, p. 238.

[49] Kosal Path, *Sino-Vietnamese Relations, 1950–1978: From Cooperation to Conflict*, unpublished PhD thesis, University of Southern California, December 2008, p. 318; Kosal Path, *Vietnam's Strategic Thinking during the Third Indochina War* (Madison: University of Wisconsin Press, 2020), chapter 1.

[50] See Lorenz M. Luthi, 'Beyond Betrayal: Beijing, Moscow and the Paris Negotiations, 1971–1973', *Journal of Cold War Studies*, Volume 11, Number 1, Winter 2009, pp. 57–107; Tuong Vu, *Vietnam's Communist Revolution: The Power and Limits of Ideology* (Cambridge: Cambridge University Press, 2017), pp. 210–211.

COMECON and side with the Soviet Union.[51] It can be said that the increasing Sino-Vietnamese animosity played into the hands of the Soviet Union, which seized the opportunity to increase its influence in Vietnam.

Moscow, on the other hand, had very little direct knowledge of the Khmer Rouge and Soviet–Khmer Rouge relations were next to non-existent.[52] Apparently, when Pol Pot reached out to the Soviets in 1966, Moscow had 'yet to decide on the forms and scale of its participation in the new Indochina war' and thus did not accord him with the respect he expected and henceforth relations never developed.[53] Apparently, when Phnom Penh fell in April 1975, a Khmer Rouge detachment summarily moved to expel Soviet diplomats from the Soviet embassy and took down the Russian flag. According to Sihanouk, 'Brezhnev's representatives never forgave the Khmer Rouge for this'. Between 1975 and 1977, 'the entire Soviet bloc made a prodigious effort to ingratiate themselves' with the Khmer Rouge leaders, 'hoping against hope that their friendliness, however spurious', would win over them. In his account, Sihanouk was making the point that Moscow had every reason to go along with what the Vietnamese decided with regard to Cambodia.[54]

We must now turn to the US. There are two points which should be mentioned at the outset. First, as Ted Osius (former US ambassador to Vietnam) reminded us in his memoir, when the Vietnam War ended in April 1975, then US President Gerald Ford 'wanted Congress and the

---

[51] Kosal Path, *Vietnam's Strategic Thinking during the Third Indochina War* (Madison: University of Wisconsin Press, 2020), p. 30.

[52] Dmitry Mosyakov, *The Khmer Rouge and the Vietnamese Communists: A History of Their Relations as Told in the Soviet Archives*, https://gsp.yale.edu/sites/default/files/gs15_-_the_khmer_rouge_and_the_vietnamese_communists_a_history_of_their_relations_as_told_in_the_soviet_archives.pdf, pp. 52, 54; *Black Paper: Facts and Evidences of the Acts of Aggression and Annexation of Vietnam against Kampuchea* (Department of Press and Information of the Ministry of Democratic Kampuchea, September 1978), or *Black Paper* for short, p. 33.

[53] Dmitry Mosyakov, *The Khmer Rouge and the Vietnamese Communists: A History of Their Relations as Told in the Soviet Archives*, https://gsp.yale.edu/sites/default/files/gs15_-_the_khmer_rouge_and_the_vietnamese_communists_a_history_of_their_relations_as_told_in_the_soviet_archives.pdf, p. 52.

[54] Norodom Sihanouk, *War and Hope: The Case for Cambodia* (New York: Pantheon Books, 1980), pp. 96–98.

American people to shift their focus from the chaos we (the Americans) had left behind ... Americans didn't want to hear about Indochina'. For twenty years, reconciliation between the US and Vietnam 'progressed slowly' and only after President Bill Clinton established full diplomatic ties in 1995 did it appear possible for both countries to 'begin anew'.[55] Second, while the first step in Sino-US rapprochement began with Nixon's visit to Beijing in February 1972, 'significant improvement in relations between China and the United States was far from inevitable'. Both countries only announced on 15 December 1978 that they would establish formal diplomatic relations on 1 January 1979.[56] However, Beijing and Moscow had a common strategic enemy: the United States.

There is no need to engage in the debate regarding whether American policies and actions in Cambodia during the Vietnam War contributed to the growth of the Khmer Rouge. It is, however, indisputable that Washington had a 'casual disregard for the fate of Laos and Cambodia when compared to the larger strategic prize of southern Vietnam', while Beijing opposed any discussion on Cambodia in an international forum for fear that an agreement reached in an international conference would necessarily involve Moscow and Hanoi, preferring to be 'the main broker'. Zhou Enlai made clear to Kissinger during the discussions between Kissinger and Le Duc Tho in Paris that 'he was the only person that could deliver Sihanouk and the Khmer Rouge'.[57] Under the Ford administration, Washington rarely commented on developments in Cambodia, except in the context of the Indochina refugee problem. During the Carter administration, Cambodia's self-imposed isolation from the rest of the world made it difficult to assess the true developments in the country. Richard Holbrooke (assistant secretary of state for East Asia and Pacific affairs) confessed that there were 'limited options available to the administration'. Despite the Carter administration's focus/emphasis on human rights, little attention was

---

[55] Ted Osius, *Nothing Is Impossible: America's Reconciliation with Vietnam* (New Brunswick: Rutgers University Press, 2022), pp. xxi–xxii.
[56] For details, see *Foreign Relations of the United States 1977–1980, Volume 13: China* (Washington, DC: United States Government Printing Office, 2013), pp. ix–x.
[57] Chris A. Connolly, 'Kissinger, China, Congress, and the Lost Chance for Peace in Cambodia', *Journal of American–East Asian Relations*, Volume 17, Number 3, 2009–2010, pp. 205–229.

paid to Cambodia. As President Carter explained, while he recognised that 'the advancement of human rights is a complicated matter that depends upon the particular political context', the lack of diplomatic relations between the US and Democratic Kampuchea made it difficult for Washington to do much.[58] In the words of Kenton Clymer, 'the administration's silence belied its rhetoric about the centrality of human rights to its foreign policy'.[59] Peter Ronaye noted that the 'imperative of improving relations with China' (which is a close ally of Democratic Kampuchea) was strongly supported by National Security Adviser Zbigniew Brzezicski 'as a means of gaining the upper hand on the Soviets diminished the importance of human rights in Cambodia for the Carter administration. Compared to Sino-American relations, Cambodia – even the genocide there – seemed more like a distraction than anything else.'[60] We now know from US State Department cables (released by WikiLeaks) that while Washington was aware of the 'horrific actions' of the Pol Pot regime, with a 21 July 1978 cable from its embassy in Laos estimating that two million people had died at its hands, the US refused overtures from Cambodia's previous leadership (Lon Nol and others) to challenge the Pol Pot government's right to represent Cambodia at the United Nations (UN). There was also fear in some US establishment quarters of 'indefinite guerilla warfare' in Cambodia should the Pol Pot regime be toppled. On 21 August 1978, for example, Senator George McGovern (who in the earlier years had opposed Washington's escalation of the Vietnam War) gave an impassioned speech to the Senate in favour of intervention, invoking the inaction during the European holocaust as an analogy. He called for 'at the very least' the possibility of military action against the Khmer Rouge regime to be tabled at the next UN Security Council meeting. He was berated by Han Hsu (of China's Liaison Office) during a correspondent lunch held for Chinese reporters two days later, accusing

---

[58] See Peter Ronayne, *Never Again? The United States and the Prevention and Punishment of Genocide since the Holocaust* (Boulder: Rowman & Littlefield Publishers, Inc., 2001), chapter 2, pp. 62, 68, 71.

[59] Kenton Clymer, *Troubled Relations: The United States and Cambodia since 1870* (DeKalb: Northern Illinois University Press, 2007), p. 168, see especially chapter 9.

[60] Peter Ronayne, *Never Again? The United States and the Prevention and Punishment of Genocide since the Holocaust* (Boulder: Rowman & Littlefield Publishers, Inc., 2001), p. 73.

the US of wanting once again to be the world's policeman. Chinese officials vehemently defended the Khmer Rouge and rejected accusations of atrocities carried out by the regime. In a subsequent cable to its embassies that had relations with Cambodia, the State Department made it clear that while the US abhorred the human rights violations in Cambodia, it would not support or condone a unilateral or multilateral intervention by any other power into Cambodia.[61]

As for Vietnam, Hanoi was keen to normalise relations with Washington after the 1973 Paris Peace Agreement, but the situation at the time was not conducive to this. While the American military might have withdrawn from Vietnam, the war had not really ended. Soon after the fall of Saigon, Prime Minister Pham Van Dong extended a formal invitation to the US to normalise relations with one precondition: Washington must fulfil its commitment/obligation to provide reconstruction aid to North Vietnam as stated in Article 21 of the 1973 Paris Peace Agreement. The Ford administration, however, was only prepared to discuss normalisation of relations without any preconditions. Aid would only be considered when the American side was satisfied that the Vietnamese were seriously addressing the missing-in-action (MIA) issue which was a high-priority concern in the US. Thus, for the first one and a half years after the fall of Saigon (May 1975–December 1976), the two sides were 'locked into their uncompromising stances'.[62] There was one further reason why the Ford administration was not forthcoming with the Vietnamese: 'Vietnamese-American normalisation would have hampered Kissinger's geopolitical strategy'. Kissinger's foremost concern was, and always had been, the balance of US–Soviet relations and the strategic importance of the China factor in the equation. As Steven Hurst put it, 'easing Chinese fears of Soviet Vietnamese collusion would have reduced the incentive to normalise with the United States on terms acceptable to Washington'.[63]

The arrival of a new president in the White House appeared to provide both sides with a fresh opportunity to revisit the issue of normalisation of relations. Under the Carter administration, the

---

[61] 'The Pol Pot dilemma', *Phnom Penh Post*, 29 May 2015; 'KR Claims angered China in '78', *Phnom Penh Post*, 1 June 2015.
[62] Steven Hurst, *The Carter Administration and Vietnam* (London: Macmillan Press, 1996), p. 23.
[63] Steven Hurst, *The Carter Administration and Vietnam* (London: Macmillan Press, 1996), p. 24.

State Department had a different perspective and approach from that of Kissinger's. Whereas Kissinger was principally focused on US–Soviet relations and Southeast Asia was to him just a subordinate or an extension of that relationship, the new secretary of state, Cyrus Vance, and Holbrooke placed ASEAN at the core of American policy in Southeast Asia. In the case of Vietnam, they saw it as a country 'trying to find a balance between over-dependence on either the Chinese or the Soviet Union', thus offering 'an opportunity for a new initiative'. It was in America's interest, Vance believed, to wean Vietnam of its dependence on China and/or the Soviet Union.[64] The Carter administration, however, shared the same position as that of his predecessor that reconstruction aid which the Vietnamese wanted could only be discussed after the MIA accounting had been satisfactory concluded. This did not appear to be a difficult task since the House Select Committee on Missing Persons in Southeast Asia, which delivered its final report in late 1976, had concluded that there were no American prisoners of war alive in Indochina. The American side was hopeful of a quick agreement. But negotiations in 1977 to bring about normalisation still failed because the Hanoi leadership was insistent that the US was legally bound to provide aid. And as a rebuke to Washington's refusal to fulfil what the Vietnamese considered to be its legal obligation, Hanoi stubbornly refused to bring the MIA accounting to a closure. The subsequent dropping of words such as 'precondition' and 'legal' and the apparent delinking of aid, MIA and normalisation were all verbal gymnastics. The bottom line was that the Vietnamese continued to expect American aid, which they badly needed, as a precondition for normalisation. After the failure of the March and May 1977 meetings, there were no more substantial discussions. In his study of the US–Vietnam negotiations during the Carter administration, Steven Hurst concluded that the best opportunity to achieve normalisation was the first six months of 1977, but the opportunity was missed.[65] In October, Nguyen Co Thach met Holbrooke during the Number National Assembly and both agreed to meet for further talks to find a compromise. Subsequently, Phan

[64] Cyrus Vance, *Hard Choices: Critical Years in America's Foreign Policy* (New York: Simon and Schuster, 1983), p. 450; Steven Hurst, *The Carter Administration and Vietnam* (London: Macmillan Press, 1996), pp. 25–28.
[65] Steven Hurst, *The Carter Administration and Vietnam* (London: Macmillan Press, 1996), p. 141.

The Fall of Saigon to Invasion of Cambodia (1975–1978) 59

Hien and Holbrooke met in Paris from 7 to 10 December 1977 but could not resolve their differences.

III

We now reach the critical year of 1978. Nobody really knew the military situation or Vietnamese intentions. In early 1978, the British, for example, were sceptical that the Vietnamese would take over the whole or part of Cambodia or install a pro-Vietnamese government, whereas the French were sure that 'an effectively united Indochina' was 'a long-standing Vietnamese ambition' and they thought there was 'little that China could do about it'.[66] The *Financial Times* on 4 March 1978 reported that observers speculated that 'if an offensive comes it must be before the onset of the monsoon at the end of May'.[67]

Tiziano Terzani (local correspondent of *Der Spiegel*), during a visit to Vietnam in early 1978, found out that several thousand Cambodian refugees in Vietnam were sent back to Cambodia between 1975 and 1976, 'as a gesture of goodwill after their victory in the South', while the Vietnamese claimed that 'they were in ignorance of the fate that awaited these people in Cambodia'. Subsequently, a 'considerable number' of Cambodians were being trained in Vietnam to be used either in the continued fighting against Cambodia or as part of a new group which the Vietnamese hoped would eventually overthrow the Pol Pot regime. According to Terzani, the Cambodians had 'virtually eliminated all those members of the Communist Party who joined before 1960 and therefore might be presumed to have come strongly under Vietnamese influence'.[68]

In June 1978, those who had been closely following the developments in Indochina noted that the Vietnamese appeared to have come out into the open in offering encouragement for the toppling of the Pol Pot regime. In Cambodia, attempts to organise Pol Pot's

---

[66] From British Embassy in Hanoi to Foreign and Commonwealth Office, London, 'SRV/Cambodia', 27 January 1978, FCO 15/2335.
[67] 'Invasion may be Hanoi's solution', *Financial Times*, 4 March 1978, FCO 15/2337.
[68] From Government Secretariat, Hong Kong to Foreign and Commonwealth Office, 'Vietnamese-Cambodian Relations', 3 April 1978, FCO 15/2337'; British Embassy in Hanoi to Foreign and Commonwealth Office, 'Vietnam-Cambodia Relations', 21 April 1978, FCO 15/2338.

overthrow by a mutiny of the Eastern Zone military forces (aligned to Vietnam) ended in a complete disaster for the anti-Pol Pot rebels in June 1978, which led to the Vietnamese to take direct control of ousting the Pol Pot regime. British officials in early July speculated that the 'next step' for the Vietnamese 'might be the settling up of liberated zones in the Eastern region of Cambodia' and reported that they would be watching for 'evidence of whether this is happening'.[69] American officials were also of the view that Hanoi 'had reached certain decisions in June' along the following lines: to take vigorous steps to eventually oust the Pol Pot regime – 'the serious haemorrhage' caused by the Kampuchean problem must be stopped and therefore opted for 'a major military, subversive and political effort', calculating that Beijing was unlikely to intervene directly; to firmly resist Chinese political and economic pressures, 'even at the risk of being provocative'; and to join COMECON and move closer to Moscow but 'offset this with an intensive diplomatic campaign to broaden Vietnam's political and economic support from non-communist countries'.[70]

Three interviews given by Pol Pot on 17 March 1978 (to a group of Yugoslavian journalists), 12 April 1978 (to the DK Press Agency) and 11 December 1978 (to Xinhua Agency) provide the Khmer Rouge perspective of the developments in 1978. According to Pol Pot, Vietnam had never given up its Indochina Federation plan once it was conceived in 1930. Hanoi's goal was 'the elimination of borders to make Kampuchea part of their country'. The objective of Hanoi's undeclared and large-scale war with Kampuchea after September 1977 was to occupy 'the eastern part of the Mekong River and the southwest zone'. After Vietnam signed the Treaty of Friendship and Cooperation with the Soviet Union (which Pol Pot described as 'expansionist Soviet Union and the Warsaw Military Alliance'), Pol Pot noted that 'in the past, Vietnam always claimed the Vietnam–Kampuchea conflicts were mere border conflict in order to cheat. Now it can cheat no longer. Everyone knows about the war.'[71]

---

[69] Foreign and Commonwealth Office, London to British Ambassador in Hanoi, 'Vietnam/Cambodia', 5 July 1978, FCO 15/2339.
[70] Secret report sent to the British 'with compliments of the American Embassy. Date unclear, possibly 8 September 1978, FCO 15/2339.
[71] For 17 March and 12 April 1978 interviews, see *Searching for the Truth*, Number 16, April 2001, pp. 2–3; 11 December 1978 interview, see *Searching for the Truth*, First Quarterly Issue, 2003, pp. 4–6.

The Fall of Saigon to Invasion of Cambodia (1975-1978)

Meanwhile, by April 1978, Sino-Vietnamese talks on the border issue had broken down. The worsening of Sino-Vietnamese relations corresponded with the rupture in Vietnam–Kampuchea relations. Chinese public statements in 1978 clearly showed that Beijing's sympathy lay with the Khmer Rouge regime. China suspended all aid to Vietnam at the end of May 1978 and recalled all their specialists in Vietnam on 3 July. Vietnam finally joined COMECON on 29 June. Finally, at the fourth session of the VWP Central Committee meeting in July 1978, a resolution was passed which identified China as Vietnam's primary enemy.

By the summer of 1978, the 'battle-lines' had widened, with Vietnam and the Soviet Union on the one side and Kampuchea and China on the other. Chinese Foreign Minister Huang Hua, in a May 1978 conversation with Brzeziński, succinctly described the Chinese perspective of the developments in Indochina as a 'problem of regional hegemony' (like Pol Pot's interpretation described earlier): Vietnam's goal was to dominate Kampuchea and Laos and establish the Indochinese Federation and 'behind there lies the Soviet Union' – so, rightly or wrongly, the Chinese saw Moscow as supporting if not directing Vietnamese aspirations. Vietnam had already achieved its dominance over Laos but was encountering difficulties in Cambodia. Vietnamese–Kampuchean tension was 'more than merely some sporadic skirmishes along the borders', it was a major conflict which 'may last for a long time' as long as Vietnam persisted in realising its goal.[72]

We will return to how Sino-Vietnamese relations led to the Chinese invasion of Vietnam in February 1979 in Chapter 3. For the present, we focus on the developments that led to the Vietnamese invasion of Cambodia in December 1978.

As mentioned earlier, Vietnam–US negotiations till the end of 1977 to normalise relations were unsuccessful. Negotiations continued into 1978. Washington had six conditions for normalisation: (1) a quick resolution of the MIA issue; (2) an end the refugee flow out of Vietnam; (3) Vietnam would not invade Cambodia (apparently the US was aware of Hanoi's plan); (4) Vietnam would distance itself from the Soviet Union; (5) there would be no discussion of the Agent Orange issue; and (6) there would be no discussion on reparation.[73]

---

[72] See Henry Kissinger, *On China* (New York: Penguin, 2011), pp. 352–353.
[73] Ted Osius, *Nothing Is Impossible: America's Reconciliation with Vietnam* (New Brunswick: Rutgers University Press, 2022), pp. 14–15.

In May 1978, Vietnam tried to resuscitate the normalisation discussions by hinting that it would drop its long-held precondition of reconstruction aid.[74] But the Vietnamese vacillated on this until late September 1978 before Nguyen Co Thach finally confirmed this. By this time, the 'window of opportunity' was already fast closing, if not already closed. In April 1978, President Carter had given permission to his National Security Adviser Brzeziński to visit Beijing, which he did in May. It was in Carter's view a 'very successful' trip.[75] Like his predecessor, Kissinger, Brzeziński's priority was the balance of US–Soviet relations and the strategic importance of China in this equation. Normalisation of relations with Vietnam was therefore secondary on his agenda. Brzeziński's view differed from the State Department, but with the support of President Carter he prevailed. Besides Brzeziński, the tensions between Vietnam and Kampuchea, Vietnam's joining of COMECON and China's opposition all worked against Vietnam. John Holdridge recalled that in September 1978, about the time that he was assigned to be the national intelligence officer for China, he became aware of 'the tremendous influence that Vietnam and Cambodia exercised on US–China relations'.[76] After the Vietnamese dropped their precondition, Washington agreed to normalise relations, but in 1979 and not before Sino-US normalisation had taken place.[77] Carter made the decision on 11 October to focus on China. Thus, by mid-October 1978, Hanoi knew that the US's priority was China and that Vietnam–US normalisation would not happen anytime soon. The Vietnamese were officially informed of the American decision by Bob Oakley (deputy assistant secretary of state) in New York in November 1978. The decision to 'shelve normalisation

---

[74] For details of Vietnam–US relations in the early post-Vietnam war years, see Steven Hurst, *The Carter Administration and Vietnam* (London: Macmillan Press, 1996) and Cecile Mentrey-Monchau, *American-Vietnamese Relations in the Wake of the War* (Jefferson: McFarland, 2006). See also the memoirs of Jimmy Carter, Zbigniew Brzezinski, Cyrus Vance, John H. Holdridge, and Desaix Anderson.
[75] Marvin Kalb and Deborah Kalb, *Haunting Legacy: Vietnam and the American Presidency from Ford to Obama* (Washington, DC: Brookings Institution Press, 2011), p. 64.
[76] John H. Holdridge, *Crossing the Divide: An Insider's Account of the Normalization of US–China Relations* (Lanham: Rowman & Littlefield, 1997), p. 179.
[77] The US and China officially normalized relations on 15 December 1978.

indefinitely', however, was not made until the Vietnamese invasion of Cambodia in December 1978. The invasion was 'the decisive blow' to normalisation.[78]

The failure of both Foreign Minister Nguyen Duy Trinh (late 1977 and early 1978) and Prime Minister Pham Van Dong (in September–October 1978) to improve relations with the ASEAN countries (see Chapter 4) compounded Vietnam's sense of insecurity and reaffirmed the view that the Soviet Union was the only country it could rely on. On 3 November, Vietnam signed the Treaty of Friendship with the Soviet Union, which was notably different from those Moscow signed with the east European countries in one important aspect. In the case of Vietnam, Moscow only committed itself to consultation in the event of an attack or threat of attack on Vietnam. The twenty-five-year Treaty of Friendship and Cooperation between the Soviet Union and Vietnam was 'the first time that the Union of Soviet Socialist Republics (USSR) has been able to establish a treaty relationship with any country in the region (Southeast Asia)'.[79] According to Stephen J. Morris, based on his research there is no direct evidence that Moscow instigated or urged the invasion of Kampuchea.[80]

That the Vietnamese would invade Cambodia some time in 1978 or the near future was widely anticipated. As noted earlier, the Americans expected it to happen, and thus one of the six conditions for Vietnam–US normalisation was a commitment from Vietnam not to invade Cambodia. Indeed, in April 1978, Hoang Tung (editor-in-chief of *Nhan Dan*) disclosed to a group of Swedish journalists that it was 'difficult for the Vietnamese leadership to stop the Vietnamese army which around the new year started a big offensive against Cambodia and could easily have taken Phnom Penh'. Hoang Tung was referring to the December 1977 military operations. 'No army wants to

---

[78] Steven Hurst, *The Carter Administration and Vietnam* (London: Macmillan Press, 1996), p. 144. For the argument that it was 'vanguard internationalism' that overrode Vietnamese leaders' 'pragmatic sense' leading to the failure of normalisation, see Tuong Vu, *Vietnam's Communist Revolution: The Power and Limits of Ideology* (Cambridge: Cambridge University Press, 2017), pp. 220–221.
[79] 'The Soviet Vietnamese Friendship Treaty', *FCO* 15/2436.
[80] Stephen J. Morris, *Why Vietnam Invaded Cambodia: Political Culture and the Causes of War* (Stanford: Stanford University Press, 1999), pp. 215–217. See also, British Embassy in Moscow to Foreign and Commonwealth Office, 'Soviet/Vietnamese Relations', 11 June 1980, *FCO* 15/2788.

fight half a battle', he added.[81] Bui Tin recalled that he (then the deputy editor of *Nhan Dan*) wrote an article in May 1978 on 'genocide' committed by the Khmer Rouge, but the editorial board hesitated to publish it. The article was eventually published in August.[82] The decision to invade Cambodia, according to Bui Tin, was not a unanimous one.[83] We now know from Kosal Path's study of top-level internal Vietnamese documents that 'from late 1977 to mid-1978 the combined political pressure of the economic crisis at home and failure in foreign and diplomacy abroad compelled Hanoi to reverse its strategy by now subordinating economic development to national defence'. As relations with Cambodia and China deteriorated, the 'military first' faction within the leadership gradually took control of the levers of power and would remain influential for much of the 1980s.[84] In August 1978, the Chinese advised Pol Pot to prepare to wage a protracted war. Nayan Chanda recalled that at a routine lunch in Hong Kong, a 'well-placed Chinese source' revealed that the Vietnamese were about to invade Cambodia, and 'when they do the Khmer Rouge will again retreat to the jungle to engage in guerrilla war'. That was precisely the Chinese advice to Pol Pot, although Pol Pot 'did not agree with the recommendation'. But the 'Vietnamese blitzkrieg' forced his hand.[85]

By late November 1978, when the rainy season had ended, most observers expected a large-scale attack of Kampuchea by the Vietnamese, although the precise timing and the nature of the campaign remained unclear. Defence analysts in Singapore, for example, were of the view that Hanoi had two options – an all-out invasion leading to the capture of Phnom Penh and the occupation of Kampuchea or 'a more prudent military option', which was to close in on the Khmer Rouge troops deployed along the border and destroy or disperse them without occupying the whole country. The destruction of

---

[81] B. E. Shinde, *Mao Zedong and the Communist Policies, 1927–1978* (New Delhi: Sangam Books, 1993), p. 113, see especially chapter 4.
[82] Bui Tin, *Following Ho Chi Minh: Memoirs of a North Vietnamese Colonel* (London: Hurst & Company, 1995), p. 117.
[83] See Bui Tin, *Following Ho Chi Minh: Memoirs of a North Vietnamese Colonel* (London: Hurst & Company, 1995); Hoang Van Hoan, *A Drop in the Ocean* (Beijing: Foreign Languages Press, 1988).
[84] Kosal Path, *Vietnam's Strategic Thinking during the Third Indochina War* (Madison: University of Wisconsin Press, 2020), p. 50, chapter 2.
[85] Nayan Chanda, 'Vietnam's invasion of Cambodia, revisited', *The Diplomat*, 1 December 2018.

this army would enable pro-Vietnamese Kampuchean armed forces to occupy Kampuchean territory with relative ease while Pol Pot's troops were engaged with the Vietnamese army. The first option was likely to provoke a major Chinese military response. No one could predict for certain whether the recently signed defence treaty between the Soviet Union and Vietnam would deter the Chinese. An all-out invasion would also likely damage Hanoi's standing in the Third World. The ASEAN states would view it as 'naked aggression' and Japan and the West would be 'greatly disturbed' and would be less inclined to give aid to Vietnam.[86]

In the end, Vietnam chose the first option, believing that 'in two weeks, the world will have forgotten the Kampuchean problem'.[87] With hindsight, they have since admitted that it was a strategic mistake.[88] Although Moscow was aware of the Vietnamese intention to invade Cambodia, the Russians neither goaded the Vietnamese into a war nor discouraged them. Soviet documents revealed that in an October 1978 meeting, the Vietnamese firmly assured Soviet representatives, who were concerned about the Chinese response to the prospective invasion, that 'China will not have time to dispatch large military units to Phnom Penh to rescue the Kampuchean regime'.[89]

Preparation for the invasion of Kampuchea began in earnest in early December. On 7 December 1978, the People's Army of Vietnam (PAVN) was given the go-ahead to activate what was called the 'General Staff's Combat Readiness Plan for Cambodia'. The Order of Battle comprised 18 divisions, 600 armoured vehicles, 137 aircraft, and as many as 250,000 men. The invasion was scheduled to begin

---

[86] R. H. Solomon (ed.), *Asian Security in the 1980s: Problems and Policies for a Time of Transition* (Cambridge: Oelgeschlager, Gunn & Hain, Publishers, Inc., 1979), chapter 7.
[87] K. Mahbubani, 'The Kampuchean Problem: A Southeast Asian Perspective', *Foreign Affairs*, Volume 62, Number 2, 1983–1984, p. 408.
[88] See David W. P. Elliot, *Changing Worlds: Vietnam's Transition from Cold War to Globalization* (New York: Oxford University Press, 2012), p. xi. For the Southeast Asian response to the invasion, see Ang Cheng Guan, *Singapore, ASEAN and the Cambodian Conflict, 1978–1991* (Singapore: NUS Press, 2013).
[89] Dmitry Mosyakov, 'The Khmer Rouge and the Vietnamese Communists: A History of Their Relations as Told in the Soviet Archives', pp. 70–71, www.isn.ethz.ch/isn/Digital-Library/Publications/Detail/?lng=en&id=46645.

on 4 January 1979, 'when the terrain was dry and the rice harvest ready'.[90] However, the Khmer Rouge caught wind of the impending invasion and launched a pre-emptive strike across the south-western border of Vietnam on 23 December, which in turn led the Vietnamese to bring forward their plan to 25 December. The Khmer Rouge's pre-emptive action 'gave Vietnam a convenient legal excuse to retaliate under international law'.[91] In the assessment of Kenneth Conboy, although the Vietnamese military overall conducted an 'efficient and effective campaign', the Khmer Rouge 'put up a tenacious fight while withdrawing, inflicting heavy losses on PAVN armoured units'.[92] The Vietnamese took Phnom Penh on 7 January 'virtually without a shot and ended the violent reign of the Khmer Rouge'.[93] However, Hanoi's plan to 'free' Sihanouk (who had been kept under house arrest by Pol Pot) so that he could head (and legitimise) a 'Cambodian liberation front' backed by the Vietnamese was foiled by Pol Pot, who released the prince on 5 January. Sihanouk left for Beijing the next day. On 10 January 1979, the pro-Vietnamese PRK was established in Phnom Penh with Heng Samrin as the head of state.

It is perhaps worth noting that the Vietnamese invasion was welcomed throughout Cambodia, particularly in the Eastern Zone. As Bunhaeng Ung recalled,

considering the relentlessness of anti-Vietnamese propaganda under the Khmer Rouge, and that every Kampuchean had learned to see Vietnam as the nation's historic enemy, the warmth with which the Vietnamese forces were welcomed came as something of a surprise, even to the Vietnamese. But it was a product of circumstances, rather than a national change of

[90] For details, see Kenneth Conboy, *The Cambodian Wars: Clashing Armies and CIA Covert Operations* (Kansas: University of Kansas Press, 2013), chapter 6.
[91] Kenneth Conboy, *The Cambodian Wars: Clashing Armies and CIA Covert Operations* (Kansas: University of Kansas Press, 2013), p. 126.
[92] Kenneth Conboy, *The Cambodian Wars: Clashing Armies and CIA Covert Operations* (Kansas: University of Kansas Press, 2013), p. 129.
[93] Nayan Chanda, 'Vietnam's invasion of Cambodia, revisited', *The Diplomat*, 1 December 2018. See also, Merle L. Pribbenow II, 'A Tale of Five Generals: Vietnam's invasion of Cambodia', *The Journal of Military History*, Volume 70, Number 2, April 2006; Ben Kiernan (guest editor), 'Thematic Issue: Conflict and Change in Cambodia', *Critical Asian Studies*, Volume 34, Number 4, December 2002, particularly, Yun Shui (author) and Paul Marks (translator), 'An Account of Chinese Diplomats Accompanying the Government of Democratic Kampuchea's Move to the Cardamom Mountains', pp. 497–519.

heart; it rested not on any real affection for historic enemies, but on the depth of hatred felt for the Khmer Rouge.[94]

Having S. Ngor (of 'The Killing Fields' fame) had the same sentiment. 'Historically, Vietnam was our enemy ... But as far as I am concerned, they were welcome as long as they stayed only a short time. They have hastened the end of the Khmer Rouge ... Better to have them around than the Khmer Rouge.'[95] As Jean-Pierre L. Fonteyne put it, that the Vietnamese invasion 'put an end to an intolerable massacre of genocidal proportions in Cambodia is beyond doubt, and for this the world should unquestionably feel indebted to Vietnam',[96] although one should stress that 'human rights' was never the consideration (which is confirmed by all the primary sources that have become available). In his study of humanitarian interventions, Nicholas Wheeler concluded that there is no evidence that Pol Pot's human rights violations played any part in the Vietnamese decision to invade Cambodia. In his words, 'Vietnam criticised these only when it became politically convenient to do so, and, had a diplomatic settlement been secured with the DK ... it would have coexisted with its murderous neighbour'.[97] Sihanouk recalled that until the end of December 1977, when the Pol Pot regime broke off diplomatic relations with Vietnam, Vietnamese state radio and press continually praised the Pol Pot regime.[98] Vietnam did not invade Cambodia to save the Cambodians from Pol Pot but rather to save itself from the perceived threat from China.[99]

The 'initial' euphoria was short-lived, lasting about a year according to Harish and Julia Mehta in their official biography of Hun Sen,

---

[94] Martin Stuart-Fox and Bunhaeng Ung, *The Murderous Revolution: Bunhaeng Ung's Life with Death in Pol Pot's Kampuchea* (Bangkok: The Tamarind Press, 1986), pp. 170, 173.

[95] Haing S. Ngor (with Roger Warner), *Surviving the Killing Fields* (London: Pan Books, 1989), p. 363.

[96] Gary Klintworth, *Vietnam's Intervention in Cambodia in International Law* (Canberra: Australian Government Publishing Service, 1989), p. xiv.

[97] Nicholas J. Wheeler, *Saving Strangers: Humanitarian Intervention in International Society* (Oxford: Oxford University Press, 2002), https://academic.oup.com/book/276, p. 105 See Chapter 3.

[98] Norodom Sihanouk, *War and Hope: The Case for Cambodia* (New York: Pantheon Books, 1980), pp. 103–104.

[99] Nguyen Co Thach's conversation with Stephen Solarz, 2 January 1981, recounted by Kishore Mahbubani, 'Cambodia: Myths and Realities', *Problems of Communism*, July–August 1984, p. 70.

'when many Cambodians felt that the Vietnamese liberators had turned into occupiers'.[100] Nevertheless, as noted in the Introduction, the question whether it was a 'liberation' or 'invasion' continues to be debated to this day.[101] Sok Udom Deth argues that one should go 'beyond the political rhetoric and characterisation of a regime as "liberator" or an "oppressor"'.[102] Jean-Pierre L. Fonteyne wondered whether a more 'understanding' attitude on the part of the ASEAN states and the major Western countries towards Hanoi's position and that of the Vietnamese-installed Heng Samrin regime 'might not have made it possible for the Vietnamese presence to end much sooner'.[103] This is a question we address in Chapter 3.

---

[100] Harish C. Mehta and Julie B. Mehta, *Strongman: The Extraordinary Life of Hun Sen* (Singapore: Marshall Cavendish Editions, 2013), p. 128.
[101] In their December 1997 interview with Hun Sen, the Mehtas used the word 'invasion' which drew 'an outraged response' from Hun Sen. See Harish C. Mehta and Julie B. Mehta, *Strongman: The Extraordinary Life of Hun Sen* (Singapore: Marshall Cavendish Editions, 2013), p. 129.
[102] See Sok Udom Deth, *The People's Republic of Kampuchea 1979–1989: A Draconian Savior?* MA thesis, Center for International Studies, Ohio University, June 2009.
[103] Gary Klintworth, *Vietnam's Intervention in Cambodia in International Law* (Canberra: Australian Government Publishing Service, 1989), p. xiv.

3 | *The Sino-Vietnamese War (February 1979)*

I

This chapter describes the immediate aftermath of the Vietnamese invasion. Apart from the ongoing war in Cambodia, the immediate and violent response to the Vietnamese invasion was the February 1979 Sino-Vietnamese war.

We described the deterioration of Sino-Vietnamese relations in Chapters 1–2, but a brief recap here is perhaps useful. China suspended all aid to Vietnam at the end of May 1978 and recalled all their specialists in Vietnam on 3 July. Vietnam finally joined COMECON on 29 June. Finally, at the fourth session of the VWP Central Committee meeting in July 1978, a resolution was passed which identified China as Vietnam's primary enemy. Meanwhile, by April 1978, Sino-Vietnamese talks on the border issue had broken down.

Private and public comments from Chinese leaders through 1978 indicated that Beijing was 'broadly prepared' for the Vietnamese invasion of Cambodia. They were, however, 'surprised by the speed' of the Vietnamese takeover.[1] When China initially decided to 'teach Vietnam a lesson' in July 1978, it was in the context of the perceived Vietnamese government's treatment of the ethnic Chinese (Hoa) living in Vietnam.[2] It was estimated way back in 1954 that the Hoa community in Vietnam controlled 90 per cent of all non-European capital investments in the country as well as holding a monopoly in the wholesale and retail trade. The Chinese population in the North was relatively small compared to the South, most of which resided in the Saigon-Cholon area in South Vietnam. Prior to reunification

---

[1] Cabinet Memorandum No. 5, 'Vietnam's Invasion of Kampuchea: Chinese and Soviet Policies and Their Implications', Office of National Assessments, 2 February 1979, National Archives of Australia, A12930, Item 5.
[2] Nayan Chanda, *Brother Enemy: The War after the War* (New York: Macmillan, 1986), p. 326.

in 1975, Saigon briefly attempted to enforce assimilation of the ethnic Chinese (followed by integration and finally citizenship), notably under the Diem government, but the escalation of the Vietnam War and the need for a stable economy precluded further attempts to force the pace of assimilation. As for Hanoi, the need to address the ethnic Chinese issue was also deferred for as long as the war of national unification was still being waged and China's support was deemed crucial towards that end. In a 1955 meeting between representatives of Hanoi and Beijing, it was agreed that Chinese nationals living in the North would be administered by Vietnam on condition that they enjoyed the same rights as the Vietnamese and that they could be encouraged but not be coerced to accept Vietnamese nationality. Lastly, the question of Chinese living in the South would be resolved through consultation between both sides after the liberation of South Vietnam.[3] In 1975, it was estimated that 85 per cent of the 1.5 million Chinese resided in the South. When the North Vietnamese forces entered Cholon in 1975, they were greeted with portraits of Mao Zedong and thousands of Chinese flags. As Sino-Vietnamese relations deteriorated, Hanoi was understandably concerned about the political implications of this Chinese population which wielded such enormous economic strength in the country. This concern and fear of a fifth column led to the urgent implementation of a series of policies, the objective of which was to ensure the political loyalty of the ethnic Chinese, which Beijing in turn saw as violating the agreements reached in 1955. Meanwhile, China had begun to recognise the potential value of the economically successful overseas Chinese for its economic development. In February 1978, at the 5th National People's Congress, Hua Guofeng made two significant statements: that China viewed overseas Chinese as part of the Chinese nation and would therefore protect their interests, and that China would welcome back and make proper arrangements to assist those overseas Chinese who wanted to return to China. From March–April 1978, Hanoi began the process of the socialist transformation of trade in the South. All these policies introduced by Hanoi and Beijing, which were uncoordinated, led to a flood of refugees

---

[3] Chang Pao-min, *Beijing, Hanoi, and the Overseas Chinese* (Berkeley: University of California, Center for Chinese Studies, 1982), p. 4; Chang Pao-min, 'The Sino-Vietnamese Dispute over the Ethnic Chinese', *China Quarterly*, Number 90, June 1982, p. 196.

The Sino-Vietnamese War (February 1979)

across the Sino-Vietnamese border. Beijing subsequently closed the entire border on 11 July 1978 to control the flow of refugees, which caused further tensions as both Vietnamese and Chinese border security sought to exercise control over the disputed border.

Beijing made great efforts to explain that the 1979 war was a limited counterattack, not unlike the many armed clashes that had taken place along the Sino-Vietnamese border since 1977. The objective of the war, it was claimed, was to secure a peaceful border with Vietnam. It further claimed that Chinese troops had been forced to launch 'a self-defensive counterattack' to safeguard China's territorial integrity in the face of incessant Vietnamese provocation. The post-war negotiations between Hanoi and Beijing in April 1979 clearly revealed that the border situation was just a convenient excuse for the Chinese invasion. During the negotiations, Hanoi presented a series of proposals specifically regarding the border: end hostilities, demilitarise the border, and resume normal transport; and settle the territorial issue based on 'respect for the borderline' established in the Sino-French Agreements of 1887 and 1895. The Chinese rejected the three-point proposal and demanded that Hanoi recognise the Paracel and Spratly islands as part of Chinese territory, the end of the persecution of Chinese nationals in Vietnam, and that neither side should station troops in other countries or join any military blocs. In a subsequent round of talks in July, the Chinese side brushed aside the border and ethnic Chinese issues and demanded that negotiations 'proceed from the crux of the matter – opposition to hegemonism'. Beijing claimed that Vietnam's invasion of Kampuchea was part of a plan to set up an Indochina Federation in coordination with the Soviet 'drive for world hegemony'.[4] As mentioned in Chapter 2, from as early as the 1950s to 1978, the Vietnamese refused to take sides in the Sino-Soviet dispute. The Sino-Soviet dispute culminated in the seven-month border skirmish in 1969 when both Chinese and Soviet troops clashed near Zhenbao Island in north-east China. Although the clashes did not escalate into an all-out war, the Chinese were extremely sensitive to any geopolitical shifts that could imperil Chinese territorial integrity, in this case, a collusion between Moscow and Hanoi. Indeed, it was in the words of Chinese scholar Yang Kuisong, 'the perception

---

[4] Grant Evans and Kelvin Rowley, *Red Brotherhood at War* (London: Verso, 1984), p. 132.

of an extremely grave threat from the Soviet Union that pushed Mao to decide to break up all existing conceptual restrictions to pursue a Sino-American rapprochement'.[5] According to the Chinese interpretation of the developments from mid-1978, the December invasion was the culmination of a plan which started with Vietnam joining the COMECON in June 1978, followed soon after in mid-August by Moscow airlifting large quantities of arms to Vietnam, after which both countries signed the Treaty of Friendship and Cooperation in November and in the same month, at the Moscow summit of Warsaw Pact countries, the Soviet Union called for joint support for Vietnam. On 3 December 1978, Hanoi facilitated the establishment of the KUFNS 'as part of their organizational preparation for their massive armed aggression'.[6]

According to Nayan Chanda, a Beijing official had told him that during one of the regular Chinese Politburo meetings in July 1978, the leadership decided in 'absolute secrecy' to 'teach Vietnam a lesson' for its 'ungrateful and arrogant behaviour'. Apparently, this issue had already been raised at the May 1978 Politburo meeting. There were some who disagreed, but Deng Xiaoping was able to make a persuasive case by arguing that (1) the limited military action would demonstrate to Moscow that China 'was ready to stand up to its bullying' and (2) Moscow would not want to get militarily involved. The Chinese idea was to frame the military action as part of a 'global antihegemonic strategy serving broader interests' (rather than a just a bilateral conflict between Vietnam and China). For this, they first needed to improve relations with the US, non-communist Asia, and the West. As to when to punish the Vietnamese, the decision would be made at the appropriate time.[7] According to American intelligence reports, the Chinese started logistic preparation for an eventual war with Vietnam soon after the Vietnamese Worker's Party Central Committee passed the resolution which identified China as Vietnam's primary enemy

---

[5] Chi-Kwan Mark, *China and the World since 1945: An International History* (London: Routledge, 2012), p. 81.
[6] The timeline was published in *Beijing Review*, 19 January 1979. See *Searching for the Truth*, Number 22, October 2001, p. 3.
[7] Nayan Chanda, *Brother Enemy: The War after the War* (New York: Colliers Books, 1986), pp. 260–261; See also Ezra F. Vogel, *Deng Xiaoping and the Transformation of China* (Cambridge, MA: The Belknap Press of Harvard University Press, 2011), pp. 526–538.

(in July 1978).[8] Wang Chenyi's research based on his reading of Chinese sources corroborates Nayan Chanda. In comparison with Deng's posture in October 1977 that the Cambodia–Vietnam conflict should be resolved by themselves, in July 1978 the Chinese stance had made a 'complete shift'.[9]

Deng Xiaoping, unlike Zhou Enlai, did not have any attachment to the Vietnamese. As Qiang Zhai put it, 'this absence of emotional ties to the Vietnamese and a visceral bitterness about what he perceived as Hanoi's ungratefulness and arrogance help explain why he had no qualms about launching a war in 1979 "to teach Vietnam a lesson"'.[10] Vietnamese Foreign Minister Nguyen Co Thach claimed that Vietnam signed the Friendship Treaty with the Soviet Union in November 1978 only after China began to concentrate its military forces on the Vietnamese border and made serious preparation for an invasion.[11] It is worth recalling that by then, it was clear that Vietnam–US normalisation would not happen, and that the only countervailing power that Vietnam could count on was the Soviet Union. To Beijing, the treaty was synonymous with having a Cuba next to her.

Apart from the May 1978 Politburo meeting, the deliberations of the Enlarged Working Conference of the Politburo (11 November–15 December 1978) merit attention. This conference has been described as marking the establishment of Deng's control over the key levers of power in the Party Central Committee. Joseph Torigian, in his study of elite power struggles in the Soviet Union and China after Mao and Stalin, described how Deng used the military, which was his 'natural

---

[8] Nayan Chanda, *Brother Enemy: The War after the War* (New York: Colliers Books, 1986), p. 323.
[9] Wang Chenyi, *Mao's Legacy and the Sino-Vietnamese War*, unpublished PhD thesis, 2017, School of Humanities, Nanyang Technological University.
[10] Qiang Zhai, *China and the Vietnam Wars, 1950–1975* (Chapel Hill: University of North Carolina Press, 2000), p. 214; Nayan Chanda, *Brother Enemy: The War after the War: A History of Indochina since the Fall of Saigon* (New York: Colliers Books, 1986), p. 261. For details of Sino-Vietnamese relations, based on Vietnamese sources, in 1977, see Kosal Path, 'The Sino-Vietnamese Dispute over Territorial Claims, 1974–1978: Vietnamese Nationalism and Its Consequences', *International Journal of Asian Studies*, Volume 8, Number 2, 2011, pp. 189–220.
[11] William J. Duiker, *Vietnam since the Fall of Saigon* (Athens, OH: Ohio University Center for International Studies, 1985), pp. 133–134. But according to Wang Chenyi, the Chinese did not deploy their forces till after the signing of the treaty.

place of dominance', to strengthen his own position in his competition was Hua Guofeng. Deng's ability to show that the military listened to him, and not Hua, 'influenced calculations within the leadership'. The decision to attack Vietnam was one example.[12] According to Nayan Chanda, the 'consolidation of Deng's position inside the party now enabled him to make an uncompromising push for foreign policy issues that had earlier provoked controversy'.[13] The foreign policy debate during the conference centred on the question whether to intervene on behalf of the Khmer Rouge against Vietnam. The hawks, such as Wang Dongxing, reportedly supported Pol Pot's request for troops. The first political commissar (navy) suggested sending a detachment of the East Sea Fleet to Cambodia to secure its territorial waters. A veteran commander of the Guangxi Military Region, Xu Shiyou, even wanted to lead his troops to attack Vietnam. Geng Biao, the Politburo member responsible for international affairs, argued that the border fighting between Vietnam and Cambodia was Moscow's ploy to bait China into sending troops into Cambodia, which would give Moscow an opportunity to mobilise world opinion against China and hinder China's modernisation goals. Thus, China should not fall for Moscow's ploy. Deng's view was that a 'self-defensive counterattack' on Vietnam instead of an intervention in Cambodia would not provoke a large-scale Soviet attack on China. It would also not invite an unfavourable international reaction or interrupt China's modernisation plans. On the contrary, it would 'demonstrate to the Soviet

---

[12] Joseph Torigian, *Prestige, Manipulation, and Coercion: Elite Power Struggles in the Soviet Union and China after Stalin and Mao* (New Haven: Yale University Press, 2022), pp. 170–189. Wang Chenyi in his unpublished PhD thesis (*Mao's Legacy and the Sino-Vietnamese War*, 2017, School of Humanities, Nanyang Technological University, p. 163), on the other hand, argued that Deng did not make the decision to attack Vietnam on his own but was entrusted to carry out the collective leadership decision to punish Vietnam. According to him, there is also no concrete evidence that Deng intentionally exploited the war against Vietnam for 'domestic profit' and to prevail over his rivals. For a contrary view, see Joshua Eisenman, 'China's Vietnam War Revisited: A Domestic Politics Perspective', *Journal of Contemporary China*, Volume 28, Number 119, 2019, pp. 729–745; see also, German Chancellor Helmut Schmidt's conversation with Hua Guofeng on the China–Vietnam conflict recounted in Helmut Schmidt, *Men and Powers: A Political Retrospective* (New York: Random House, 1989), pp. 312–313. The power struggle in China during this period remains murky.

[13] Nayan Chanda, *Brother Enemy: The War after the War* (New York: Colliers Books, 1986), p. 328.

Union and Vietnam, China's determination, and ability to break their encirclement'.[14]

According to US sources, from the end of the Vietnam War in 1975 till early 1978, the Chinese appeared to support US–Vietnamese normalisation 'in the hope that it would counter Soviet influence in Hanoi'. By August 1978, the attitudes 'have been generally negative'. For example, on 3 November 1978, Vice-Premier Li Xiannian 'recited in an irritated fashion China's belief that it is no use trying to draw Vietnam economically or politically away from the USSR', and asserted that any US economic aid to Vietnam would relieve Moscow of a 'great burden' while having 'no effect on Vietnam's close ties to the USSR'.[15]

From this account, although the dispute over Hanoi's treatment of ethnic Chinese and the border tensions generated a certain momentum that set the two countries on a collision course, it was, above all, Vietnam's decision to invade Cambodia with the tacit support of Moscow which finally led to the Sino-Vietnamese war in February 1979. The decision to punish Vietnam was made as early as May 1978. What was left undecided was the timing and the form 'the lesson' would take.[16] The ethnic issue, while it certainly contributed to the deterioration of the bilateral relations, was more a symptom of the soured relationship than the actual cause of the war. Chinese sources also revealed that in the wake of the signing of the Treaty of Friendship and Cooperation between Vietnam and the Soviet Union, the Central Military Commission (CMC) issued the 'Instructions on the Issue of Sino-Vietnamese border defence' on 21 November 1978. The CMC convened on 23 November to study and discuss the implementation of the 'Instructions', following which several PLA units were deployed to the Sino-Vietnamese border. However, at the end of November 1978,

---

[14] Nayan Chanda, *Brother Enemy: The War after the War* (New York: Colliers Books, 1986), p. 329; see also Ezra F. Vogel, *Deng Xiaoping and the Transformation of China* (Cambridge, MA: The Belknap Press of Harvard University Press, 2011), pp. 526–538.

[15] *Foreign Relations of the United States 1977–1980, Volume 13: China* (Washington, DC: United States Government Printing Office, 2013), Document 155.

[16] In his unpublished PhD thesis, Wang Chenyi argues that the Chinese leadership contemplated a war with Vietnam soon after Vietnam signed the Treaty of Friendship and Cooperation with the Soviet Union. See Wang Chenyi, *Mao's Legacy and the Sino-Vietnamese War*, unpublished PhD thesis, 2017, School of Humanities, Nanyang Technological University, chapter 4.

the Chinese leadership had yet to decide on a large-scale war against Vietnam. The decision to wage a war against Vietnam was made on 8 December (soon after the establishment of the KUFNS on 3 December, which was viewed as an 'unequivocal message' that a Vietnamese invasion of Cambodia was imminent and on an unprecedented scale) and the instructions were for all units to arrive at their designated areas by 10 January 1979. The PLA would transit from covert manoeuvring to open deployment.[17]

II

As mentioned earlier, one of the preconditions for China to punish Vietnam was the need to first improve relations with the US, non-communist Asia, and the West. Thus, while the discussions on how to respond to the Indochina situation was going on, Deng visited Thailand, Malaysia, and Singapore from 5 to 14 November 1978,[18] and then the US from 29 January to 5 February 1979. The decision to punish Vietnam had already been taken when Deng visited the three Southeast Asian countries; only the timing and method of punishment remained to be decided. By the time Deng visited the US, only the timing of the punishment was left to be confirmed. Deng's motives for these series of visits were of course broader than the issue of Indochina and Sino-Vietnamese relations. For this study, we focus on Deng's Indochina agenda.

Lee Lai-to noted that Deng's visit to the ASEAN states showed that the Chinese policy of 'Sino-Vietnamese solidarity' had been replaced by a growing emphasis on the non-communist ASEAN states in China's fight against Soviet 'strategic encirclement'.[19] Economic interests aside,

---

[17] Wang Chenyi, *Mao's Legacy and the Sino-Vietnamese War*, unpublished PhD thesis, 2017, School of Humanities, Nanyang Technological University.

[18] For a discussion of this visit, see Lee Lai-to, 'Deng Xiaoping's ASEAN Tour: A Perspective on Sino-Southeast Asian Relations', *Contemporary Southeast Asia*, Volume 3, Number 1, June 1981, pp. 58–75.

[19] Lee Lai-to, 'Deng Xiaoping's ASEAN Tour: A Perspective on Sino-Southeast Asian Relations', *Contemporary Southeast Asia*, Volume 3, Number 1, June 1981, p. 72. Vice-Premier Li Xiannian visited the Philippines in March 1978 and was apparently given a 'hearty Filipino reception'. Deng's visit came after Soviet deputy Foreign Minister Nikolai Firyubin's visit to ASEAN countries in October 1978 and Vietnamese Prime Minister Pham Van Dong's visit in September–October 1978.

Beijing's hope was for the non-communist ASEAN states to either take its side or remain neutral in the Sino-Soviet conflict.[20] Of the countries visited, Thailand and the US were the most significant.

Thailand established diplomatic relations with China on 1 July 1975, not long after the fall of Saigon. Then, led by Prime Minister Kukrit Pramoj, Bangkok decided to normalise relations with Beijing in the hope that the Chinese could help counter the potential threat of Hanoi. Bangkok was concerned about a unified Vietnam, and its influence on Laos and its connection with the Khmer Rouge in Cambodia, which Thailand shares common borders with. As Sihanouk noted, 'when the Khmer Rouge said they could walk all over the Thais, they were not exaggerating'.[21] More on this later. Bangkok also hoped that the Chinese could be induced to reduce its support for the communists based in Thailand. Finally, there was the prospect of economic benefits from improving relations with China.

By the time of Deng's five-day visit from 5 to 9 November 1978, Thailand had a new prime minister, Kriangsak Chamanan (1977–1980), who had earlier visited Beijing in March 1978 with the objectives of strengthening relations with China and getting Chinese assistance in smoothing Thai–Cambodian relations. During Deng's return visit, aside from bilateral relations, 'the Cambodian issue was central to their discussion'.[22] Deng's objective was to rally support for Cambodia and to warn about Vietnam's hegemonic tendency. As Lee Lai-to put it, 'Thailand, located at the doorstep of Indochina, naturally had become all the more significant in Chinese foreign policy in forestalling the influence of the "Cuba of Asia" and Soviet "hegemony"'.[23] Both Kriangsak and Deng apparently saw eye-to-eye on the Cambodian issue. Kriangsak supported the idea of keeping Cambodia independent and free from

---

[20] Lee Lai-to, 'Deng Xiaoping's ASEAN tour: A Perspective on Sino-Southeast Asian Relations', *Contemporary Southeast Asia*, Volume 3, Number 1, June 1981, p. 72.
[21] Norodom Sihanouk, *War and Hope: The Case for Cambodia* (New York: Pantheon Books, 1980), p. 81.
[22] Jittipat Poonkham, *A Genealogy of Bamboo Diplomacy: The Politics of Thai Détente with Russia and China* (Canberra: ANU Press, 2022), p. 257. For details of Sino-Thai relations from 1975, see chapters 6 and 7.
[23] Lee Lai-to, 'Deng Xiaoping's ASEAN Tour: A Perspective on Sino-Southeast Asian Relations', *Contemporary Southeast Asia*, Volume 3, Number 1, June 1981, p. 62. Vietnam has also been denounced by Deng as the 'Cuba of the Orient'.

outside influence and asked Deng to convey to the Cambodian leadership that Thailand would not allow its territory to be used as a base 'to create trouble for Cambodia'. In return, Beijing, in Sihanouk's words, 'did its best to get Pol Pot, Ieng Sary, and Son Sen to stop fooling around on the Thai frontier and concentrate their war effort more seriously on the Kampuchean–Vietnamese border', of which they took heed.[24] Deng was happy that Thailand was willing to develop friendly relations with countries regardless of their socio-political systems. Jittipat Poonkham noted that Deng's visit 'marked a significant turning point in Thai –Chinese relations amid the deteriorations of Sino-Vietnamese relations and Vietnamese–Cambodian relations'.[25]

Although Malaysia was the first of the ASEAN countries to establish diplomatic relations with China in May 1974 under then Prime Minister Tun Razak, there had not been any substantial developments in the bilateral relations due mainly to China's continual support of the Malayan Communist Party (MCP). Deng's visit, 'though welcomed by Malaysia, lacked that enthusiasm and spontaneity as seen in Bangkok'.[26] There was little publicity, deliberately so, and we still do not know much about the discussions during the visit from 9 to 12 November 1978. Apparently, the Malaysian side failed to 'elicit any likelihood of change in China's stand on party-to-party relations' (with regard to the MCP) and Kuala Lumpur was also 'less receptive' to Deng's 'anti-Vietnam or anti-Soviet attitude'. Prime Minister Hussein Onn said that 'Malaysia wanted to be left in peace, free from any form of interference, subversion, or incitement, that Malaysia wanted a policy of equidistance from all major powers',[27] which was good enough for Deng.

Deng's visit to Singapore (12–14 November 1978) – the only country of the three which did not have formal diplomatic relations with

---

[24] Norodom Sihanouk, *War and Hope: The Case for Cambodia* (New York: Pantheon Books, 1980), p. 82.
[25] Jittipat Poonkham, *A Genealogy of Bamboo Diplomacy: The Politics of Thai Détente with Russia and China* (Canberra: ANU Press, 2022), p. 260.
[26] Lee Lai-to, 'Deng Xiaoping's ASEAN tour: A Perspective on Sino-Southeast Asian Relations', *Contemporary Southeast Asia*, Volume 3, Number 1, June 1981, p. 67.
[27] Chandran Jeshurun, *Malaysia: Fifty Years of Diplomacy 1957–2007* (Kuala Lumpur: The Other Press, p. 166); Lee Lai-to, 'Deng Xiaoping's ASEAN Tour: A Perspective on Sino-Southeast Asian Relations', *Contemporary Southeast Asia*, Volume 3, Number 1, June 1981, p. 68.

The Sino-Vietnamese War (February 1979)

China but had maintained close economic ties – was also very low key at the time, although since the end of the Cold War, this visit has often been highlighted as a showcase of the bilateral relations. Singapore (with its majority Chinese population), while keen to advance economic relations with China, was wary of being perceived as too close to China and arousing 'suspicion' from its neighbours, particularly Indonesia.[28] This was the first meeting between Deng Xiaoping and Prime Minister Lee Kuan Yew. Deng warned that Vietnam, with the support of the Soviet Union, was preparing to invade Cambodia. Lee responded by saying that China wanted the ASEAN countries to unite with China to isolate the 'Russian bear', but Singapore's neighbours wanted Singapore to unite with them to isolate the 'Chinese dragon'. They feared China because of Beijing's support for the communist insurgencies in Southeast Asia.[29] Lee Kuan Yew, in his memoir, recalled that when Deng visited Singapore, a possible Vietnamese invasion of Kampuchea was very much on the Chinese leader's mind (and on Lee's as well). He probed Deng on the Chinese response if indeed the Vietnamese were to invade Cambodia. From Deng's response, he concluded that China would not sit idly by.[30]

From 29 January to 5 February 1979, Deng Xiaoping visited the US, not long after both countries normalised relations.[31] There was thus much more than Indochina on the agenda, as can be seen from the declassified documents pertaining to this visit, but clearly one of Deng's immediate interests was to either obtain US support or neutrality for its impending attack on Vietnam. The Carter administration was aware of that, but the Americans also knew that they lacked the leverage to deter a Sino-Vietnamese conflict and did not want to be implicated should Beijing launch an attack on Vietnam soon after Deng's US visit. The Carter administration was concerned that Chinese

---

[28] Lee Lai-to, 'Deng Xiaoping's ASEAN Tour: A Perspective on Sino-Southeast Asian Relations', *Contemporary Southeast Asia*, Volume 3, Number 1, June 1981, p. 71.
[29] Tommy Koh, 'Building on Deng, LKY legacy', *The Straits Times*, 12 November 2018.
[30] Lee Kuan Yew, *From Third World to First, the Singapore Story: 1965–2000* (Singapore: Times Edition, 2000), pp. 661–662.
[31] The following account is gleaned from *Foreign Relations of the United States 1977–1980, Volume 13: China* (Washington, DC: United States Government Printing Office, 2013), Documents 196, 197, 199, 201–207, 208, 212–221, 226, 231, 239, 252, 264, 265, 270, 275, 278, 312, 313.

action against Vietnam would conjure 'visions of attack on Taiwan'. So, while they made it clear to Deng that while Washington strongly condemned the Vietnamese invasion of Cambodia, they could not support the Chinese retaliation, 'which could widen or escalate the fighting', they also tried very hard to assure Deng that they would consult closely with the Chinese and Japanese in the coming months on the Cambodia issue, work together with the Chinese at the UN, and warn Moscow not to take advantage of the situation in Cambodia to set up military bases in Vietnam (further damaging US–Soviet relations), and that they would not recognise Vietnam until they withdrew from Cambodia. All these assurances were made in the hope of dissuading the Chinese from taking military action.

Deng, on the other hand, as in Bangkok, Kuala Lumpur, and Singapore, reiterated his view that Vietnam was the 'Cuba of the East' and '100 per cent' so. 'If we do not pay attention to this', Deng warned, 'the role of Vietnam will greatly exceed that of Cuba', given that Vietnam had a population of fifty million and a large military force. Carter urged for restraint. However, Deng was adamant that Vietnam needed to be punished but assured Carter that the Chinese side only 'intend a limited action' and Chinese troops 'will quickly withdraw ... We'll deal with it like a border incident.' Deng argued that 'if we do not punish them, their violent actions will continue on a greater scale. They will expand their activities also on China's borders ... Some punishment over a short period of time will put a restraint on Vietnamese ambitions.' Given that 'the lesson will be limited to a short period of time', he did not expect that there would be 'a problem of a chain reaction'. While it was 'inconceivable for the Soviets not to react at all', he anticipated that it would not be 'a large reaction'. In Deng's calculation, given that it was winter, large-scale military operations in northern Vietnam would not be easy. Thus, if Chinese action 'is quickly completed', both the Vietnamese and Soviets 'won't have time to react'. In the worst-case scenario that the Vietnamese side could mobilise their forces quickly, the Chinese could 'hold out'. What Deng wanted from the Americans was just 'moral support in the international field'. While the Americans could not support Deng's proposed 'punitive strike against the Vietnamese' (which Deng had expected), Carter said that they could give the Chinese 'intelligence briefings' regarding Soviet troop movements. Deng also asked for US aid to Cambodia to be channelled through Thailand. Asked by Carter whether Bangkok could accept and relay such aid to the Cambodians, Deng said yes and suggested light weapons. According to Deng, Bangkok was sending a senior officer to the Thailand–Cambodia border 'to keep communications more secure'. When the Chinese launched their attack on Vietnam, Carter had wished that Deng had not told him of his intention in advance, which placed the Americans in a 'difficult situation'. In his words, 'our degree of knowledge should be minimised. And we should not emphasise we have been discussing the issue. We do not wish to be deeply involved in this conflict, though we recognise its dangers.'

The Chinese launched their attack on 17 February 1979. Whether Hanoi expected the Chinese attack remains unclear. According to Hoang Tung (who until 1982 was editor of *Nhan Dan*), he did not expect the attack by China – 'we may have feared it, but we didn't expect it would come so quickly. We did our best to delay it but we failed ... This war, started by the Chinese, greatly upset us. It was closely linked with the US–China collusion.'[32] In his study of Vietnam's communist revolution, Tuong Vu showed that Hanoi's belief in 'vanguard internationalism' was the reason for the leadership's failure to anticipate the Chinese attack.[33] The Hanoi leadership was pleased to see the fall of the Gang of Four in October 1976, and although (unlike Ho Chi Minh) Le Duan had never been close to the Chinese leadership, he expected that Sino-Vietnamese relations could be improved under Deng.[34] It was not to be. The Sino-Vietnamese war affected Le Duan's hope and ability to pursue his 'three revolutionary tidal waves' ideology (a globalist socialist revolutionary movement, the workers' movement in capitalist countries, and national liberation movements in colonised countries with Vietnam as the vanguard).[35] Vietnamese historian Hoang Minh Vu believed the Vietnamese leadership expected the attack 'even if officially they said they did not'.

---

[32] Hoang Tung, D. B. Ngu, and Kathleen Gough, 'A Hanoi Interview', *Contemporary Marxism*, Numbers 12–13, Southeast Asia, Spring 1986, p. 49.
[33] Tuong Vu, *Vietnam's Communist Revolution: The Power and Limits of Ideology* (New York: Cambridge University Press, 2017), pp. 228–235.
[34] Stephen J. Morris, *Why Vietnam Invaded Cambodia: Political Culture and the Causes of War* (Stanford: Stanford University Press, 1999), p. 181.
[35] Khue Dieu Do, '"Victory of the Aggregate Strength of the Era": Le Duan, Vietnam and the Three Revolutionary Tidal Waves', in Marc Opper and Matthew Galway (eds), *Experiments with Marxism-Leninism in Cold War Southeast Asia* (Canberra: Australia National University Press, 2022).

According to Hoang, 'everything points towards a yes'. He gave three reasons. First, Vietnam signed the security guarantee with the Soviet Union in November 1978 before invading Cambodia. 'This was clearly planned with an understanding that a Chinese invasion was a possibility, even a probability'. Second, the two sides had been clashing at the borders since as early as 1977. By mid-1978, the Chinese had closed the borders, 'a move widely understood as a prelude to a formal war. Chinese troop movements to the border could not have been unnoticed by the Vietnamese.' Third, the Vietnamese response to the invasion was 'immediate, measured, and systematic. There was no general panic, or incoherent troop movements.'[36] According to Ha Hoang Hop, Vietnam thought the Chinese would attack in March and so was 'unprepared in February. When Chinese troops crossed the border, neither the government nor the military knew.' The counterattack by the main force only came three days later. The First Army Corp was stationed in Ninh Binh. Half of the First Army Corp had been sent to the border with Cambodia in the South. The division closest to the border was stationed in Thai Nguyen. Vietnam asked the Soviet Union to send military aircraft to help carry six divisions from Military Region 7 to Hanoi. With the help of Soviet military aircraft, they transported soldiers from the First Army Corp, Fourth Army Corp, and others from Ho Chi Minh City to Hanoi, 'so they were able to catch up'.[37]

---

[36] Correspondence with Hoang Minh Vu, 12 September 2023. Hoang's analysis is broadly corroborated by an article entitled 'On the eve of the war, Xu Shiyou said, I wrote to Deng Xiaoping because the Vietnamese were still free to come and go at the border', https://min.news/en/military/1d239dfc4f01ed25b72b13b2495f1d83.html, 20 November 2023, accessed on 20 November 2023. Apparently, although the borders were closed early in 1978, the closure was not sufficiently tight until December 1978. Xu (commander of the Guangzhou Military Region, who was ordered to command Guangxi) said that, 'with so many Vietnamese still active in Pingxiang, there will no secrecy for our troops' actions'. On 25 December 1978, the entire border of Guangxi was finally closed. By 31 December, 'all participating troops of the Guangzhou Military Region had arrived at the designated area, completing the strategic deployment. The cadres and soldiers are ready to fight, waiting for the order.' The author of this account only described himself/herself as a 'master of history and a university lecturer, focusing on the history of the Sino-Vietnamese War'.

[37] Ha Hoang Hop (Associate Senior Fellow at the ISEAS-Yusof Ishak Institute) is an expert on Vietnam's security and defence. I wish to thank Dr Ha for sharing this information with me on 12 September 2023.

On the same day of the Chinese offensive, President Carter wrote to Brezhnev to let him know that Washington was not in collusion with Beijing and urged the Soviet Union to exercise restraint, saying that Washington was prepared to cooperate with Moscow to seek a solution to the conflict. Publicly, when asked whether Deng Xiaoping raised the issue of an attack on Vietnam when he was in the US, the answer was 'no', and all press questions pertaining to the Sino-Vietnamese war were to be addressed by the Department of State, not the White House or Department of Defence.

For the US, with regard to the Sino-Vietnamese war, Washington's policy was to minimise its impact on US bilateral relations with both China and the Soviet Union and to deter Moscow from escalating the conflict. The longer-term goal was to secure the withdrawal of Vietnam from Cambodia and China from Vietnam, establish an independent and neutral Cambodia, and reassure both the ASEAN countries and Japan.

While the ASEAN countries felt that Vietnam could not be let off without repercussions, none could officially support the Chinese action for the same reason that they could not support Vietnam's invasion of Kampuchea.[38] The Vietnamese Foreign Ministry Minister Vo Dong Giang noted that in hindsight, the speed and intensity of ASEAN reaction to the Vietnamese invasion of Cambodia was partly affected by feelings that they had been deceived by Pham Van Dong, who had assured the ASEAN states during his visit that Hanoi would not interfere in the internal affairs of its neighbours. Giang revealed that Hanoi 'had not foreseen the strong reaction to the invasion'. The ASEAN reaction to the Chinese invasion of Vietnam was, however, 'somewhat ambivalent'.[39] S. R. Nathan (permanent secretary, Singapore's Ministry of Foreign Affairs) recalled that having strongly opposed the Vietnamese invasion of Cambodia, the ASEAN countries had a problem in 'coming to terms' with the Chinese invasion. ASEAN 'could not reasonably endorse' the Chinese action. But fortuitously, the Chinese troops withdrew a month after the attack 'and so ASEAN was let off the hook'.[40] Singapore was of the view that 'by combining diplomatic

---

[38] Interview with S. Dhanabalan, 1994, *Senior ASEAN Statesmen* (Oral History Centre, National Archives of Singapore, National Heritage Board, 1998).
[39] 'Vo Dong Giang on Cambodia', 16, 24, and 28 June, FCO 15/3510.
[40] S. R. Nathan, *An Unexpected Journey: Path to the Presidency* (Singapore: Editions Didier Millet, 2011), p. 386.

moves with military pressure against Vietnam, China had brought about the isolation of Vietnam and her economic impoverishment'.[41] In his memoir, Lee Kuan Yew, who found the Vietnamese particularly tough even in defeat, wrote that he was thankful that the Chinese had punished the Vietnamese.[42] But in fact, a few days before the Chinese invasion, Lee had expressed 'deep concern' about the possibility of Chinese military action to Donald Hawley (British high commissioner to Malaysia). Lee feared that if China took military action against Vietnam, the Soviet Union might feel obliged to intervene as well. He hoped that the British 'would take the initiative in urging caution on the Chinese and that the European Community (which "counted politically with China") would do the same'.[43] In the wake of the attack, Mushahid Ali, who was then deputy director (international) covering China at the Ministry of Foreign Affairs (MFA), recalled that Singapore was concerned about how far and for how long China would pursue its 'punishment' of Vietnam and the repercussions. Thailand was less troubled by the Chinese action.[44] Whatever the reservations some quarters of the Thai leadership might have had regarding China, they needed the support of Beijing (and Washington) against the Vietnamese. On the other hand, the attack 'enhanced the suspicions' Malaysia and Indonesia already had of Beijing. Kuala Lumpur and Jakarta were also concerned about the growing Sino-Thai relationship.[45] Ghazali Shafie (Malaysian minister of home affairs), in a November 1979 speech on 'Security and Southeast Asia', analysed the Chinese strategy in this way: Beijing was trying 'to get the Soviets committed further and further into the bottomless pit in which the United States found herself once in Vietnam'. They needed to make the Soviets 'bend and bleed' for aiding the Vietnamese until they could not withstand the strain anymore and then they 'would lose Indochina altogether'. When that

---

[41] 'The Vietnam War: Round 3', in Linda Goh (ed.), *Wealth of East Asian Nations: Speeches and Writings by Goh Keng Swee* (Singapore: Federal Publication, 1995), p. 312.
[42] Lee Kuan Yew, *From Third World to First, the Singapore Story: 1965–2000* (Singapore: Times Editions, 2000), p. 353.
[43] From British High Commission in Kuala Lumpur to Foreign and Commonwealth Office, London, 'China and Vietnam', 12 February 1979, FCO 973/35.
[44] Email correspondence with Mr Mushahid Ali, 20 January 2011.
[45] Nicholas Tarling, *Regionalism in Southeast Asia: To Foster the Political Will* (London: Routledge, 2006), p. 181.

happened, 'China would be free to pursue her own "hegemonism" in Asia'.[46] Malaysian Deputy Prime Minister Seri Mahathir Mohammed said: 'Perhaps China's invasion did have a salutary effect on Vietnam but it also demonstrated unequivocally the willingness of China to act regardless of the usual norms of world opinion.'[47] Despite Chinese efforts to reassure the ASEAN countries, S. R. Nathan commented to British High Commissioner Henning that 'they would all remain wary of China' and that 'Singapore, in sympathy with her ASEAN partners, was taking a rather more cautious line to China than they did at the time of China's punishment of Vietnam'.[48]

On 5 March, China announced the beginning of its troop withdrawal from Vietnam, having achieved its objective. All Chinese troops were withdrawn by 16 March. Although the Soviet Union did not come to the aid of the Vietnamese during the war, Moscow did beef up its military divisions at the Soviet–China border.[49] The Soviet military presence in Vietnam accelerated after, most visibly, the Soviet presence in Cam Ranh Bay.[50] In 1979, Moscow signed a twenty-five-year lease on the former American naval base, which became the Soviet Union's first military base in Southeast Asia.

Since the February 1979 invasion, there has been much discussion of whether the Chinese offensive was a success or a failure. Was the

---

[46] *Malaysia: International Relations, Selected Speeches by M. Ghazali Shafie* (Kuala Lumpur: Creative Enterprise Sendiran Berhad, 1982), p. 297. See also speech by the Minister of Home Affairs to the Malaysian Armed Forces Staff College at the Officers Ministry of Defence, Kuala Lumpur, 8.30 pm, 9 June 1980, in *Malaysia: International Relations, Selected Speeches by M. Ghazali Shafie* (Kuala Lumpur: Creative Enterprise Sendiran Berhad, 1982), pp. 311–321; See also Nayan Chanda's interview with Chinese Vice-Foreign Minister Han Nianlong in Nayan Chanda, *Brother Enemy: The War after the War* (New York: Harcourt Brace Jovanovich, 1986), p. 379.

[47] *Foreign Affairs Malaysia*, Volume 12, Number 2, June 1979 (Kuala Lumpur: Ministry of Foreign Affairs), pp. 226–227, cited in Jyotirmoy Banerjee, 'Indonesia, Malaysia and the Indochina Crisis: Between Scylla and Charybdis', *China Report*, Volume 17, Number 1, 1981, pp. 41–54, n. 62.

[48] From British High Commission, Singapore to Governor Hong Kong, 19 March 1980, FCO 15/2674.

[49] Ha Hoang Hop, 12 September 2023. According to Hop, the Soviet Union immediately sent thirty-two divisions to the Russia–China border when the Chinese invaded.

[50] K. K. Nair, *ASEAN–Indochina Relations since 1975: The Politics of Accommodation*, Canberra Papers on Strategy and Defence, Number 30, 1984 (Canberra: ANU Press, 1984), pp. 129–130.

Chinese punitive action a failure which showed up Chinese military weakness and Beijing's lack of influence over Vietnam, as most observers concluded?[51] Lee Kuan Yew, Henry Kissinger (former national security adviser and secretary of state during the Nixon administration), and the late-Ezra Vogel did not think so. In Lee's assessment, the Western press may have 'summed up the Chinese punitive action as a failure', but in fact it 'changed the history of East Asia'. There were important outcomes to the Chinese action: (1) Hanoi got the message that China would attack if they went beyond Cambodia on to Thailand and (2) Moscow was saddled with the burden of supporting Vietnam until 1991.[52] Henry Kissinger noted that 'for years afterward, Vietnam was forced to support considerable forces on its northern border to defend against another possible Chinese attack'.[53] Ezra Vogel noted that at times, as many as 800,000 Vietnamese soldiers were stationed at the Chinese border in case of a Chinese assault. In his words, 'given the relative populations of China and Vietnam, roughly twenty to one, Vietnamese efforts to protect their border over that next decade were a heavy drain on resources'.[54]

Deng Xiaoping told Roy Jenkins (president of the European Commission) not long after the invasion that Chinese troops could extricate themselves from Vietnam 'whenever they wanted' – the local commanders were under direct and close control from Beijing and would pull out when they were ordered to. Deng added that China could live with criticism of her action from the Third World. Asked

---

[51] See, for example, Ruan Ming, *Deng Xiaoping: Chronicle of an Empire* (Boulder: Westview Press, 1992), pp. 54, 229–230. According to Ruan Ming (who was deputy director of the Theoretical Research Department in the Central Party School of the Chinese Communist Party until he was expelled from the party in 1983), the punitive war against Vietnam had three historic consequences: (1) it caused China to lose its status as a major world military power; (2) the war was a military failure and 'it only achieved success in international politics by virtue of the fact that the Soviet Union failed to act'; and (3) domestically, the war consolidated the 'dogmatist and militarist factions and effectively terminated the alliance of the free democratic forces in and outside the Party' (which Deng initially supported).
[52] Lee Kuan Yew, *From Third World to First: The Singapore Story: 1965–2000* (Singapore: Singapore Press Holdings, 2000), pp. 669–670; Henry Kissinger, *On China* (New York: Penguin, 2011), p. 376.
[53] Henry Kissinger, *On China* (New York: Penguin, 2011), p. 373.
[54] Ezra F. Vogel, *Deng Xiaoping and the Transformation of China* (Cambridge, MA: The Belknap Press of Harvard University Press, 2011), pp. 534–535.

whether the Chinese were not finding the Vietnamese 'difficult adversaries', Deng replied that China had not fought a war for twenty years and that one only learned to fight by fighting. According to Deng, there was no aircraft used during the war, which was restricted to machine guns and tanks. Both sides were using the same type of tanks. As for the Soviets, Beijing did not expect a 'total war' or even a 'division-level attack' by Soviet troops on the Xinjiang border, although they were prepared if it happened. More likely would be 'limited border incursions, which would not unduly concern' the Chinese.[55] The Australian assessment was that Moscow has 'customarily been reluctant' to commit its combat troops overseas and thus would unlikely send troops to Vietnam. The number of Soviet military advisers could increase, and Moscow would also supply Vietnam with military equipment the Vietnamese needed. But 'any substantial growth in the USSR's military presence in Vietnam, in particular, if the USSR were to gain access to naval facilities there, would be of direct strategic concern to Australia' (and to the non-communist Southeast Asia states as well).[56]

Deng did not expect that the short February 1979 attack would force Vietnam to withdraw from Cambodia. Asked by former British Prime Minister Edward Heath if he thought Vietnam had learned their lesson, Deng replied 'not' – 'the lesson had been a limited one, because of the opposition shown by the US and Japanese governments when he had told them in advance that China was taking this action ... China reserved this right to teach the Vietnamese another lesson ... but would be very prudent'.[57] As he told US Vice-President Walter Mondale in August that year, 'Vietnam is not yet in enough of a difficult position to accept a political solution. Perhaps later, when the difficulties the Vietnamese are facing increase to an unbearable extent, then the time would be appropriate for them to accept'.[58] Asked by Malcolm MacDonald (president, Great Britain-China Centre) what he thought

---

[55] From British Embassy in Peking to Foreign and Commonwealth Office, London, 24 February 1979, FCO 973/35.
[56] Cabinet Memorandum No. 5, 'Vietnam's Invasion of Kampuchea: Chinese and Soviet Policies and Their Implications', Office of National Assessments, 2 February 1979, National Archives of Australia, A12930, Item 5.
[57] 'Extract from Meeting between Vice-Premier Deng Xiaoping and Mr Heath on 17 September 1979', FCO 15/2580.
[58] Ezra F. Vogel, *Deng Xiaoping and the Transformation of China* (Cambridge, MA: The Belknap Press of Harvard University Press, 2011), pp. 534–535. See also, Henry Kissinger, *On China* (New York: Penguin, 2011), chapter 13.

would be needed to get Vietnam to withdraw from Cambodia, Deng said that it would require a combination of negotiation and 'military action'. He anticipated that 'the struggle in Cambodia would be long and hard but if persisted, it would bring the Vietnamese to a state of collapse'.[59] In a September 1979 conversation with Heath, Chinese Foreign Minister Huang Hua said that 'the dispute would continue for a long time to come' and that 'there was therefore the need for high sustained pressure, political, economic and military on Vietnam'.[60]

Indeed, the twelve-year occupation of Kampuchea was 'costly and futile' for Hanoi, and with hindsight the Vietnamese have since admitted that it was a strategic mistake.[61] Deng Xiaoping, who pushed for the 'punishment' of Vietnam in 1979, would have felt vindicated. As Lee Kuan Yew observed, the Chinese have 'a long view'.[62] Seen from both Deng's and Lee's perspectives, China's exercise of influence in invading Vietnam was certainly a success. China's short-term 'red line' and long-term message for the invasion was indeed achieved, thus showing up China's power over Vietnam. This was even though the Chinese military was then weaker than the battle-beaten Vietnamese military and was generally assessed to have performed less well than the Vietnamese during the brief war.

Indeed, by the mid-1980s, Vietnam came under increasing pressure for overreliance on the Soviet Union as Mikhail Gorbachev embarked on domestic reforms. As its strategic options narrowed, Hanoi had to reassess its relationship with China. In a February 1985 speech marking the 55th anniversary of the founding of the VCP, Le Duan said that friendship between China and Vietnam would have to be restored. Mikhail Gorbachev, in a landmark speech delivered in Vladivostok in

---

[59] From British Embassy in Peking to Foreign and Commonwealth Office, 'Sino-Vietnamese Relations', 21 March 1979, FCO 15/2578; 'Record of a Meeting with Vice Premier Deng Xiaoping at the Great Hall of the People, Peking, on Wednesday 21 March at 10.00 A.M.', FCO 15/2579.

[60] From British Embassy in Peking to various other embassies, 'Sino-Vietnamese Relations', 10 September 1979, FCO 15/2580.

[61] See David W. P. Elliot, *Changing Worlds: Vietnam's Transition from Cold War to Globalization* (New York: Oxford University Press, 2012), p. xi. For the Southeast Asian response to the invasion, see Ang Cheng Guan, *Singapore, ASEAN and the Cambodian Conflict, 1978–1991* (Singapore: NUS Press, 2013).

[62] Graham Allison and Robert D. Blackwill, with Ali Wyne, *Lee Kuan Yew: The Grand Master's Insights on China, the United States, and the World* (Cambridge, MA: MIT Press, 2012), p. 11.

July 1986, spoke of the need of both the Soviet Union and Vietnam to improve relations with China. In that same speech, he also emphasised that the future of Kampuchea had to be decided within Kampuchea. With the introduction of Perestroika and Glasnost, it was obvious that Moscow was neither willing nor able to continue bankrolling the Vietnamese indefinitely.[63] In its effort to wean itself from its dependency on the Soviet Union, the Vietnamese simultaneously pursued a two-pronged strategy. First, a 'multi-directional orientation' – reaching out to the West and in particular to the US – which was spearheaded by Nguyen Co Thach. Unfortunately for Thach, Washington was not ready to respond to Hanoi's overture. Second, reaching out to China, the remaining pillar of socialism/communism led by General Secretary Nguyen Van Linh, whose priority was defending the socialist state, especially in the wake of the Tiananmen Incident (June 1989) and the developments in eastern Europe.[64] However, we are running ahead of this narrative. The 1980s and how the Third Indochina War eventually ended are covered in Chapters 4 and 5.

---

[63] See Bill Hayton, *Vietnam: Rising Dragon* (New Haven: Yale University Press, 2010) and 'Chengdu 1990: Nguyen Co Thach and Vietnam's Normalisation with China', Lewis Stern's Vietnam Blog, http://vietpoliticsblog.blogspot.sg/2012_07_01_archive.html, accessed on 7 October 2013.

[64] 'Chengdu 1990: Nguyen Co Thach and Vietnam's Normalisation with China', Lewis Stern's Vietnam Blog, http://vietpoliticsblog.blogspot.sg/2012_07_01_archive.html, accessed on 7 October 2013.

4 Regional Responses to the Vietnamese Invasion

I

This chapter revisits the efforts, mostly spearheaded by ASEAN – fighting and talking – which took up much of the 1980s, to bring the Third Indochina War to an end. Recalling the Third Indochina War, Jusuf Wanandi noted that 'remaining in Cambodia was not an option of Vietnam. A political solution needed to be reached. It was clear that, a little over a decade after its creation, this would be ASEAN's first real test.'[1]

We must begin our narrative with Thailand given that it was the front-line state of ASEAN. Of the five ASEAN member states, Thailand had the most complex relations with both Vietnam and Cambodia. Without going too far back, Bangkok had a difficult relationship with Cambodia (even when it was under Sihanouk). At the end of the Vietnam War, Thailand made efforts to reorientate its foreign policy towards China, Vietnam, and Cambodia. Indeed, as early as 1973, Bangkok, in its capacity as ASEAN (rotating) Chair, extended an invitation to the North Vietnamese to send an observer to the ASEAN Ministerial Meeting in Pattaya, which Hanoi rejected because of Thai involvement in the Vietnam War on the side of the Americans. ASEAN again invited the North Vietnamese the following year and was again rejected. Thailand (and the Philippines) eventually established diplomatic relations with Vietnam in 1976 after the reunification, much later than Indonesia (1964), Malaysia, and Singapore (1973). Thailand initiated the recognition of the Khmer Rouge government on 18 April 1975, one day after the Khmer Rouge captured Phnom Penh. S. R. Nathan recalled that Bangkok sought a decision by 07.00 hours Bangkok time of the following morning after the fall

[1] Jusuf Wanandi, *Shades of Grey: A Political Memoir of Modern Indonesia 1965–1998* (Singapore: Equinox Publishing, 2012), p. 133.

of Phnom Penh for a joint ASEAN announcement to recognise the Khmer Rouge government.[2] As mentioned in Chapter 3, Thailand established diplomatic relations with China in July 1975.

Until 1976, Vietnam (as well as Laos) continued to treat Thailand and the other ASEAN states with hostility despite ASEAN's gestures to engage with the Indochinese states. But in July 1976, the Vietnamese appeared to have changed their attitude. Vietnamese Deputy Foreign Minister Phan Hien visited Kuala Lumpur, Manila, Jakarta, Singapore, Rangoon, and Vientiane. The destinations were deliberately chosen so as not to give the impression that it was a tour of ASEAN, which Hanoi still viewed as an American-creation. Nothing substantial materialised from Phan Hien's visit, although most observers viewed the swing through the region as an indication of Vietnam softening its position towards ASEAN. During Phan Hien's visit to Manila, Vietnam established diplomatic relations with the Philippines even though Manila still hosted American military bases.

Between 20 December and 12 January 1978, Vietnamese Foreign Minister Nguyen Duy Trinh visited the ASEAN capitals (except Singapore). The visit took place against the backdrop of the fighting between Vietnam and Cambodia that, in the words of an Indonesian, 'aroused old fears of an aggressive, Vietnam-dominated, Indochina'. Apparently, besides the 'fraternal socialist countries', Hanoi was 'privately disappointed' that it could not win much support for the Vietnamese case.[3]

In end-July 1978, Phan Hien again visited Kuala Lumpur and Singapore as well as Bangkok (which he gave a miss in 1976). In a charm offensive, Prime Minister Pham Van Dong visited the ASEAN states in September 1978, where he expressed willingness to shelve its own concept of 'Freedom, Independence and Neutrality' to discuss the ASEAN concept of 'Zone of Peace, Freedom and Neutrality', offered a non-aggression pact, and assured that Hanoi would not interfere in the internal affairs of regional countries, which turned out to be untrue. In the case of Thailand, Dong assured the Thais that Hanoi would discontinue its involvement in the Thai communist insurgency

---

[2] Ang Cheng Guan, *Singapore, ASEAN and the Cambodian Conflict 1978–1991* (Singapore: NUS Press, 2013), pp. 6, 9.
[3] From British Embassy in Hanoi to Foreign and Commonwealth Office, London, 'SRV/Cambodia', 20 January 1978, FCO 15/2334; 27 January 1978, FCO 15/2335.

movement, but in 1979 a splinter Thai communist movement was formed – the Thai Isarn Liberation Party – based in Laos and drawing support from Vietnam, which in turn aroused 'Thai feelings about a continuing claim to the sixteen northeastern provinces of Thailand'.[4] In hindsight, all these visits seen in the context of developments in Indochina (as described in Chapters 1–3) can be interpreted as Hanoi trying to win support against Cambodia and China. A few months after the September visits, Vietnam invaded Cambodia, which 'left the lasting impression, particularly in ASEAN capitals and Japan, that Hanoi's preinvasion diplomacy had been a duplicitous stratagem'.[5]

Returning to our main narrative, despite Thai efforts, rapprochement with Vietnam was difficult.[6] According to the Khmer Rouge leadership, diplomatic relations with Thailand were 'too problematic'.[7] The Thais were still recovering from the rapid fall of Saigon, described as 'a traumatic experience', when the December 1978 invasion in one stroke removed the 'territorial buffer' between Thailand and Vietnam, which Cambodia had served, made possible by the French colonisation of Cambodia that had persisted after the country became independent under Sihanouk (who disliked the Vietnamese). As Bernard Gordon noted, 'in the Thai view, a de facto Indochinese federation dominated by Hanoi places Vietnamese power along Thailand's south-eastern border, at some points only 120 miles from Bangkok'.[8] Roy D. Morey

---

[4] Sarasin Viraphol, 'Domestic Considerations of Thailand's policies towards the Indochinese States', 15 July 1982, FCO 15/3307 and FCO 15/3308.
[5] William S. Turley and Jeffrey Race, 'The Third Indochina War', *Foreign Policy*, Number 38, Spring 1980, p. 102; Ang Cheng Guan, *Singapore, ASEAN and the Cambodian Conflict 1978–1991* (Singapore: NUS Press, 2013), pp. 12–14; Thu-huong Nguyen-vo, *Khmer–Viet Relations and the Third Indochina Conflict* (Jefferson: McFarland and Company, 1992), pp. 120–121.
[6] Sok Udom Deth, *A History of Cambodia–Thailand Diplomatic Relations 1950–2020* (Glienicke: Galda Verlag, 2020), pp. 82–83.
[7] David Chandler, Introduction *'My' Cambodia 1960–1962*, www.levandehistoria.se/sites/default/files/material_file/skriftserie-8-beneath-a-beautiful-piece-of-cloth.pdf, p. 23, accessed on 21 September 2022. For details, see Sok Udom Deth, *A History of Cambodia–Thailand Diplomatic Relations 1950–2020* (Glienicke: Galda Verlag, 2020). According to Sok Udom Deth, the ups and downs of Thailand–Cambodia relations between 1975 and 1978 was very much dependent on the government in power in Thailand. On the other hand, the Khmer Rouge, although communist, pursued a 'neutralist policy' toward Thailand.
[8] Bernard K. Gordon, 'The Third Indochina Conflict', *Foreign Affairs*, Fall 1986, p. 70.

(who was deputy Number Development Programme resident representative from 1978 to 1981) recalled how the mass movement of Cambodian refugees crossing the Thailand–Cambodia border created 'an enormous headache for the Thais because they were not equipped to handle hundreds of thousands of refugees'. An even larger concern was the fear that the Vietnamese military would push the Khmer Rouge across the border and 'then keep pushing on to Bangkok'.[9]

Chinese Foreign Minister Huang Hua told Richard Holbrooke that the Vietnamese occupation of Cambodia was a threat to Thailand, 'where seven Vietnamese divisions are poised on the border'. 'If Thailand goes', he said, 'the rest of ASEAN will fall like dominoes'.[10] The Thai diplomat Sarasin Viraphol noted that the 'Indochina problem' was not an 'academic one, but one which involves directly Thailand's vital security interests'. One basic difficulty, Viraphol highlighted, was 'the fact that Thailand accepts the necessity of coexistence with the Indochina states, and yet they are deemed as a potential threat, if not actual, source to Thailand's security'.[11]

After the Vietnamese invasion, Thailand once again became strategically important as Bangkok 'provided key support to the Khmer Rouge – beyond physical sanctuary along the border, or secret diplomatic aid'.[12] We may recall from Chapter 3 that while in the US, Deng and Carter spoke about what Thailand could do. It is well known that the national security adviser during the Carter administration, Zbigniew Brzeziński, encouraged the Chinese support of Pol Pot. 'Pol Pot was an abomination. We could never support him, but China could.' Brzeziński also encouraged the Thais to help the Khmer Rouge. The US 'winked, semi-publicly at the Chinese and Thai aid to the Khmer Rouge'.[13] We now know from WikiLeaks that

---

[9] Roy D. Morey, *The United Nations at Work in Asia: An Envoy's Account of Development in China, Vietnam, Thailand and the South Pacific* (Jefferson: McFarland & Company, Inc. Publishers, 2014), p. 91.
[10] *Foreign Relations of the United States 1977–1980, Volume 13: China* (Washington: United States Government Printing Office, 2013), Document 252.
[11] Sarasin Viraphol, 'Domestic Considerations of Thailand's policies towards the Indochinese States', 15 July 1982, FCO 15/3307 and FCO 15/3308.
[12] Ben Kiernan, 'Cambodia's Twisted Path to Justice' (1999), www.historyplace.com/pointsofview/kiernan.htm, accessed on 19 September 2022.
[13] See 'United States Policy on the Khmer Rouge regime, 1975–1979', https://gsp.yale.edu/case-studies/cambodian-genocide-program/us-involvement/united-states-policy-khmer-rouge-regime-1975, accessed on 19 September 2022.

in 1979, a secret meeting took place between Brzeziński, a deputy foreign minister from China, and Thai Prime Minister Kriangsak Chomanand at U-Tapao Airbase, where they agreed to help rebuild Pol Pot's army – China would provide the arms while Thailand would 'serve as a facilitator and transit country to funnel those arms to the Khmer Rouge and provide them sanctuary'. The US, on the other hand, would provide medicine and food 'via its influence over international agencies'.[14]

There was, however, the concern in some quarters that Thailand was 'being drawn into an armed confrontation with Vietnam by playing into the Chinese hands ... a general wariness that Thai policy may have been unnecessarily bellicose and appeared concurrently too closely identified with Peking'. At the same time, these critics felt that supporting the Kampuchean resistance with Chinese-supplied arms was the correct move 'in step with the maintenance of Thailand's security interests'.[15] Throughout the decade-long Third Indochina conflict, the Thais continuously debated the relative gravity of the Vietnam and China threat, how much time and resources to devote to the Indochina problem, whether Thailand could extricate itself from the Indochina problem, and whether Thailand could avoid an open split in ASEAN by maintaining a tough stance, among other issues.[16] For example, on the one side, there was a 'powerful lobby led particularly by Kukrit (Pramoj) and Thanat (Khoman)', which argued for abandoning the Khmer Rouge and 'accepting the reality of Vietnamese influence over Cambodia' but still regarded the withdrawal of Vietnamese troops as a prerequisite for any settlement. On the other, there were Prem Tinsulanonda (prime minister from 1980 to 1988) and Siddhi Savetsila (foreign minister from 1980 to 1990) who stuck to the ASEAN approach.[17] In summary, generally for the Thais, while China 'posed no obvious short-term threat' to the country, they believed China to be 'the greatest threat to their security' in

---

[14] 'The hypocrisy: "why didn't they arrest him 20 years ago?"', *Phnom Penh Post*, 24 April 1998.
[15] Sarasin Viraphol, 'Domestic Considerations of Thailand's policies towards the Indochinese States', 15 July 1982, FCO 15/3307 and FCO 15/3308.
[16] Sarasin Viraphol, 'Domestic Considerations of Thailand's policies towards the Indochinese States', 15 July 1982, FCO 15/3307 and FCO 15/3308.
[17] From British Embassy in Bangkok to British Embassy in Hanoi, 'Soviet-Vietnamese Relations', 15 May 1980, FCO 15/2788.

the long term. Bangkok would also not countenance 'a Cambodian solution which acknowledges a Vietnam sphere of influence'.[18]

Next to Thailand, Singapore played a particularly active role, despite not being a front-line state. For Singapore, the invasion and occupation were perceived as an existential threat to the country. In the words of its minister of defence, Goh Keng Swee, this was 'a life-and-death struggle, the outcome of which will have profound effect on the Republic'. S. R. Nathan (permanent secretary, Singapore's MFA) elaborated: 'The Kampuchean issue was central to Singapore's policy. The principle involved was that no foreign military intervention should be allowed to overthrow a legally constituted regime. If this principle was violated, it would create a dangerous precedent ... Singapore had to work on the worst possible outcome ... Singapore could not compromise.'[19] As Jusuf Wanandi put it, 'Singapore, long nervous about its neighbours to the immediate north and south, was also upset. To them, Vietnam abused the principle of sovereignty, opening a Pandora's Box for the small island state.'[20]

As for Malaysia and Indonesia, as well as the Philippines (and from 1984, Brunei), ASEAN solidarity dictated that they backed Thailand as a front-line member state. That said, each country had its own dynamics and concerns. Malaysia (and Thailand) 'faced the full brunt of the huge exodus of refugees from Indochina', which arrive in three waves. Prime Minister Hussein Onn was the first ASEAN leader who met newly elected President Carter in September 1977. His meeting with US officials focused mainly on the refugee issue as well as ascertaining the continued US presence in the region.[21]

The first wave of refugees began to land on Malaysian shores after the fall of Saigon in April 1975. The second wave was brought about by

---

[18] From British Embassy in Bangkok to Foreign and Commonwealth Office, London, 'Cambodia: Thai Long-Term Thinking', 23 December 1981, FCO 15/2876. See also, Jittipat Poonkham, *A Genealogy of Bamboo Diplomacy: The Politics of Thai Détente with Russia and China* (Canberra: ANU Press, 2022), p. 257. For details of Sino-Thai relations from 1975 to 1980, see chapters 6 and 7.
[19] Ang Cheng Guan, *Singapore, ASEAN and the Cambodian Conflict 1978–1991* (Singapore: NUS Press, 2013), p. 5.
[20] Jusuf Wanandi, *Shades of Grey: A Political Memoir of Modern Indonesia 1965–1998* (Singapore: Equinox Publishing, 2012), p. 137.
[21] Chandran Jeshurun, *Malaysia: Fifty Years of Diplomacy 1957–2007* (Kuala Lumpur: The Other Press, 2007), p. 143.

the fighting between Vietnam and Cambodia, which culminated in the December 1978 invasion. The third wave came after the Chinese invasion of Vietnam in February 1979.[22] According to Chandran Jeshurun, by early 1979 the situation had become so serious – with ASEAN 'quite clearly having very little to offer by way of an initiative through diplomatic channels for a resolution' of the Indochina crisis – that in March 1979, Kuala Lumpur and Jakarta reached an understanding whereby the Hussein Oon government would make a diplomatic approach to China and the Indonesians would do so with Vietnam 'in an attempt to prevent further escalation of the fighting'. Jeshurun believed that this was the first attempt by Indonesia to launch a bilateral initiative with Malaysia.[23] The second was the often-cited 'Kuantan Declaration' (to illustrate ASEAN disunity), which came out of a meeting between President Suharto and Prime Minister Hussein Oon in Kuantan in March 1980, which essentially asked 'Vietnam to decouple its links with the Soviet Union as well as China to stay out of Kampuchea'. Some Malaysian politicians questioned the logic 'of this impossible formula as a means of contributing to regional peace', criticising the declaration as 'inimical to ASEAN solidarity'; one Malaysian member of parliament even said that it created new tensions between Malaysia and Singapore. According to Chandran Jeshurun, there are few indications as to the origins of this Jakarta–Kuala Lumpur initiative, although Foreign Minister Tengku Rithauddeen and General Benny Moerdani (of Indonesia) were shuttling between their capitals and Hanoi in the months leading up to the Kuantan meeting. In the words of Jeshurun, 'it appears that their fingerprints were all over this document'.[24] The 'Kuantan Declaration', if implemented, would have likely led to a compromise and a 'significant degree of Vietnamese hegemony over Kampuchea'. Jakarta and Kuala Lumpur failed to convince Thailand and Singapore.

In June 1980, the Vietnamese, in the pursuit of anti-Vietnamese Khmer resistance elements, attacked Ban Non Mak Moon, north of

---

[22] Johan Savavanamuthu, *Malaysia's Foreign Policy: The First Fifty Years – Alignment, Neutralism, Islamism* (Singapore: ISEAS, 2010), pp. 167–168; Chandran Jeshurun, *Malaysia: Fifty Years of Diplomacy 1957–2007* (Kuala Lumpur: The Other Press, 2007), pp. 144–146.
[23] Chandran Jeshurun, *Malaysia: Fifty Years of Diplomacy 1957–2007* (Kuala Lumpur: The Other Press, 2007), p. 144, n. 80.
[24] Chandran Jeshurun, *Malaysia: Fifty Years of Diplomacy 1957–2007* (Kuala Lumpur: The Other Press, 2007), p. 144.

Aranyaprathet, which muted discussions on the Kuantan approach. The incursion affirmed Vietnam's threat to Thailand and disrupted Vietnam's Foreign Minister Nguyen Co Thach's efforts to 'exploit differences between "hard line" Singapore and Thailand and "soft line" Malaysia and Indonesia' (although Thach never gave up trying).[25]

The Americans assured Kuala Lumpur that 'relations with the ASEAN countries were every bit as important to the US as their rapport with China'. According to Murray Zinoman (political counsellor, US embassy in Kuala Lumpur), 'the last thing the Malaysians wanted was the destruction of Vietnam, which in a stable situation they saw as the only really viable buffer against China' and that 'it was difficult for the State Department and other Foreign Ministries throughout the world to understand Malaysia's obsession with the threat from China since it was determined by the domestic political situation' in the country.[26] The Malaysian embassy in Hanoi also believed that the Vietnamese were 'disenchanted with the Soviets' and 'would like to get rid of the Soviets'. ASEAN thus needed 'to provide the Vietnamese with a face-saving way out which they could take at an appropriate time'.[27]

That said, as Lee Poh Ping noted, 'the Malaysian approach has been basically that of subscribing to a united ASEAN position ... The importance Malaysia attaches to ASEAN is clear.'[28] Zakaria Haji Ahmad made a similar point. In his words, 'Malaysia's position in ASEAN remains a commitment that will be hard to dislodge ... That the Malaysian government hosted the formation of the Coalition Government of Democratic Kampuchea (CGDK) in June 1982 is an indication of "action" rather than verbal deliberations.'[29] The behind-the-scenes negotiations to form the CGDK were cobbled together in

---

[25] Ang Cheng Guan, *Singapore, ASEAN and the Cambodian Conflict 1978–1991* (Singapore: NUS Press, 2013), pp. 33, 73, 161.
[26] From British High Commission, Kuala Lumpur to Foreign and Commonwealth Office, London, 'Visit by the United States Assistant Secretary of State', 13 November 1981, FCO 15/2876.
[27] From British High Commission, Singapore to Wellington, 'From Minister of Foreign Affairs – ASEAN Dialogue', 18 June 1982, FCO 15/3309.
[28] Lee Poh Ping, 'The Indochinese Situation and the Big Powers in Southeast Asia: The Malaysian View', *Asian Survey*, June 1982, pp. 516–523, p. 516. See also, Rajmah Hussain, *Malaysia at the United Nations: A Study of Foreign Policy Priorities, 1957–1987* (Kuala Lumpur: University of Malaya Press, 2010), chapter 8.
[29] Zakaria Haji Ahmad, 'The Domestic Bases of Malaysia's Foreign Policy under the 2-M Government', 15 July 1982, FCO 15/3307 and FCO 15/3308.

Singapore. Overall, Kuala Lumpur decided to let the other ASEAN member states take the lead, 'having realised that its attempt to play the role of an honest broker was doomed to fail'. Wisma Putra was also 'severely constrained in steering a shrewd course through the web of regional politics' because of Prime Minister Mahathir's 'adamant insistence on totally transparent policies that did not allow for any calculated pre-emptive strategies'.[30]

In Indonesia, Indonesia's Foreign Ministry, under Mochtar Kusumaatmadja, backed Thailand and Singapore, whereas 'the more powerful Defence Ministry', under General Benny Moerdani, 'was more sympathetic towards Vietnam because they saw it as a strategic issue'. In the assessment of some quarters in Indonesia and Malaysia, China was the longer-term threat and Vietnam was strategically important in the region to balance China. In a conversation with the British high commissioner to Singapore, John Dunn Hennings, on 12 February 1980, Lee Kuan Yew explained that the Indonesians tended to see China as the greater threat to ASEAN in a shorter term than did Singapore because of their memory of the role the overseas Chinese had played in the Community Party of Indonesia. Lee revealed that he had done what he could to persuade the Indonesians that 'unless communities of Chinese overseas were given a sense of really belonging to the state in which they lived they would inevitably hark towards China'. That was the Singapore situation fifteen years previously but 'not so now'. Thus, Singapore did not have 'too many qualms' about allowing Beijing to establish a trade office in Singapore, which could potentially become an embassy in the future. Not that Beijing would not try to influence when they could and 'keeping an eye on them would mean extra work', but he was confident that the Chinese would not be able to cause any 'real trouble'. Some Malaysians also viewed Vietnam sympathetically as being 'apprehensive of China' and thought they could be 'lured to become more independent of the Soviet Union' and serve as a 'bulwark against China', according to Lee. In Lee's assessment, there was no need to worry about China for the 'next ten years or more'. China had no interest in destabilising ASEAN 'for so long as her dispute with the Soviet Union and her squabble with Vietnam continued'. In the longer term, China could become a threat

---

[30] Chandran Jeshurun, *Malaysia: Fifty Years of Diplomacy 1957–2007* (Kuala Lumpur: The Other Press, 2007), pp. 147–148.

but 'it was useless to speculate at this distance in time about how that threat might present itself or allow that speculation to lead to an under-estimate of the threat posed by the Soviet Union and Vietnam'. Lee, according to Hennings, 'was dismissive of the Thais saying only that they remained Thais and by implication defective in their analysis of their country's best policy'.[31]

Jusuf Wanandi recalled that in the end, 'it came down to Suharto ... he said yes to Mochtar. ASEAN was our priority; and that was it. Benny was forced to withdraw a little because of the public support he had given Vietnam, and that had confused ASEAN.'[32] There was also the issue of East Timor, which Indonesia invaded in December 1975, hanging over the Indonesian neck. Because Indonesia was still under international pressure over the controversial invasion, Jakarta much preferred 'a more regionalist-accommodative approach' compared to Thailand's and Singapore's 'internationalist-confrontational' approach towards Vietnam. Jakarta, whenever it saw the opportunity, tried to 'restrict the influence of great powers and external parties in the management of order in the region and regarded this as the key to managing the conflict'. For example, the Jakarta Informal Meetings (JIMs) initiated by Indonesia in the latter part of the 1980s (see Chapter 5).[33]

It is no secret that the ASEAN states were not completely united in dealing with Cambodian issue. But to expect perfect unity is perhaps asking too much. As Lee Kuan Yew said in 1980, there were no signs that ASEAN was divided, because member states identified their immediate and intermediate threats differently.[34] In mid-1982, according to Lee, Singapore shared 90 per cent of Thailand's objectives. Singapore managed to persuade Malaysia to share about 80 per cent of the objectives. Indonesia gave just about 50 per cent support

---

[31] From British High Commission, Singapore, to Foreign and Commonwealth Office, London, 13 February 1980, FCO 15/2674.
[32] Jusuf Wanandi, *Shades of Grey: A Political Memoir of Modern Indonesia 1965–1998* (Singapore: Equinox Publishing, 2012), pp. 138–139.
[33] Aryanta Nugraha, *Indonesia's Foreign Policy in the Making of Regional International Society in Southeast Asia*, unpublished PhD thesis, Flinders University, 2022, p. 212, chapter 6. See also, Juwono Sudarsono, 'Current Indonesian Foreign Policy Making', 15 July 1982, FCO 15/3307 and FCO 15/3308.
[34] Ang Cheng Guan, *Lee Kuan Yew's Strategic Thought* (London: Routledge, 2013), p. 59.

and the Philippines about 55–60 per cent,[35] enough for a consensus that Cambodia was 'the greatest diplomatic success of ASEAN's first quarter century'. 'The nature of ASEAN', as Lee Poh Ping explained, 'is such that while constituent countries strive hard for a united approach, this does not preclude the existence of diverse national views.'[36] For example, the proposal for Indonesia to continue to 'act as a conduit for dialogue to Vietnam' was put forward by Singapore (often described as one of the most hard line ASEAN member states with regard to the Cambodia issue), 'indicating an acknowledgement of the need for continued dialogue, or at least of the public need for an appearance of flexibility'.[37] President Suharto was 'very anxious that any notion of disharmony should be dispelled'.[38]

II

Having discussed ASEAN, we now need to shift our attention to Sihanouk, one of the most pivotal, if not the most important, character in this whole episode. Readers may recall from Chapter 1 the sporadic discussions between Zhou Enlai and Henry Kissinger in the early 1970s regarding getting Sihanouk to return to Phnom Penh as head of state. If that had worked out, perhaps the Khmer Rouge might had been constrained. We will never know.

The possibility of Sihanouk playing a role in a political settlement was mentioned at different times and in different conversations in the aftermath of the Vietnamese invasion, although no one could be sure whether the prince could be persuaded to collaborate again with the Khmer Rouge after what he had suffered in their hands. In January 1979, Sihanouk, who was in New York presenting the Democratic Kampuchea's case before the United Nations, surprised everyone by turning against the Khmer Rouge, charging them with mass murder, and even calling for the expulsion of the Khmer Rouge from the UN.

---

[35] Ang Cheng Guan, *Singapore, ASEAN and the Cambodian Conflict 1978–1991* (Singapore: NUS Press, 2013), p. 162.
[36] Lee Poh Ping, 'The Indochinese Situation and the Big Powers in Southeast Asia: The Malaysian View', *Asian Survey*, June 1982, p. 516.
[37] From Australian High Commission in Canberra to various Embassies/High Commissions, 4 June 1984, FCO 15/3880.
[38] From Australian High Commission in Canberra to Foreign and Commonwealth Office, London, 10 August 1984, FCO 15/3998.

In his 27 and 28 August 1979 conversations with US Vice-President Mondale in Beijing, Deng Xiaoping told Mondale that the Chinese had been persuading Pol Pot to let Sihanouk play the role of head of state, but Sihanouk had not accepted the position. Sihanouk's mindset at this point of time, according to what Deng had gleaned from conversations with the prince, was that 'he now considers Pol Pot as his arch enemy rather than the Vietnamese' and he persisted in thinking that 'he is the person who can negotiate with Pham Van Dong', which Deng thought was 'unrealistic'. Sihanouk's plan was to 'exclude the main force of resistance in Kampuchea' (the Khmer Rouge) and set up 'another government in exile'. Deng believed that Sihanouk may 'have some political influence within Kampuchea' but 'he does not really have strength'. According to Deng, Sihanouk's view that 'any political settlement must not include Pol Pot' was an 'unrealistic approach' because 'whatever may happen in the future, at least for the present it would weaken the Pol Pot's forces, which are almost the sole force in resisting Vietnam's position and support the Heng Samrin regime in Kampuchea'. Sihanouk's supporters in Europe, particularly France, were in disarray. Sihanouk was cognizant of that and thus he had stated publicly that 'in view of the disintegration' among his former followers, he was stepping back from politics. Deng believed that Sihanouk was 'just showing his displeasure' and he could change his mind. In Deng's assessment, while Sihanouk was entitled to his own opinions, 'as a national leader ... his views are too narrow and too near-sighted'. While it was understandable why Sihanouk categorically refused to have dealings with Pol Pot, 'his words and deeds only abet Vietnamese aggression and the Heng Samrin puppet regime'. In any case, Deng felt that the Vietnamese were 'not yet in enough of a difficult position to accept a political solution'.[39] The US, according to Mondale, was also 'unsure' of what Sihanouk's role might be but agreed with Deng that 'he should be encouraged to follow a course which could make it possible for him to play a role ... the installation of a genuinely non-aligned government and the removal of foreign troops from Kampuchea'.[40] Lee Kuan Yew had a similar view as Deng and Mondale. Paris, on the other hand, did not think Sihanouk could play a significant

[39] *Foreign Relations of the United States 1977–1980, Volume 13: China* (Washington: United States Government Printing Office, 2013), Documents 264 and 265.
[40] *Foreign Relations of the United States 1977–1980, Volume 13: China* (Washington: United States Government Printing Office, 2013), Document 265.

role. Bangkok also had reservations about Sihanouk's 'reliability' but encouraged 'the emergence of a Khmer united front ... principally as a political move aimed at securing the Democratic Kampuchean seat at the UN'. The Thais also did not expect 'the military performance of a united front to improve immediately'.[41]

In a 7 September 1979 conversation with former British Prime Minister Edward Heath, Chinese Foreign Minister Huang Hua said that China did not entirely oppose a political solution in Cambodia but 'at present the idea was not realistic'. Huang Hua said that Sihanouk wanted to negotiate and strike a compromise with Vietnam in pursuit of at least a partial withdrawal of Vietnamese troops. In the Chinese view, this was an 'unacceptable gamble'. Describing Sihanouk as 'an old friend and patriot', and that 'despite divergences the Chinese respected and favoured his national salvation front to oppose Vietnamese occupation', he explained that Sihanouk 'had no real forces at home and if an election were held as he suggested under UN auspices, the result would be Vietnamese control'.[42]

In early 1980, Sihanouk lambasted ASEAN's continued recognition of Democratic Kampuchea and not including an assurance in UN Resolution 35/6 that the Khmer Rouge would not return to power. He also criticised Beijing for its military aid to the Khmer Rouge and the Thais for colluding with the Chinese. At the same time, he acknowledged that the Chinese role was critical to resolving the Kampuchean problem.[43]

In January 1981, ASEAN decided that it should help nurture a credible alternative or 'Third Force' to assume the leadership of Democratic Kampuchea to prevent the Khmer Rouge from returning to power. While supporting the 'legality of Democratic Kampuchea', ASEAN was cognisant of the fact that its links with Pol Pot created 'problems', thus the need for a leader with 'popular appeal' willing to form a 'wider based' government.[44]

---

[41] From British Embassy in Bangkok to Foreign and Commonwealth Office, London, 23 February 1981, FCO 15/2874.
[42] From British Embassy in Peking to various other Embassies, 'Sino-Vietnamese Relations', 10 September 1979, FCO 15/2580.
[43] For details, see Ang Cheng Guan, *Singapore, ASEAN and the Cambodian Conflict 1978–1991* (Singapore: NUS Press, 2013), chapter 3.
[44] From British High Commission, Kuala Lumpur to Foreign and Commonwealth Office, London, 'ASEAN Senior Officials Meeting Manila, 5–7 January', 21 January 1981, FCO 15/2874.

The shortlist came down to either Sihanouk or Son Sann, who once served as prime minister under Sihanouk in 1967–1968.[45] Both had their strengths and weaknesses. Sihanouk, still revered in Cambodia as the 'god-king' had the charisma which Son Sann (described as 'not really a political animal') lacked.[46] In 1980–1981, Sihanouk was living in Pyongyang. (According to Sihanouk, the US was unwilling to grant him political asylum when he requested in January 1979, while France 'placed unacceptable conditions' on an eventual political asylum.)[47] According to S. R. Nathan, while Son Sann 'was gaining credibility as a leader of a third force in Kampuchea', ASEAN 'still hoped, almost against hope, that Sihanouk would play a role'. Son Sann too needed persuading. He felt that he could not cooperate with the DK 'as yet' as he had far fewer forces compared to the Khmer Rouge. Nathan assured him that 'we – would look to see where to mobilise the practical support – money and weapons – for him'.[48] However, not every ASEAN country was keen on providing the resistance with arms and/or financial assistance so it was agreed that such support would be left to the discretion of individual ASEAN member states. No ASEAN country was opposed to arms being supplied.[49]

Meanwhile, China, through various envoys, travelled to Pyongyang in 1980 and 1981 to persuade Sihanouk. Eventually, Sihanouk agreed to meet Khieu Samphan and a DK delegation in March 1981 to discuss the formation of a united front, 'following new ideas proposed' by Deng and Lee Kuan Yew, who had met in Beijing to discuss the Cambodia conflict. In his letter to Lee Kuan Yew on 28 May 1981, Deng Xiaoping said that he had recently met Sihanouk and suggested to him 'to try his best to bring about an early trilateral meeting of

[45] John Gittings, 'Son Sann', *The Guardian*, 23 December 2000; 'Cambodian Statesman Son Sann Dies at 89', *Washington Post*, 20 December 2000; 'Son Sann dies at 89', *Phnom Penh Post*, 22 December 2000.
[46] From British High Commission, Singapore to Foreign and Commonwealth Office, London, 7 April 1981, FCO 15/2875.
[47] For Sihanouk's account of how he eventually agreed to join the CGDK, see Julio A. Jeldres (translated), *Shadow over Angkor, Volume 1: Memoirs of His Majesty King Norodom Sihanouk* (Phnom Penh: Monument Books, 2005).
[48] From British High Commission, Singapore to Foreign and Commonwealth Office, London, 'ASEAN Senior Officials Meeting: Manila, 5–7 January', 15 January 1981, FCO 15/2874.
[49] From British High Commission in Kuala Lumpur to Foreign and Commonwealth Office, London, 'ASEAN Foreign Ministers' Informal meeting: Cambodia', 13 May 1981, FCO 15/2876.

the Kampuchean patriotic forces and Singapore is a suitable venue. This desire is shared by Prince Sihanouk.' In his letter, Deng exhorted Lee to exert his influence 'to help bring about the meeting so the united front of Kampuchea and coalition government can be established as soon as possible'. Beijing would 'play its part by actively coordinating its efforts with those of the ASEAN countries'.[50]

Following a visit to Singapore in September 1981, Sihanouk (National United Front for an Independent, Neutral, Peaceful and Cooperative Cambodia (FUNCINPEC)), however, agreed to join the coalition, which would include Son Sann (Khmer People's National Liberation Front (KPNLF)) and the Khmer Rouge, albeit reluctantly throughout the 1980s. In June 1982, Lee Kuan Yew told Sihanouk that there were considerable reservations about Sihanouk from several ASEAN countries, and he advised the prince to visit not just Singapore and Malaysia – the two countries most supportive of a 'Third Force' coalition government – but Jakarta and Manila as well, to consolidate the support of ASEAN.[51] The CGDK was eventually formed on 22 June 1982 in Kuala Lumpur, nearly three years after the Vietnamese invasion. The establishment of the CGDK was critical to ASEAN's strategy of isolating and pressurising Vietnam and as a means of forcing Hanoi to the negotiating table. As Lee Kuan Yew put it, 'without the formation of the coalition government, we would not have been able to move'.[52] Singapore was convinced that the Vietnamese believed that time was on their side. Neither economic pressures nor 'the strains of occupying Cambodia' would bring about a Vietnamese withdrawal. Thus, the conclusion Singapore drew was that 'ASEAN has to be equally steadfast and determined, and has to make clear it will not be divided, nor deflected from its present strategy'.[53]

---

[50] The letter is reprinted in Julio A. Jeldres (translated), *Shadow over Angkor, Volume 1: Memoirs of His Majesty King Norodom Sihanouk* (Phnom Penh: Monument Books, 2005), p. 239.
[51] Julio A. Jeldres, 'The Eminent Role of King Father Norodom Sihanouk in the Peace Process for Cambodia 1979–1991', *Khmer Times*, 22 October 2021; Ang Cheng Guan, *Singapore, ASEAN and the Cambodian Conflict 1978–1991* (Singapore: NUS Press, 2013), chapter 3.
[52] Ang Cheng Guan, *Singapore, ASEAN and the Cambodian Conflict 1978–1991* (Singapore: NUS Press, 2013), p. 57.
[53] From British High Commission, Singapore to Chanceries in Bangkok, Kuala Lumpur, Jakarta, Hanoi and Manila, 28 July 1983, FCO 15/3510. Conversations in Kuala Lumpur, Jakarta, and Manila showed the similar view.

It is fair to say that had Sihanouk not agreed to head the CGDK, the whole strategy would likely fall apart. The encouragement of political support for the CGDK and the provision of material assistance to the non-communist resistance was among 'the principal ways of sustaining pressure, rather than as leading towards the achievement of a "military solution"'. The Singaporeans (as well as the other ASEAN states) were under no illusions about the capability of the CGDK forces but hoped that the coalition could 'make life difficult and unpleasant for the Vietnamese, thus encouraging them to look for a way out'.[54] As for the US, Washington's attitude had been for much of the 1980s, to quote Patricia Byrne (US ambassador to Burma), 'ASEAN had the lead in this problem (Cambodia)'.[55] Washington welcomed the CGDK as 'a means of harnessing the Khmer Rouge and transferring legitimacy to Son Sann and Sihanouk' – Son Sann had popular support among the Cambodian exile community while Sihanouk was popular with the Cambodian peasantry and well known internationally.[56] According to John Negroponte (US deputy assistant secretary of state for East Asian and Pacific affairs), the US was 'prepared to give moral support to such a coalition'.[57] US policy objectives, as Negroponte described, were: the security of Thailand, the complete withdrawal of Vietnamese forces from Cambodia, and the restoration of self-determination for the Cambodians. In reply to the awkward question of US support for Pol Pot, Ambassador Morton Abramowitz replied that the immediate priority was the withdrawal of Vietnamese forces from Cambodia. And, if the Vietnamese 'were ever to decide that they were prepared to come to the negotiating table ... in the context of an overall political settlement ... ways and means should

---

[54] From British High Commission, Singapore to Chanceries in Bangkok, Kuala Lumpur, Jakarta, Hanoi and Manila, 28 July 1983, FCO 15/3510. Conversations in Kuala Lumpur, Jakarta, and Manila showed the similar view. See also, British High Commission to Singapore to Foreign and Commonwealth Office, London, 'The Singapore View', 29 November 1983, FCO 15/3511.
[55] From British Embassy in Rangoon to Foreign and Commonwealth Office, London, 'Conversation between the US Ambassador and the Burmese Foreign Minister on 2 February', 13 February 1981, FCO 15/2864.
[56] British Embassy in Washington DC to Foreign and Commonwealth Office, London, 'Son Sann's Visit to Washington', 9 December 1981, FCO 15/2865.
[57] British Embassy in Bangkok to Foreign and Commonwealth Office, London, 'John Negroponte: Visit to Thailand (26–29 March)', 6 April 1981, FCO 15/2865.

obviously and can obviously be found to insure' that 'some other political outcome takes place other than the restoration' of Pol Pot.[58] Unlike Carter, the Reagan administration (1981–1989) had 'fewer qualms about providing aid' to the CGDK, although there remained no clear policy towards Southeast Asia, particularly in the first few years of the administration. Publicly, Washington continued to refuse any commitment of aid but there were some amounts of covert funding to Son Sann's KPNLF through Thailand from 1982. The objective was simply to 'bleed Vietnam white'. The administration never had any illusions that the coalition could achieve military victory over the Vietnamese.[59]

So long as the DK remained a coalition partner, inevitable as it might be, it would remain 'ASEAN's Achilles heel', which the Vietnamese continued to target.[60] Beijing supported the Khmer Rouge to the hilt and Washington during this period was at one with Beijing in wanting 'to bleed Vietnam white and destroy her economically'. The ASEAN countries, on the other hand, were to various degrees not comfortable with the Khmer Rouge and certainly not supportive of destroying Vietnam (given that every country had their private reservations about China). All these differences played out at the International Conference on Kampuchea at the Number in New York (13–17 July 1981).[61] Other than a speech by US Secretary of State Alexander Haig, the Americans 'played virtually no public part and absented themselves from both Working and the later small Drafting Group', essentially deferring to the Chinese.[62] There was the view (and concern) among the ASEAN leaders that Washington

---

[58] British Embassy in Bangkok to Foreign and Commonwealth Office, London, 'John Negroponte: Visit to Thailand (26–29 March)', 6 April 1981, FCO 15/2865.
[59] Ang Cheng Guan, *Singapore, ASEAN and the Cambodian Conflict 1978–1991* (Singapore: NUS Press, 2013), pp. 76–77. US covert aid was disclosed by Charles Babcock and Bob Woodward in the *Washington Post* in July 1985.
[60] From British Embassy in Hanoi to various Embassies and High Commissions, 'Vietnam: Cambodia and US–Chinese Relations', 7 July 1981, FCO 15/2881.
[61] For (British) accounts of what transpired behind the scenes, see correspondences in 'Cambodia: International Conference', FCO 15/2882 and FCO 15/2884.
[62] From Foreign and Commonwealth Office, London to British Embassy in Bangkok, 'International Conference on Cambodia', 31 July 1981, FCO 15/2884.

was disposed to go along with Beijing on the Cambodia issue because they wanted to appease the Chinese over US provision of arms to Taiwan, and that the 'Taiwan problem' had constrained the US ability to influence Beijing on other issues as well.[63] The ASEAN states, particularly Indonesia and Malaysia (which we mentioned earlier) were 'vocal in warning Washington to be cautious, to exercise scepticism about some aspects of Chinese policy, and to avoid providing US support for the PRC, for instance on the Indochina question, just because China is taking an anti-Soviet position'.[64] The Carter administration (1977–1981) was more prone to playing the 'China card'. ASEAN's concern was much lessened during the Reagan administration, which adopted a policy of 'greater realism' towards China.[65]

As the British diplomat Derek Tonkin opined, the solution was for ASEAN 'to oust the DK from the UN', but it was clear that the ASEAN countries could not or would not take this step.[66] The Chinese gave preferential treatment to the Khmer Rouge such as that Thai Premier Prem Tinsulanonda had to urge Beijing to provide more aid to the non-communist partners of the coalition to ensure that the CGDK remained united (which the Chinese said they were prepared to do). Beijing also took 'great pains' to explain to the ASEAN leaders that they would limit their support for communist parties in the ASEAN countries 'to the political and moral'.[67]

It is perhaps useful to end this account with the words of Sihanouk. In an interview in late 1984, Sihanouk said:

We have to put aside things of the past. We have to put aside the Khmer Rouge case and concentrate on fighting against the Vietnamese. Otherwise, one day there will be five million Vietnamese in Cambodia. Cambodia will

---

[63] From British Embassy in Washington to Foreign and Commonwealth Office, London, 'Vietnam/Cambodia', 6 April 1982, *FCO* 15/3195.
[64] Robert C. Horn, 'Southeast Asian Perceptions of US Foreign Policy', *Asian Survey*, Volume 25, Number 6, June 1985, p. 688.
[65] Robert C. Horn, 'Southeast Asian Perceptions of US Foreign Policy', *Asian Survey*, Volume 25, Number 6, June 1985, p. 688.
[66] From British Embassy in Hanoi to various Embassies and High Commissions, 'Vietnam: Cambodia and US-Chinese Relations', 7 July 1981, *FCO* 15/2881.
[67] From British Embassy in Bangkok to various Embassies and High Commissions, 'Cambodia and Prospects for Movement', 1 December 1982, *FCO* 15/3193.

be lost to the Cambodians, and Cambodia will be a colony of Vietnam. So we have to fight. If we are not with the Khmer Rouge, we have no means to fight as nationalists, because China would not provide ammunitions, weapons, or financial aid. ASEAN would provide nothing, would give nothing to the nationalists, because we would just be rebels ... That is the reason why ASEAN told Son Sann and his followers, told Sihanouk and his followers, please enter the legal framework of Democratic Kampuchea so that we can help you. Then, we can help not rebels, but a legal state recognised by the United Nations.[68]

Sihanouk, however, continued to hold the view that so long as China and others continued to support the Khmer Rouge, the latter would 'always be a major obstacle to a negotiated solution to the Kampuchean problem'. He believed that 'only Sihanouk can negotiate with the Vietnamese'.[69] According to Julio A. Jeldres (senior private secretary to Sihanouk), despite agreeing to join the CGDK and head the coalition, Sihanouk's 'main objective remained to reach a political compromise with Vietnam through an international conference, a process which would allow Vietnam not to lose face'.[70]

Although public statements by the Vietnamese and their supporters dismissed the significance of the coalition, according to Sarasin Viraphol, 'privately, Vietnamese leaders have shown far greater concern at this political move by ASEAN, which amongst other things, is likely to ensure continued ASEAN success at maintaining the Democratic Kampuchea seat in the United Nations while enhancing the critical voice against Vietnam in the international arena'.[71] Indeed, at the United Nations in October 1982, the number of countries voting in favour of the CGDK credentials increased to ninety countries from seventy-seven (who had voted in favour of Democratic Kampuchea's credentials) in the previous year, and 105 countries compared to 100 in 1981 voted in favour of the resolution co-sponsored by ASEAN and

---

[68] David Ablin, Marlowe Hood, and Norodom Sihanouk, '"The Lesser Evil": An Interview with Norodom Sihanouk', *New York Review of Books*, 14 March 1985.
[69] Prince Norodom Sihanouk, *War and Hope: The Case for Cambodia* (New York: Pantheon Books, 1980), pp. 129–130, chapter 21.
[70] Julio A. Jeldres, 'The eminent role of King Father Norodom Sihanouk in the peace process for Cambodia 1979–1991', *Khmer Times*, 22 October 2021.
[71] Sarasin Viraphol, 'Domestic Considerations of Thailand's Policies towards the Indochinese States', 15 July 1982, *FCO* 15/3307 and *FCO* 15/3308.

several other countries calling for the withdrawal of all foreign forces from Cambodia.[72]

When all is said and done, the CGDK was but a 'loose' coalition and the Khmer Rouge remained the key military element in the anti-Vietnamese struggle.[73]

[72] 'NATO Experts Working Group on Eastern and Southern Asia', Brussels, 16–18 February 1983, *FCO* 15/3510.
[73] Foreign and Commonwealth Office, London, 'Cambodia: Annual Review for 1981', *FCO* 15/3183.

5 The Long-Drawn Endgame

I

'Wars are easy to start and hard to end', as Stephen Walt observed.[1] How did the other ASEAN countries envisage the Cambodia problem would end? Based on their words and actions throughout the decade, it is reasonable to conclude that their thinking did not deviate far from Singapore's. Singapore did not envisage an eventual military solution to the Kampuchean problem. As Nathan said, it was a political, rather than a military, war which was being waged in Kampuchea.[2] Defence Minister Goh Keng Swee made a similar point. The Vietnamese, he said, would have to seek a political settlement in Cambodia.[3] The biggest problem was how to prevent civil war and banditry as all the Cambodian factions had large military forces. Minister for Foreign Affairs S. Rajaratnam explained that 'all wars must end and end through a political act. The political warfare in Kampuchea needed to be maintained. The Vietnamese would only give up the fight when they were convinced that they were not winning the war, and it would be a matter of time before losing it.'[4] Nathan believed that an international conference on Cambodia was the only solution to the conflict, but in his words, 'one had to drift towards it ... Each party,

---

[1] Stephen M. Walt, 'Why wars are easy to start and hard to end', *Foreign Policy*, 29 August 2022, https://foreignpolicy.com/2022/08/29/war-military-quagmire-russia-ukraine/, accessed on 8 November 2022.

[2] Notes of conversation between First Permanent Secretary and Edith Lenart, journalist for *The Economist* and *Sunday Times* (Paris), 18 December 1979 (Secret).

[3] 'The Vietnam War: Round 3', in Linda Goh (ed.), *Wealth of East Asian Nations: Speeches and Writings by Goh Keng Swee* (Singapore: Federal Publication, 1995), p. 312.

[4] Notes of meeting between Minister and Madam Ieng Thirith, Minister of Social Affair of DK, Delegate Lounge of the UN in Geneva, 27 May 1980.

particularly Vietnam, had first to feel the cost of the war.'[5] All very prescient indeed.

A political settlement, the late Michael Leifer (often considered as the most astute scholar of the international politics of Southeast Asia) opined, might be expected to come about in two ways – one side prevailing conclusively in battle (which did not look like a likely scenario in the case of the Cambodian conflict) or a 'military stalemate', which would impose 'unacceptable costs on one or other of the warring parties', thus opening the possibility of a political settlement.[6] The latter alternative was a view shared by Henry Kissinger, who wrote in a different context that 'stalemate is the most propitious condition for settlement'.[7] This is referred to as 'ripeness theory' in the field of conflict studies, describing a situation 'when the conflict's escalation leaves the belligerents with little choice but working out a solution together'.[8]

In a November 1982 lecture (given to the Royal Society for Asian Affairs) about the Indochina Conflict, Leifer prognosticated that 'the interlocking pattern of conflict in Indochina makes the early prospect of political settlement seem unlikely'. As the conflict entered its fourth dry season, 'the struggle is no nearer resolution'. 'An ideal settlement', according to Leifer, 'would take the form of the political reconstitution of the government in Kampuchea in such a manner that it would be acceptable to Vietnam and to China and Thailand. To pose a solution in these terms is to beg the question because one has done no more than identify the central, and so far, insuperable problem.'[9] Emory Swank (US ambassador to Cambodia, 1970–1973, who visited Vietnam in early 1983 when he was head of the Cleveland Council of World Affairs) wrote: 'Because I admire the non-communists in the

---

[5] Quoted in Ang Cheng Guan, *Singapore, ASEAN and the Cambodian Conflict 1978–1991* (Singapore: NUS Press, 2013), p. 30.
[6] Michael Leifer, 'The Third Indochina Conflict', *Asian Affairs*, Volume 14, Number 2, June 1983, pp. 125–131, pp. 127, 130.
[7] Henry Kissinger quoted in the *New York Times*, 12 October 1974.
[8] Stephanie Benzaquen-Gautier, 'The relational archive of the Khmer Republic (1970–1975): revisiting the "coup" and the "civil war" in Cambodia through written sources', *South East Asia Research*, 5 November 2011, pp. 450–468, https://doi.org/10.1080/0967828X.2021.1989987, accessed on 8 November 2022.
[9] The November 1982 lecture was published in Michael Leifer, 'The Third Indochina Conflict', *Asian Affairs*, Volume 14, Number 2, June 1983, pp. 125–131.

coalition, I deeply regret that I must conclude, following a recent study mission to Vietnam and Cambodia, that their aspirations to achieve a broadened government in Phnom Penh and a timetable for withdrawal of Vietnamese forces are probably illusory.' Swank, in his conversations with Vietnamese and Khmer leaders, found them intransigent and unwilling or unable to contemplate any compromise.[10] Deng reportedly said in 1984 that he did not understand why some people were calling for the removal of Pol Pot. In his view, while Pol Pot 'made some mistakes in the past', he was now 'leading the fight against the Vietnamese aggressors'.[11] Hu Yaobang (general secretary of the CCP) apparently told a Bulgarian diplomat, Stanko Todorov, in 1985 that the claim that the Pol Pot regime had killed several million people was 'nothing but a lie' and that the Vietnamese were killing more people than the number killed in the period between 1975 and 1978.[12] Thailand's foreign minister described Pol Pot's deputy, Son Sen, as a 'very good man'.[13]

Writing in 1984, David Chandler predicted that it would be 'more of the same for Cambodia' in 1985. He also did not think the CGDK, 'separated by chasms of animosity for more than 20 years, will make their marriage of convenience more durable in 1985'.[14] Indeed, British sources noted that 'coordination between the three CGDK factions ... remained poor in 1986'.[15] Also in 1985, US Secretary of State George Schulz advised ASEAN diplomats 'to be careful in drafting peace proposals or the Vietnamese might accept them'.[16]

[10] Emory Swank quoted in 'Cambodia: the rebirth of a nation', *Far Eastern Economic Review*, 17 March 1983, pp. 34–50. See David W. P. Elliot, 'Vietnam in Asia: Strategy and Diplomacy in a New Context', *International Journal*, Volume 38, Number 2, Spring 1983, pp. 287–315, n. 50.
[11] 'Who supported the Khmer Rouge?', *Counterpunch*, 16 October 2014, www.counterpunch.org/2014/10/16/who-supported-the-khmer-rouge/, accessed on 9 November 2022.
[12] Email correspondence from Balaz Szalontai to Tobias Rettig, 29 May 2013, Vietnamese Studies Group.
[13] Ben Kiernan, 'Cambodia's twisted path to justice', *History Place*, www.historyplace.com/pointsofview/kiernan.htm, accessed on 9 November 2022.
[14] David Chandler, *Facing the Cambodian Past: Selected Essays 1971–1994* (Sydney: Allen & Unwin, 1996), pp. 292–293. See also, 'Cambodia: Annual Review for 1986', FCO 15/4902.
[15] 'Cambodia: Annual Review for 1986', FCO 15/4902.
[16] 'Who supported the Khmer Rouge?', *Counterpunch*, 16 October 2014, www.counterpunch.org/2014/10/16/who-supported-the-khmer-rouge/, accessed on 9 November 2022.

The Long-Drawn Endgame 113

This is perhaps an appropriate place to turn our attention to the PRK perspective on the developments during this period, which we know much less than those of the other protagonists in the conflict. From the limited sources and mostly recounted by Cambodian cadre historians, the PRK's account of the war during this period was that during the rainy season of 1984 (from mid-May to October), both the CGDK and the PAVN were 'locked in a stalemate with both sides unable to launch major operations'.[17] During the 1984–1985 dry season (October–April), in fact as soon as the rain stopped, to the surprise of many analysts the Vietnamese, supported by troops from the Vietnamese-installed PRK, launched the '16-Camps Campaign' – a series of offensives against the CGDK bases which succeeded in pushing the CGDK forces into Thailand,[18] but they were not decisive in the war.[19] The PRK history described the '16-Camps Campaign' as a 'turning point' for all four factions in the Cambodian civil war as well as the Vietnamese. The Khmer Rouge 'returned to its traditional guerrilla tactics', the KPNLF and FUNCINPEC 'also switched to guerrilla tactics, as well as increasing their cooperation', and the Vietnamese 'found it timely to transfer responsibilities' to the PRK forces (the KPRP).[20] Vietnam apparently realised that its army could not stay in Cambodia for much longer and wanted to meet with China and the ASEAN states to resolve the Cambodian issue. In March 1985, Soviet Foreign Minister Eduard Shevardnadze, on the other hand, proposed a meeting between Hun Sen and Sihanouk, which made the former 'very

---

[17] Boraden Nhem, *The Chronicle of a People's War: The Military and Strategic History of the Cambodian Civil War, 1979–1991* (London: Routledge, 2018), p. 82.
[18] For Vietnam's K-5 (military) Plan to seal of as much of the Cambodia–Thailand border as possible to prevent Khmer Rouge infiltration, see Sok Udom Deth, *A History of Cambodia–Thailand Diplomatic Relations 1950–2020* (Glienicke: Galda Verlag, 2020), pp. 126–128.
[19] Lau Teik Soon, 'Shifting Alignments in Regional Politics', in *Southeast Asian Affairs 1986* (Singapore: ISEAS, 1986), pp. 3–11. Writing in 1985, Lau was of the view that the war had become protracted and there was 'likely little likelihood of an early end to the military conflict'. For details on the fighting, see Boraden Nhem, *The Chronicle of a People's War: The Military and Strategic History of the Cambodian Civil War, 1979–1991* (London: Routledge, 2018), pp. 82–90.
[20] For details, see Boraden Nhem, *The Chronicle of a People's War: The Military and Strategic History of the Cambodian Civil War, 1979–1991* (London: Routledge, 2018), pp. 85–90, chapter 4.

happy' because that would 'put him on an equal footing' with the prince. Hanoi, however, 'did not want' Hun Sen (who had just been promoted to prime minister in January 1985) to meet with Sihanouk for fear that Hun Sen 'would not be able to resist Prince Sihanouk'. Washington and Beijing also 'vehemently opposed any peace talks'.[21]

Ben Kiernan described the situation in 1986: 'While 140,000 Vietnamese troops remained in-country, there was little chance of the PRK regime being overthrown. But 30,000 Khmer Rouge troops remained, and they were making a sustained effort to de-stabilise the PRK with massive Chinese support.'[22] Resistance against the Vietnamese was dependent on the Khmer Rouge.

As for the other partners of the CGDK, there had been a serious rift within Son Sann's KPNLF since mid-1985, leading to the creation of a splinter group led by Suk Sutsakhan (commander-in-chief of the KPNLF) who wanted to oust Son Sann from his leadership role.[23] The royalist party, FUNCINPEC, did not have a credible fighting force and its relations with the KPNLF was also tenuous.

II

The consensus among those who closely followed the conflict was that 'the reality on the ground ... the essential political facts in Cambodia have changed little since the Khmer Rouge was ousted in 1979'.[24] The stalemate over Cambodia would last till around 1986–1987, when there was a flurry of political and diplomatic activities aimed at finding a political solution to end the war. There were, however, small but uncoordinated tell-tale signs of change in the air as early as 1984–1985, despite the fighting, which became clearer on hindsight.

---

[21] Pov Sok, *Samdech Hun Sen: Supreme Founder and Father of Peace of Cambodia* (Phnom Penh: Ponleu Khmer Printing and Publishing House, 2021), pp. 406–407. This book is a publication of the Khmer Writers' Association.

[22] Ben Kiernan quoted in Richard Broinowski, *The Vote for Cambodia: Australia's Diplomatic Intervention* (Deakin: Australia Institute of International Affairs, 2021), p. 54.

[23] See Robert Shaplen, *Bitter Victory: A Veteran Correspondent's Dramatic Account of His Return to Vietnam and Cambodia Ten Years after the End of the War* (New York: Harper & Row, Publishers, 1986), pp. 215–216.

[24] Bernard K. Gordon, 'The Third Indochina War', *Foreign Affairs*, Fall 1986, p. 71.

The Long-Drawn Endgame 115

Indeed, from about late 1984, the Hanoi leadership was beginning to feel the grind of its occupation of Cambodia and was beginning to search for an exit strategy. The veteran journalist Robert Shaplen, who visited Vietnam and Cambodia in September 1984, detected 'a beginning interest in reaching a compromise on the Cambodian question'. Shaplen recalled that in the spring of 1984 (after years of 'repeated requests for a visa ... being ignored or rejected'), with the assistance of the Permanent Mission to the Number in New York, he received permission to travel to Hanoi via Bangkok. To his 'pleasant surprise' on arrival in Hanoi, he was allowed to remain in Vietnam for five weeks and spend week in Cambodia, where 'virtually all my requests to see people and visit places were met', including 'an illuminating four-hour talk with Le Duc Tho'. Shaplen's visit could not have been coincidental as 'the Politburo was just beginning to rethink the Vietnamese role in Cambodia and ... the abysmal failures of the national economy and half-hearted attempts at reform finally led to an effort to set things right'. In his conversation with Le Duc Tho, which he described as 'long and frank', Shaplen noted that Tho was 'tolerant and almost forgiving' when speaking about the Chinese, and 'careful, as Le Duan has been in expressing criticism of the Soviet Union'.[25] In February 1985, in a speech marking the 55th anniversary of the founding of the VCP, Le Duan declared that he was 'firmly convinced that friendship between China and Vietnam will have to be restored. This cannot be otherwise.'[26] It is worth remembering that almost a decade previously, Le Duan had described China as Vietnam's principal enemy. Nguyen Co Thach also wrote to his Chinese counterpart Wu Xueqian, thanking the Chinese for their help in the past and suggested 'secret talks in order to restore our friendship'. Also in February 1985, Le Duc Tho attended the French Communist Party Congress in Paris, which was unprecedented, and it was believed that he had secretly met with the Chinese while there. Notably, Le Duc Tho's speech at the congress did not

---

[25] See Robert Shaplen, *Bitter Victory: A Veteran Correspondent's Dramatic Account of His Return to Vietnam and Cambodia Ten Years after the End of the War* (New York: Harper & Row, Publishers, 1986), pp. 2–3, 136–137.
[26] Excerpts from Le Duan's speech at the commemorative meeting for the 55th CPV anniversary in Hanoi on 2 February 1985, BBC, *Summary of World Broadcasts*, Part 3: *The Far East*, FE/7867/B/1.

malign China but instead called for 'all parties concerned to sit down together to seek a peaceful solution to the problems concerning the three Indochinese countries'. There was no official response from the Chinese side, but at the fortieth anniversary of Vietnam's independence in September 1985, Beijing did send a congratulatory message which expressed hopes for the normalisation of relations. Beijing was evidently adopting a wait-and-see attitude. In November that year, the Vietnamese attended an international trade fair in Beijing. This was described to Shaplen by a Vietnamese official as comparable to the 'Ping-Pong diplomacy', a reference to the beginning of the thaw in Sino-US relations in the 1970s. Robert Shaplen further reported that when he met the Vietnamese delegation at the United Nations in 1985, he found them 'more willing, if not eager, to reach a political solution prior to 1990'. The view was that the sooner they (the Vietnamese) could extricate from Cambodia, the sooner they could 'concentrate on our own economic development'. The Vietnamese officials at the Number believed that in Vietnam 'the conditions for a political solution are ripening' and that 'there is now agreement on the broad principles'.[27] Kosal Path's recent research (which we referred to in Chapter 2) revealed that after four years of military mobilisation and confrontation, in Vietnam the 'economic-firsters' gradually came back into the forefront. From 1983, the economic threat facing Vietnam 'loomed even larger than the military one'. The old guard were gradually persuaded of the need 'to reconsider the costs of the two-front war and change the course of Vietnam's foreign policy'. Hanoi was compelled to reduce the costs of its occupation of Cambodia as well as abandon 'the idea of Vietnam-led economic regionalism in Indochina', which it was no longer able to finance by 1985. This led to the Doi Moi (renovation) policy adopted at the 6th Party Congress in December 1986, which marked 'the most transformative transition in Vietnam's modern political history from the Marxist central-planning model to a market-oriented economy'.[28] By August 1985, it was public knowledge that Hanoi

---

[27] Robert Shaplen, *Bitter Victory: A Veteran Correspondent's Dramatic Account of His Return to Vietnam and Cambodia Ten Years after the End of the War* (New York: Harper & Row, Publishers, 1986), pp. 137–138, 201.
[28] Kosal Path, *Vietnam's Strategic Thinking during the Third Indochina War* (Madison: University of Wisconsin Press, 2010), see chapters 5 and 6, pp. 165, 167, and 202.

intended to withdraw their troops from Cambodia by the end of 1990,[29] although ASEAN and others did not believe it.

Sihanouk was willing 'to talk without preconditions' but acknowledged (in an October 1985 conversation) the difficulty of getting the 'various sponsors ... to agree ... The Chinese and the Thais are still more interested in having the war continue, in relying on us, the coalition forces, to bleed the Vietnamese.'[30]

Meanwhile, Sino-Soviet relations were also showing signs of morphing, dating back to early 1982 and culminating in the summit between Deng Xiaoping and Mikhail Gorbachev in 1989.[31] But the starting point most relevant to this study is perhaps Soviet First Deputy Premier Ivan Arkhipov's visit to China in December 1984–January 1985. This was the highest-level visit by a Soviet official since the border clash in 1969 which brought both countries to the brink of war. Described as an 'old friend' of China dating back to the 1950s, the visit was 'unexpectedly warm and friendly', although it did not mean the Sino-Soviet relation turned the corner. But the relations were clearly thawing. As David Bonavia observed, 'the past year (1984) has seen great atmospheric improvements in Sino-Soviet relations, and progress in trade links, but no fundamental solutions of the big foreign policy issues that divide the two countries'. Worth noting also was the very much reduced tension on the Sino-Soviet border, which was a 'sharp contrast to the situation on the Sino-Vietnamese border, where there are daily shoot-outs and prisoners are taken if rival patrols meet in the ill-defined frontier zone'.[32] Beijing continued to insist that any meaningful improvement of Sino-Soviet relations would require overcoming the 'three major

---

[29] See Communique of the Eleventh Conference of the Foreign Ministers of Kampuchea, Laos, and Vietnam, Phnom Penh, 16 August 1985.
[30] Robert Shaplen, *Bitter Victory: A Veteran Correspondent's Dramatic Account of His Return to Vietnam and Cambodia Ten Years after the End of the War* (New York: Harper & Row, Publishers, 1986), pp. 200–201. Shaplen had a long conversation with Sihanouk in New York in October 1985.
[31] See Qian Qichen, *Ten Episodes in China's Diplomacy* (New York: HarperCollins Publishers, 2005), chapter 1, which recalls the normalization of Sino-Soviet relations. Qian was vice-minister of foreign affairs in 1982, rising to become China's foreign minister from 1988 to 1998. Liu Xiaohong, *Chinese Ambassadors: The Rise of Diplomatic Professionalism since 1949* (Seattle: University of Washington Press, 2001), pp. 156–157.
[32] 'Superpower links are the prime concern', *Far Eastern Economic Review*, 21 March 1985, p. 94. For Arkhipov's visit, see also Qian Qichen, *Ten Episodes in China's Diplomacy* (New York: HarperCollins Publishers, 2005), chapter 1.

barriers': Soviet troops withdrawing from both Afghanistan and the Chinese border and Moscow ceasing its support of Vietnam's occupation of Cambodia.[33] Hanoi was, in the words of Richard Nations, 'apparently under no illusion that the long-term trend of Sino-Soviet normalization can only leave it isolated and weakened'.[34] Hanoi was reportedly told that the Arkhipov visit would go ahead in 1985 'regardless of the level of hostility on the Sino-Vietnamese border'.[35]

Here is where we must introduce Mikhail Gorbachev, who became the general secretary of the Communist Party of the Soviet Union in March 1985. Whereas US initiatives dominated the first half the 1980s and Soviet policies were mostly reactive, a consequence of the three successive deaths of Leonid Brezhnev, Yuri Andropov, and Konstantin Chernenko between November 1982 and March 1985, 'the final years of the Cold War ... were dominated by Soviet leader Mikhail Gorbachev'.[36] There is consensus that Gorbachev's rise to power was critical in bringing the Third Indochina War to an end.[37] Gorbachev's ascension to power, in the words of Richard H. Solomon (assistant secretary of state for East Asian and Pacific affairs, 1989–1992), 'led to a fundamental shift in Soviet foreign policy, away from the expansionist initiatives of the Khrushchev and Brezhnev eras toward normalisation relations with the United States and China'.[38] Qian Qichen

---

[33] 'Superpower links are the prime concern' and 'The Indochina factor: when pragmatism fails', *Far Eastern Economic Review*, 21 March 1985; Qian Qichen, *Ten Episodes in China's Diplomacy* (New York: HarperCollins Publishers, 2005), p. 17.

[34] 'The Indochina factor: when pragmatism fails', *Far Eastern Economic Review*, 21 March 1985, p. 99.

[35] 'The Indochina factor: when pragmatism fails', *Far Eastern Economic Review*, 21 March 1985, p. 99.

[36] David S. Painter, *The Cold War: An International History* (London: Routledge, 1999), p. 104; Leszek Buszynski, 'Soviet Foreign Policy and Southeast Asia: Prospects for the Gorbachev Era', *Asian Survey*, Volume 26, Number 5, May 1986, pp. 591–609; Carlyle Thayer, 'The Soviet Union and Indochina', paper presented at the 4th World Congress for Soviet and East European Studies, Harrogate, England, 21–26 July 1990. I wish to thank Professor Carlyle Thayer for sharing this paper with me.

[37] See, for example, Robert Shaplen, *Bitter Victory: A Veteran Correspondent's Dramatic Account of His Return to Vietnam and Cambodia Ten Years after the End of the War* (New York: Harper & Row, Publishers, 1986), p. 221.

[38] Richard H. Solomon, *Exiting Indochina: US Leadership of the Cambodia Settlement and Normalisation with Vietnam* (Washington, DC: United States Institute of Peace Press, 2000), p. 15.

recalled that in the effort to unfreeze Sino-Soviet relations, all three Soviet leaders (Brezhnev, Andropov and Chernenko) had avoided 'the three major barriers', dwelling instead on the 'trivial' (developing trade and economic cooperation), until Gorbachev took over. Initially, Gorbachev also showed no inclination of removing the 'three barriers'.[39]

In October 1985, Deng Xiaoping conveyed through the Romanian President Nicolae Ceausescu, who was visiting China, an oral message to Gorbachev that normalisation of Sino-Soviet relations 'depended on the removal of the three barriers, and that this should start with the withdrawal of Vietnamese troops from Cambodia. Once this issue was resolved, the other disputes would be easier to settle.' Deng proposed a meeting at the highest level between the two countries and was even willing to travel to meet Gorbachev to reach an understanding on getting Vietnamese troops to withdraw from Cambodia. In November 1985, Moscow replied that the oral message was received and that 'the time was ripe for holding a Sino-Soviet meeting at the highest level and for normalizing relations'.[40]

On 28 July 1986, Gorbachev delivered what is famously known as the 'Vladivostok speech' (because it was delivered in the port city of Vladivostok on the far eastern part of the Soviet Union). It was a very long speech but most relevant to this study is what Gorbachev said about the Third Indochina War – that it was an issue between China and Vietnam and depended on the normalisation of Sino-Vietnam relations, and that all Moscow could do was to hope that China and Vietnam would resume their dialogue and reach an amicable settlement. The future of Cambodia should be decided by Cambodians.[41] Qian Qichen (China's foreign minister from 1988 to 1998) recalled that after the Vladivostok speech, the special envoys of China and the Soviet Union no longer avoided the topic of Cambodia in their political consultation.[42] As Ken Berry noted, although Gorbachev's statement

---

[39] Qian Qichen, *Ten Episodes in China's Diplomacy* (New York: HarperCollins Publishers, 2005), p. 17.
[40] Qian Qichen, *Ten Episodes in China's Diplomacy* (New York: HarperCollins Publishers, 2005), pp. 17–18.
[41] For the full text of the Vladivostok speech (28 July 1986), see *Contemporary Southeast Asia*, Volume 8, Number 3, December 1986.
[42] Qian Qichen, *Ten Episodes in China's Diplomacy* (New York: HarperCollins Publishers, 2005), p. 37.

on the Cambodia issue 'looked fairly thin and (in hindsight) little more than a statement of the obvious fact', the statement 'broke the international ice to the extent that Cambodia was thereafter used as the reason for subsequent meetings between China and the Soviet Union, between Thailand and Vietnam, and eventually between China and Vietnam, rather than as before, a motive for *not* talking'. Gorbachev's statement 'may also have given Vietnam and Cambodia at least pause to consider that they would not always be able to call upon the Soviet Union for unquestioning support'.[43] Relations between Hanoi and Moscow have indeed cooled considerably since Gorbachev took power in March 1985. It is no wonder that in Vietnam, Gorbachev 'remains a divisive figure'. Apparently, the VCP 'hated' Gorbachev and considered him 'a traitor'. There were some – 'the more modern-minded party members' – who wanted to follow the Gorbachev path to bring 'democracy and liberal spirit' to Vietnam, but they were too weak and were 'cracked down by the Vietnamese Communist Party'. Gorbachev's policies 'forced Vietnam to reform because he took away aid'.[44]

It is worth noting here that Le Duan, who as general secretary of the VCP oversaw the breakdown of Vietnam–Cambodia–China relations, died on 10 July 1986. Lee Kuan Yew, according to Sihanouk, hoped that with the death of Le Duan and the older generation of leaders such as Truong Chinh and Pham Van Dong getting older, there would appear a new and younger generation of leaders capable of seeing the dangers of overdependence on the Soviet Union and the 'happiness, prosperity, the development of ASEAN nations', think of the future of Vietnam and the benefits of cooperating with countries such as the ASEAN states. Truong Chinh died in September 1988. Sihanouk, however, did not expect the younger generation of Vietnamese leaders 'to be more reasonable, less tough, or less ambitious than the older generation in Hanoi'.[45]

The veteran Thai journalist Kavi Chongkittavorn, then a young reporter, was at Vladivostok on 26 July 1986 to report on Gorbachev's major foreign policy speech. He described Gorbachev as 'the game

---

[43] Ken Berry, *Cambodia: From Red to Blue – Australia's Initiative for Peace* (Canberra: Allen & Unwin, 1997), p. 7.
[44] 'In Vietnam, Gorbachev remains a divisive figure', *Radio Free Asia*, 1 September 2022.
[45] Transcript of Prince Sihanouk's Press Briefing at the Japanese Suite, Mandarin Hotel, 5 August 1986, 4.00 pm, FCO 15/4544.

changer in bringing an end to the Cambodian conflict'. He believed that Southeast Asia 'owed him for giving peace a chance', and that historians have to revisit Gorbachev's legacy in Southeast Asia, particularly 'the crucial years of 1987–1988 when the Vladivostok speech gradually took hold and impacted developments on the ground'. Kavi recalled that during the 1980s, news about the Soviet Union often dominated the front pages of regional newspapers but they mostly covered the threats posed by communism and linked that to Moscow. The Gorbachev era also saw the gradual decline of the Soviet military presence in the region as Moscow turned its attention towards its domestic affairs. Soviet–US relations were also experiencing a thaw, beginning with the Geneva Summit on 19–20 November 1985 between Reagan and Gorbachev, the first summit between the two superpowers in more than six years. Despite not producing any tangible results, the Geneva Summit has been described as 'a breakthrough point for American–Soviet relations ... largely predicated on the personal connection forged between Gorbachev and Reagan'.[46] The two leaders had three more summit meetings between 1986 and 1988 where they progressively reached agreements on a wide-ranging set of issues, although it should be said that none dealt directly with the Cambodia issue since it was never a priority issue for Washington in their relations with Moscow. Kavi further recalled Soviet Foreign Minister Eduard Shevardnadze's very first visit to Bangkok in March 1987, which excited the Thai authorities for they knew that 'there would be some dramatic policy shifts in the internecine Cambodian conflict'.[47] Unfortunately, the Soviets did not live up to expectations. Although Gorbachev's Vladivostok speech was significant, the Americans and Thais, in their encounters with Shevardnadze, concluded that while Moscow 'appeared to be re-examining their policy ... they have reached no conclusions, nor come up with new ideas. They seemed to recognize that their involvement in Vietnam was not doing them any good, except for their naval facilities in Cam Ranh Bay.' While in Bangkok, Shevardnadze 'had nothing new to say'. The feeling in some quarters (the UK, US, Thailand, and Singapore) was that there was

---

[46] 'Reagan and Gorbachev: the Geneva Summit', www.atomicheritage.org/history/reagan-and-gorbachev-geneva-summit, acceded on 1 December 2022.

[47] 'Thanks to Gorbachev, SE Asia found peace', *Bangkok Post*, 6 September 2022.

little change in either Vietnamese or Soviet policies on Cambodia.[48] Lee Kuan Yew's analysis was that the Soviets wanted to keep their naval and air bases in Vietnam while seeing Vietnam exit Cambodia. But for the time being, Moscow was not prepared to loosen its hold on Vietnam and lose their access to the bases.[49]

The Indians, who had close connections with both Moscow and Hanoi, had a different view. According to the Indian side, the Vietnamese were genuinely interested in a resolution; for example, they now did not insist on Heng Samrin as being the sole representative of the Cambodians and other 'representatives' could play a role. Nguyen Co Thach has asked the Indians to convey that to the ASEAN countries. Jakarta agreed that that represented a shift in the Vietnamese position; however, Bangkok and Singapore did not think so. Also, after a 'fifteen-year silence', Sihanouk contacted the Indian government and informed New Delhi that Vietnam told him that they would wish India to be one of the 'guarantors of any international settlement on Cambodia'. According to Indian Deputy Foreign Minister Natwar Singh, 'the Vietnamese ... were sending signals of flexibility ... The Vietnamese wanted the war to end; it was expensive, unpopular, and causing their isolation in the international community. The crucial figure in ASEAN was Dr. Mochtar. If he could be convinced of Vietnamese flexibility, he could probably carry his ASEAN colleagues.' As for Moscow, Natwar Singh was of the view that 'the West should not overestimate Russian influence in Vietnam'. Singh recounted how, when he visited other communist countries, 'within five minutes of his arrival, he would hear praises of the Russians; the Vietnamese, by contrast, never mentioned them'. The Russians had been encouraging the Vietnamese to improve their relations with China 'but had achieved little; the Vietnamese were in no hurry to do this'.[50] That was as much as Moscow was prepared to do. The Russians 'would not take any initiative vis-à-vis the Vietnamese'.[51]

[48] Record of a meeting between Mr Tim Renton MP, Minister of State for Foreign and Commonwealth Affairs, and Mr Natwar Singh, Indian Deputy Foreign Minister, 15.15, Tuesday, 29 April 1987, FCO 15/4914.
[49] Ang Cheng Guan, *Singapore, ASEAN and the Cambodian Conflict, 1978–1991* (Singapore: NUS Press, 2013), pp. 98–99.
[50] Record of a meeting between Mr Tim Renton MP, Minister of State for Foreign and Commonwealth Affairs, and Mr Natwar Singh, Indian Deputy Foreign Minister, 15.15, Tuesday, 29 April 1987, FCO 15/4914.
[51] FM Lou Coreu to All Coreu Routine, 12 August 1986, 'Discussion with Prince Sihanouk in Bangkok, FCO 15/4544.

III

A 'bargaining space', to borrow H. E. Goemans' phrase, which is a 'necessary condition for war termination',[52] appeared to be opening, albeit very slowly. To briefly recap, the Third Indochina conflict can be broadly broken down into four interconnected components: (1) mutual threat perceptions of Vietnam and Cambodia, which would require reaching agreements between Heng Samrin's PRK and the components of the CGDK, particularly the Khmer Rouge; (2) Sino-Vietnamese relations; (3) mutual threat perceptions of Vietnam and Thailand/ASEAN, which would require agreements between Vietnam, the PRK, and the ASEAN states; and (4) superpower rivalries, particularly between China and the Soviet Union, which would require an improvement in Beijing–Moscow and Moscow–Washington relations.

We have noted that for (3), there has been movements in improving relations. Sino-Vietnam relations, however, had not kept up with the pace of improvement in Sino-Soviet and US–Soviet relations. Finally, both Hanoi and Sihanouk were still feeling for a way forwards. Sihanouk was somewhat pessimistic in 1986 when he said he did not expect the Cambodian problem to be resolved in his lifetime, 'though this would not diminish his determination'.[53] The war would only end when all three components fell into place. The following account reconstructs how the pieces came together, culminating in the Paris Peace Accords of 1991.

There was no shortage of initiatives to solve the conflict. Rather than going through all the failed plans, it is perhaps more useful to explain why these initiatives – such as the Malaysian proposal of 'proximity talks' (April 1985), CGDK's 'Eight-point Plan' (March 1986), and Indonesia's 'cocktail party' (July 1987)[54] – were non-starters from the

---

[52] See H. E. Goemans, *War and Punishment: The Causes of War Termination and the First World War* (New Jersey: Princeton University Press, 2000).
[53] FM Lou Coreu to All Coreu Routine, 12 August 1986, 'Discussion with Prince Sihanouk in Bangkok', FCO 15/4544.
[54] 'Shultz opposes Cambodia talks plan', *Washington Post*, 6 July 1985; *The Eight-Point Peace Proposal of the Coalition Government of Democratic Kampuchea and International Support*, https://cambodiatokampuchea.files .wordpress.com/2015/08/1986_8-point.pdf, accessed on 1 December 2022; 'Cambodia: Annual Review for 1986', FCO 15/4902; Ang Cheng Guan, *Singapore, ASEAN and the Cambodian Conflict, 1978–1991* (Singapore: NUS Press, 2013), pp. 88–97, 101–107.

beginning. Any plan or proposal that could imply recognition of the PRK and/or the Cambodia conflict as merely as civil war (rather than Vietnamese aggression) would be rejected by those who opposed the Vietnamese invasion. Any plan or proposal that suggested Vietnam act on behalf of the PRK and/or which involved the Khmer Rouge as a negotiating party would be rejected by Vietnam and her supporters. Over the years (until 1987), the Vietnamese position had remained substantially unchanged: 'the resistance group (without Pol Pot) should reach an accommodation with the PRK' before anything else.[55]

What eventually moved the dial? There was no one single event that led to a change of tack but rather several developments, which began in 1984–1985 (described earlier) but crystallised and/or accelerated after Gorbachev's July 1986 Vladivostok speech and eventually coalesced together over the next few years.

One critical development was a reassessment of Hun Sen, once a junior Khmer Rouge commander in the Eastern Zone, who escaped to Vietnam in June 1977 and in January 1985 became the prime minister of the PRK at the age of thirty-three. He was seen, rightly or wrongly, as a Vietnamese 'puppet'.[56] In his meeting with Robert Shaplen in late 1984, Hun Sen told him that 'we need the Vietnamese forces here only to help us defend ourselves until we are strong enough ourselves. If we don't need them, we'll tell them to go, and they'll withdraw. All foreign forces should withdraw from Southeast Asia, including the Americans in the Philippines.' Hun Sen described Sihanouk as 'temperamentally like a cloud after a rain', although both he and the Vietnamese would come round to accept the indispensability of Sihanouk. In the PRK official history, Hun Sen revealed that he had attempted to hold secret talks with Sihanouk in 1984 but failed '[b]ecause of the opposition from China and the Khmer Rouge'.[57]

According to Shaplen, other than Pol Pot specifically and his immediate associates, Hun Sen 'seemed to leave the door open for reconciliation with other ranking members of the Khmer Rouge and for them

---

[55] 'Cambodia: Annual Review for 1986', FCO 15/4902.
[56] See Harish C. Mehta and Julie B. Mehta, *Strongman: The Extraordinary Life of Hun Sen, from Pagoda Boy to Prime Minister of Cambodia* (Singapore: Marshall Cavendish, 2013).
[57] Pov Sok, *Samdech Hun Sen: Supreme Founder and Father of Peace of Cambodia* (Phnom Penh: Ponleu Khmer Printing and Publishing House, 2021), pp. 199, 369.

to be included in talks', including Khieu Samphan,[58] which eventually happened in October 1987 when the PRK put forth its five-point peace proposal and showed its willingness to enter into talks with Khieu Samphan, the nominal head of the Khmer Rouge and foreign minister of the CGDK.[59]

In March 1985, Bill Hayden (Australia's minister for foreign affairs and trade) met Hun Sen secretly in Ho Chi Minh City. Over a two-hour meeting, Hayden 'made up his mind that Hun Sen was a genuine Cambodian patriot, not a puppet'.[60] By 1986, the PRK, while it had not brought prosperity to Cambodia, had survived and 'established some identity of its own' and was seen in some quarters as a 'feasible alternative' to the Khmer Rouge, with or without Pol Pot.[61] Whether others agreed with Hayden or not is perhaps not important, but it is worth noting that one of the critical concessions made by the CGDK in its 'Eight-Point Plan' of 17 March 1986 was accepting the participation of the Heng Samrin regime in the interim quadripartite government, which meant having to negotiate with the 'tough' and 'brash' Prime Minister Hun Sen. Indeed, in April 1987, *The Economist* stated in an editorial that the only possibility for Cambodians to live in peace was for 'expatriates led by Sihanouk to swallow hard and talks to Cambodians under Hun Sen'.[62]

---

[58] Robert Shaplen, *Bitter Victory: A Veteran Correspondent's Dramatic Account of His Return to Vietnam and Cambodia Ten Years after the End of the War* (New York: Harper & Row, Publishers, 1986), pp. 219–220, 226.

[59] 'DPM Prak Sokhonn shares historical truth related to Paris Peace Agreement', *AKP Phnom Penh*, 23 October 2021. According to Prak Sokhonn, Hun Sen was the first to express his intention to meet Sihanouk to discuss the five-point declaration he had put forth in October 1987. The five points were: (1) organise a Sihanouk–Hun Sen meeting; (2) complete withdrawal of Vietnamese troops from Cambodia; (3) organise an election with international observers to form a coalition government that adheres to the principles of neutrality and non-alignment; (4) negotiate with Thailand on border and refugee matters; and (5) convene an international conference to ensure all agreements would be adhered to.

[60] Richard Broinowski, *The Vote for Cambodia: Australia's Diplomatic Intervention* (Canberra: Australia Institute of International Affairs, 2021), pp. 52–53.

[61] Robert Shaplen, *Bitter Victory: A Veteran Correspondent's Dramatic Account of His Return to Vietnam and Cambodia Ten Years after the End of the War* (New York: Harper & Row, Publishers, 1986), p. 278.

[62] Richard Broinowski, *The Vote for Cambodia: Australia's Diplomatic Intervention* (Canberra: Australia Institute of International Affairs, 2021), p. 55.

Hun Sen also had to temper his hard line attitude towards Sihanouk and the CGDK. As prime minister, he had to oversee the economic reforms in Cambodia, which had so far been linked to Hanoi and Moscow. Vietnam was already beginning to implement its Doi Moi ('renovation') policy in 1986 ahead of watershed Sixth Party Congress (15–18 December 1986). The one term that captured the major themes running through the Congress was the word 'renovation'.[63] As Kosal Path noted, 'Cambodia's economic reforms were largely influenced by a combination of external pressures and learning from the reforms taking place in Vietnam and the Soviet Union'. Hanoi had counselled the PRK to pursue economic reform, especially when Moscow 'curtailed its aid commitment to the PRK, pushing the regime to think about economic self-sufficiency and a political solution to the Cambodian conflict'.[64] The Sixth Party Congress, however, had little to say with regard to foreign policy. The political report repeated the standard view, which was that Vietnam would welcome a settlement of the Cambodian conflict on the condition that it excluded the Pol Pot clique and that negotiations must be with the PRK.[65]

Turning to Sihanouk, from very early in the conflict he had advocated a peace proposal which involved (1) the disarming of all Cambodian warring factions; (2) a UN peacekeeping force to ensure peace in Cambodia; and (3) a general election supervised by the UN. In August 1980, Sihanouk invited US Congressman Stephen Solarz to Pyongyang where he was then residing to discuss his proposal. He gave Solarz a copy of his proposal (written in French). Julio Jeldres met Sihanouk for the first time, also in Pyongyang, and before he left, Sihanouk asked him to help translate the proposal for a peace

---

[63] See Carlyle Thayer, 'Vietnam's Sixth Party Congress: An Overview', *Contemporary Southeast Asia*, Volume 9, Number 1, June 1987, pp. 12–22; William J. Duiker, 'Vietnam Moves toward Pragmatism', *Current History*, April 1987, pp. 148–151; Le Hong Hiep, 'Performance-based Legitimacy: The Case of the Communist Party of Vietnam and Doi Moi', *Contemporary Southeast Asia*, Volume 34, Number 2, 2012, pp. 145–172.

[64] Kosal Path, *Vietnam's Strategic Thinking during the Third Indochina War* (Madison: University of Wisconsin Press, 2010), pp. 199–200; Robert Shaplen, *Bitter Victory: A Veteran Correspondent's Dramatic Account of His Return to Vietnam and Cambodia Ten Years after the End of the War* (New York: Harper & Row, Publishers, 1986), pp. 219–220.

[65] William J. Duiker, 'Vietnam Moves toward Pragmatism', *Current History*, April 1987, p. 179.

The Long-Drawn Endgame 127

settlement from French to English and, 'if possible, pass it on to government officials in Australia', which Jeldres eventually did through a retired Australian ambassador to Chile, Noel Deschamps.[66]

Sihanouk was not able to gain the support of China or ASEAN. We may recall that the Chinese were of the view that Sihanouk's proposal, while sound, was premature. Sihanouk was subsequently persuaded to lead the CGDK, but he remained 'unconvinced' by the Khmer Rouge/CGDK preconditions. Sihanouk's 'main objective', Jeldres recalled, 'remained to reach a political compromise with Vietnam through an international conference, a process which would allow Vietnam not to lose face. At the same time, he insisted that the very survival in the international jungle of 20th century world demanded two things: internal unity and external neutrality. Any breach of either would pose mortal threat to Cambodia.' In February 1981, Sihanouk met François Mitterrand, then leader of the French Socialist Party, who was visiting Pyongyang. Sihanouk called for the urgent convening of an international conference, preferably hosted by Paris. Mitterrand was supportive of Sihanouk's solution to end the conflict and promised that if he were elected president,[67] he would work towards organising an international conference.

Sihanouk continued to promote his proposal whenever he had the opportunity to do so. He felt hemmed in by China and his coalition partners. Apparently, Hanoi had signalled its interest to talk with Sihanouk, and Hun Sen had been trying to meet Sihanouk to discuss the modalities to end the conflict since 1984. But his coalition partners and backers rejected all negotiations with Phnom Penh unless the Vietnamese troops withdrew completely from Cambodia, 'a posture' which Sihanouk felt was 'too rigid'. In the later part of 1987, Sihanouk found an opportunity to act more independently in his endeavour to resolve the Cambodia conflict,[68] which troubled ASEAN, and Thailand

---

[66] Michelle Vachon, 'King Norodom Sihanouk and Cambodia in the Cold War', https://cambodianess.com/article/king-norodom-sihanouk-and-cambodia-caught-in-the-cold-war, accessed on 7 December 2022.
[67] François Mitterrand was president of France from May 1981 to 1995.
[68] The above account is gleaned from various articles written by Julio Jeldres, former senior private secretary to King Father Norodom Sihanouk: 'The eminent role of King Father Norodom Sihanouk in the peace process for Cambodia 1979–1991', *Khmer Times*, 22 October 2021; 'The King Father Norodom Sihanouk: an eminent statesman and an accomplished musician', *Khmer Times*, 31 October 2022.

in particular, 'which continued to regard Sihanouk as the pivotal figure in its Cambodia strategy, but was frustrated by its inability to control the prince'.[69]

The situation from late 1987 was very fluid. Each of the players appeared to be shifting positions but there was no evidence of any substantial change. The next two years witnessed much posturing among the various protagonists, with everyone trying to extract the maximum possible advantage prior to any settlement. Whereas, in the recent past, the parties were adamantly unwilling to negotiate with each other unless their respective preconditions were met, we begin to see a series of talks taking place without preconditions. An exploratory phase was evidently underway.

Most notable and significant was the series of bilateral meetings between Sihanouk and Hun Sen, the first on 2–4 December 1987, which was 'the first, albeit small indication of flexibility among the major protagonists', but substantive negotiations was expected to be a long way off.[70] The significance of this first meeting was that Sihanouk and Hun Sen had emerged as co-equals of any future agreements. Sihanouk had broken off from the ASEAN leash. The CGDK had been sidelined and both the KPNLF and the Khmer Rouge were left with 'the stark choice of joining Sihanouk or waging a struggle on their own'. The PRK had established its legitimacy. As most of the protagonists accepted the talks, ASEAN had little option but to support it as well. Their main concern was that the Vietnamese were not given a free pass.[71]

In PRK history, 2 December is a significant date. It was the day the KPNLF was formed in 1978. It was (and we do not know if this was deliberate or a coincidence) also the first day of the 'first peace talks' between Hun Sen and Sihanouk in Fere-en-Tardenois. In the view of Hun Sen, 'without December 2, 1987, there would have been no

---

[69] See Ang Cheng Guan, *Singapore, ASEAN and the Cambodian Conflict, 1978–1991* (Singapore: NUS Press, 2013), p. 106.

[70] 'Cambodia: Annual Review 1987', 19 February 1988, *FCO* 15/5237. For the PRK account of the origins of the Sihanouk and Hun Sen talks and the first bilateral meeting between them, see Pov Sok, *Samdech Hun Sen: Supreme Founder and Father of Peace of Cambodia* (Phnom Penh: Ponleu Khmer Printing and Publishing House, 2021), pp. 410–411.

[71] Ang Cheng Guan, *Singapore, ASEAN and the Cambodian Conflict, 1978–1991* (Singapore: NUS Press, 2013), p. 103.

The Long-Drawn Endgame

Paris Peace Agreement of October 23, 1991'.[72] Indeed, the agreement reached at this meeting would serve as the framework for subsequent negotiations. The main issues of contention were over (1) dismantling the Khmer Rouge military structure (which Sihanouk refused) and the PRK structure (which Hun Sen refused) prior to the general elections; and (2) whether a coalition government should be formed before the elections (which Sihanouk wanted) or after the elections (which Hun Sen preferred).[73] The twists and turns, and the minute details of the bargaining, need not delay us here, except to say that whatever decisions Sihanouk made at his meeting with Hun Sen, he had to be able to consider the views and get the support of Son Sann and Khieu Samphan. The December meeting was followed by a second in January 1988 in Saint Germain-en-Laye which Sihanouk described as a 'very small step in a very long road'. At this second meeting, Hun Sen proposed the creation of a 'high-level national unification council'. This proposal was discussed again at the first JIM in July 1988. Although no agreement was reached, the proposal would eventually materialise as the Supreme National Council (SNC) in 1990.[74] Meanwhile, a third meeting between Hun Sen and Sihanouk, initially scheduled for the end of April 1988 in Pyongyang, was postponed till November 1988.

The third Sihanouk–Hun Sen meeting was followed by a fourth in May 1989, shortly before the International Conference on Cambodia in Paris (30 July–30 August 1989). The main issue which Sihanouk and Hun Sen had to resolve was the nature of the provisional quadripartite government, and tied to that how to prevent a return of the Khmer Rouge.[75] As Stephen Chee noted,

---

[72] Pov Sok, *Samdech Hun Sen: Supreme Founder and Father of Peace of Cambodia* (Phnom Penh: Ponleu Khmer Printing and Publishing House, 2021), pp. 130, 132, 210–214, 343, 347–362. Chhay Sophal, *Hun Sen, War and Peace in Cambodia and Southeast Asia* (Phnom Penh: Publisher unstated, 2020), pp. 182–191, also contains snippets of information on the first meeting between Sihanouk and Hun Sen. See also, 'DPM Prak Sokhonn shares historical truth related to Paris Peace Agreement', *AKP Phnom Penh*, 23 October 2021. See note 59 on Hun Sen's intention to meet Sihanouk to discuss the five-point declaration.
[73] From Tokyo to FCO, 27 January 1988, FCO 15/5267.
[74] 'DPM Prak Sokhonn shares historical truth related to Paris Peace Agreement', *AKP Phnom Penh*, 23 October 2021. See also, Pov Sok, *Samdech Hun Sen: Supreme Founder and Father of Peace of Cambodia* (Phnom Penh: Ponleu Khmer Printing and Publishing House, 2021), pp. 198, 345–347, 366–367, 370.
[75] For details, see Ang Cheng Guan, *Singapore, ASEAN and the Cambodian Conflict, 1978–1991* (Singapore: NUS Press, 2013), chapter 4; Harish C.

the crux of the Kampuchean problem lay in the internal aspects, that is power sharing among the four contending factions and the mechanism for policing the peace after a settlement. Despite world abhorrence over the Pol Pot regime and consensus that the clique should not be allowed to return to power, it seemed unrealistic that the 30,000–40,000 Khmer Rouge force could be denied participation in a transitional national reconciliation government without a civil war.[76]

Singapore's Foreign Minister S. Rajaratnam's advice to Son Sann is worth recalling. He told Son Sann that for the first ten years, mobilisation of support on the Cambodian question focused on Vietnam. However, in the second decade, negotiations would need to involve the question of the Khmer Rouge. This, he said, 'would complicate the whole game'. The new task for the CGDK, he advised Son Sann, would be to create a coalition of patriotic forces including the PRK, otherwise civil war would soon break out. Rajaratnam admitted that he did not know how this could be done. However, he was optimistic, as both the Soviet Union and China, having decided to settle the Cambodian problem, wanted a peaceful Cambodia so that they could concentrate their resources on economic development within their own countries.[77] The time had come to envision and prepare an overall plan. Lee Kuan Yew advised Son Sann to consider three points: (1) whether Son Sann could work with Sihanouk or even Ranariddh; (2) whether Son Sann could work together with Sihanouk and Hun Sen to prevent the Khmer Rouge from returning to power; and (3) to try to familiarise himself with the PRK structure and determine which elements he might be able to win over from the PRK's ranks.[78]

The JIMs, of which there were two, commonly abbreviated as JIM and JIM II, were held in July 1988, and February 1989 respectively. Spearheaded by Indonesia, which had always wanted to pursue a regional solution to resolving the conflict rather than let extra-regional

Mehta and Julie B. Mehta, *Strongman: The Extraordinary Life of Hun Sen, From Pagoda Boy to Prime Minister of Cambodia* (Singapore: Marshall Cavendish, 2013), pp. 154–170; 'Sihanouk eases stand on talks to settle Cambodian conflict', *Los Angeles Times*, 1 May 1989.

[76] Stephen Chee, 'Southeast Asia in 1988: Portents for the Future', in *Southeast Asian Affairs 1989* (Singapore: ISEAS, 1989), p. 22.

[77] Notes of meeting between PM Son Sann and Senior Minister, MFA (Singapore), 2 August 1988.

[78] Notes of conversation between PM and Son Sann, President of the KPNLF and Prime Minister of CGDK, Istana, 1 August 1988.

powers call all the shots, the JIMs are often cited as one of the most, if not the most significant ASEAN initiative to end the Cambodia war. Foreign Minister Ali Alatas positioned the JIM as a 'preparatory meeting for an eventual international conference'.[79] The JIM brought together, for the first time since the invasion of Kampuchea, representatives of the CGDK and PRK into an 'intra-Kampuchean discussion' essentially to unpack the components of the framework of a political settlement (particularly preventing the return of the Khmer Rouge) and to decouple that as much as possible from the 'external issue of the Vietnamese invasion in 1979' – the subject of the second stage of the meeting which brought together all parties, including Vietnam, Laos, and ASEAN.[80]

Looking at the glass as half-empty, JIM failed to achieve any substantial breakthrough, which was unsurprising. As Sihanouk said, 'such a complex issue could not be resolved at a first meeting'. At the very least, everyone involved agreed that only negotiations could bring an end to the conflict.[81] Although not directly connected, it is worth assessing the JIM initiative alongside the Sihanouk–Hun Sen meetings described earlier, coming as it did after two Sihanouk–Hun Sen meetings (December 1987 and January 1988) which were inconclusive and a third initially scheduled for the end of April 1988 that had to be postponed. Sihanouk did not attend the JIM, although he was in Jakarta as a guest of President Suharto. However, everyone knew that he was deeply involved behind the scenes. There was no communiqué issued at the end of the JIM, but it was agreed that a working group of senior officials would continue to examine the issues for a subsequent meeting. In the view of Ali Alatas, the very fact that all the parties involved in the conflict participated in the 'unprecedented talks were

---

[79] For details of the JIM meetings, see Ang Cheng Guan, *Singapore, ASEAN and the Cambodian Conflict, 1978–1991* (Singapore: NUS Press, 2013), p. 108; 'International Meetings on the Cambodian Problem', FCO 15/5283 (complete folder).

[80] Richard Broinowski, *The Vote for Cambodia: Australia's Diplomatic Intervention* (Canberra: Australia Institute of International Affairs, 2021), p. 56. For details of the JIM meetings, particularly the differences among the ASEAN states, see Ang Cheng Guan, *Singapore, ASEAN and the Cambodian Conflict, 1978–1991* (Singapore: NUS Press, 2013), pp. 107–122; Stephen Chee, 'Southeast Asia in 1988: Portents for the Future', in *Southeast Asian Affairs 1989* (Singapore: ISEAS, 1989), pp. 15–23.

[81] 'Cambodia: Annual Review 1987', 19 February 1988, FCO 15/5237.

itself a success', and although no agreement was reached, 'there was a remarkable convergence of views on the key issues and basic principles of a political settlement'.[82]

The JIM also showed up the differences within ASEAN, particularly Jakarta and Bangkok. As the JIM was an Indonesian-led ASEAN initiative, ASEAN member states were obliged to partake in the JIM process. Bangkok, and to an extent Singapore, was unhappy that Indonesia appeared to have bent backwards to accommodate the Vietnamese. We may recall that Jakarta had been sympathetic to Vietnam all along. Some in Indonesian policy-making circles were concerned that Indonesian interests would be sacrificed by an informal Sino-Thai alliance, and Singapore believed that Suharto would still give priority to ASEAN interests. Thailand, on the other hand, felt that Jakarta was usurping its lead role (as ASEAN's front-line state) in resolving the Cambodia conflict and would not accept any solution that did not remove the Vietnamese threat to Thailand. Bangkok was also critical of Sihanouk's manoeuvres. The Thais were of the view that Sihanouk's approach, rather than leading to a political settlement, would only split the CGDK, legitimise the PRK, and deflect international pressure on Vietnam.

JIM II took place in February 1989 (shortly after the third Sihanouk–Hun Sen meeting in November 1988, which also failed to achieve any breakthrough), even though the CGDK as well as some ASEAN member states were not enthusiastic about holding it, preferring the meeting to be postponed. Jakarta persisted and everybody went along, albeit half-heartedly. The chairman's statement issued at the end of the meeting described a framework for political settlement which was seen as very partial to the Vietnamese and the PRK.[83]

JIM II was also complicated by developments in Thailand. We may recall that there was a long-running debate in Thai circles on the approach to managing the Cambodia conflict which would best serve Thai national interest. There was an ongoing rivalry between Chatichai Choonhavan (who became prime minister in August 1988 after his Thai Nation Party won the 1988 Thai general election) and

---

[82] Stephen Chee, 'Southeast Asia in 1988: Portents for the Future', in *Southeast Asian Affairs 1989* (Singapore: ISEAS, 1989), p. 22.

[83] Ang Cheng Guan, *Singapore, ASEAN and the Cambodian Conflict, 1978–1991* (Singapore: NUS Press, 2013), pp. 118–122. For details of the JIM II, see also, 'Cambodia: Jakarta Informal Meeting', FCO 15/5648 (whole folder).

his advisers and Foreign Minister Siddhi and the Foreign Ministry for control of Thai policy towards Indochina. The new pro-business, democratically elected civilian government led by Chatichai declared his goal of turning Indochina 'from battlefield to a marketplace'. As Jittipat Poonkham noted, this 'significantly redefined the framing of Thailand's national interest. It in turn deemphasized national security to affirm Thailand's status as an aspiring regional economic power.'[84] Kraisak Choonhavan, who served as an adviser to his father the prime minister, and who had been placed in charge of the negotiations with Cambodia, said that Thailand should stop supporting the Khmer Rouge. In his words, 'Thailand must take the initiative if China doesn't change its stand toward the Khmer Rouge'.[85] Changes were also afoot in the Thai military when General Chaovalit Yongchaiyuth, on two occasions, described the Cambodian dispute as an internal conflict or civil war, and that Vietnam did not constitute a threat to Thailand.[86] Thai–Soviet relations were also changing, with Foreign Minister Siddhi Savetsila's visit to Moscow in May 1987.

In January 1989, Prime Minister Choonhavan received Hun Sen in Bangkok, much to the unhappiness of the CGDK as well as certain quarters in Bangkok. The meeting, though presented as a private visit, had all the semblances of a working visit by a head of state,[87] marking the 'first concrete step' towards the realisation of his goal 'to turn Indochina from a battlefield into a trading market'.[88] It is worth

---

[84] Jittipat Poonkham, *A Genealogy of Bamboo Diplomacy: The Politics of Thai Détente with Russia and China* (Canberra: ANU Press, 2022), p. 291. See also, Tita Sanglee, 'Revisiting Thailand's involvement in the Cambodian conflict', *The Diplomat*, 19 January 2022.

[85] Cited in Elizabeth Becker, 'The Progress of Peace in Cambodia', *Current History*, April 1989, p. 172.

[86] For a discussion of Thailand's new thinking and the similarities and differences between Chatichai and the Thai military, see 'Thailand: ambitious thinking behind Indochina, Burma link – the Golden Land', *Far Eastern Economic Review*, 23 February 1989; Michael Vickery, 'Cambodia (Kampuchea): History, Tragedy, and Uncertain Future', *Bulletin of Concerned Asian Scholars*, Volume 21, Numbers 2–4, 1989, p. 55.

[87] See discussion in Michael Vickery, 'Cambodia (Kampuchea): History, Tragedy, and Uncertain Future', *Bulletin of Concerned Asian Scholars*, Volume 21, Numbers 2–4, 1989, pp. 35–58.

[88] 'Thailand: Ambitious Thinking behind Indochina, Burma Links – The Golden Land', *Far Eastern Economic Review*, Volume 143, Number 8, 23 February 1989, p. 11.

noting that Chatichai's policy was not confined to Cambodia but included Laos and Burma (now Myanmar). Also worth noting is that Hun Sen, during his first meeting with Sihanouk at Fere-en-Tradenois in December 1987, told Sihanouk that he was more concerned about Thailand, given their unresolved territorial issues (specifically Preah Vihear) than Vietnam. In his words, 'the danger of the territory isn't from Vietnam, but Thailand'.[89]

Chatichai's new policy had 'disturbing consequences for ASEAN ... Although Chatichai has reiterated that ASEAN remains the "cornerstone" of Thai foreign policy, his initiatives and his ideas seem to point in another direction.'[90] More importantly, the visit also deviated from the agreement to focus on the ASEAN-initiated JIM process (which was very much driven by Indonesia) reached at the fifth meeting of the ASEAN Senior Officials Meeting Working Group on the Kampuchean Problem. Singapore's S. Rajaratnam (one of ASEAN's founding fathers) expressed concern that the Chatichai's move would negatively impact ASEAN's credibility. Those who opposed the new Thai approach within Thailand included, most prominently, Foreign Minister Siddhi Savetsila and another founding father of ASEAN, Thanat Khoman. Tej Bunnag recalled: 'By that time Air Chief Marshal Siddhi was really out on a limb. He was not representing the mainstream of government policy, and not long afterwards, he was no longer Foreign Minister.'[91]

Lee Kuan Yew's view was that Chatichai's actions led Hanoi to drag out the Paris Peace Talks for another three years until 1991.[92] Lee may be right. China, the US, and some ASEAN countries were indeed concerned that the new Thai policy would make it easier for Hanoi to retain its control of Cambodia.[93] Although the third round

---

[89] Pov Sok, *Samdech Hun Sen: Supreme Founder and Father of Peace of Cambodia* (Phnom Penh: Ponleu Khmer Printing and Publishing House, 2021), pp. 360–362.
[90] See Leszek Buszynski, 'New Aspirations and Old Constraints in Thailand's Foreign Policy', *Asian Survey*, Volume 29, Number 11, November 1989, pp. 1057–1072.
[91] Anuson Chinvanno (interviewed and edited), Thai Diplomacy: In Conversation with Tej Bunnang (2022), p. 94, https://isc.mfa.go.th/en/content/thai-diplomacy-in-conversation-with-tej-bunnag?cate=5f204a5928600c5315 17cb75, accessed on 7 November 2023; Tita Sanglee, 'Revisiting Thailand's involvement in the Cambodian conflict', *The Diplomat*, 19 January 2022.
[92] Lee Kuan Yew, *From Third World to First: The Singapore Story 1965–2000* (Singapore: Times Edition, 2000), pp. 334–335.
[93] Michael Richardson, 'Thailand embraces Indo-China', *Pacific Defence Reporter*, June 1989, pp. 21–22.

The Long-Drawn Endgame 135

of Sihanouk–Hun talks in November 1988 did not reach any agreement, the sense was that Hun Sen was just intransigent in hopes of extracting the maximum possible advantage before agreeing to a settlement. It was anticipated that there would be tough bargaining ahead, but it was only a matter of time before a resolution would be reached. It was not just the ASEAN member states that were upset; China and the US were also not supportive of Chatichai's new policy direction. Tej Bunnag, who was then Thai ambassador to China, recalled that he 'had a difficult time explaining to the Chinese that we had changed our policy'.[94] The Chinese made it clear that they would not support any regional development schemes until the Vietnamese withdrew from Cambodia.[95]

JIM I would be remembered for, at the very least, bringing together all the regional parties for the first time, but JIM II is simply forgettable, overshadowed by both regional and extra-regional developments, the latter of which we now turn to.

Before doing so, it is worth summarising the observations of Claude Martin (director for Asia and the Pacific, Quai d'Orsay) following his visit to the region, which gives a good picture of the situation and the thinking of the key protagonists in 1987–1988.[96] Martin was struck by the extent of economic decline in Vietnam after a hiatus of nine years. It was clear to him that the country was 'getting steadily poorer' and there was 'no end in sight' – 'Everyone talked about reform, but nobody did anything about it'. The Vietnamese leaders still did not understand the need for and the nuts and bolts of economic reform but they recognised that 'a withdrawal from Cambodia was crucial', 'they wanted the PRK to remain in place and they also feared a return of the Khmer Rouge'. Martin had the impression from his conversation with Nguyen Co Thach that the Vietnamese would move back into western Cambodia if the Khmer Rouge returned, particularly

---

[94] Anuson Chinvanno (interviewed and edited), Thai Diplomacy: In Conversation with Tej Bunnang (2022), p. 94, https://isc.mfa.go.th/en/content/thai-diplomacy-in-conversation-with-tej-bunnag?cate=5f204a5928600c5315 17cb75, accessed on 7 November 2023. For Tej Bunnang's recollections and views of Thailand, ASEAN, and the Cambodia conflict, see pp. 88–94.
[95] Michael Richardson, 'Thailand embraces Indo-China', *Pacific Defence Reporter*, June 1989, pp. 21–22.
[96] The following is summarised from Record of Meeting at the FCO between Mr McLaren, Australia, and M. Claude Martin, Director for Asia and the Pacific, Quai D'Orsay, Tuesday 26 July 1988, FCO 15/5264.

if they threatened Phnom Penh. Martin also believed that Hanoi attended the JIM 'only under pressure from the Soviet Union' – 'they did not have the will to negotiate seriously'. Nguyen Co Thach maintained that being present would be 'sufficient to establish Vietnamese and PRK goodwill'. There was a consensus that Sihanouk was key to any settlement. Martin was of the view that Sihanouk 'would want power and would not be content with being a figurehead', but Hun Sen had his 'sensitivities'. In his conversation with Sihanouk, Martin noted that Sihanouk was furious that the Khmer Rouge, in their effort to shore up their position before any settlement, were attacking the non-communist resistance, particularly Armée Nationale Sihanoukiste (ANS) troops. Regarding Sihanouk's resignation as president of the CGDK, seen as a 'tactical' move, the prince explained that he judged that he should distance himself from the CGDK, especially from the Khmer Rouge, before the JIM started. Sihanouk knew that Beijing 'had used him in the past as their political card just as they have used the Khmer Rouge as their military card'.[97] He hoped that his resignation would put pressure on the Thais and Chinese to sever their links with the Khmer Rouge. The British (Robin McLaren) shared that the Chinese were still not ready to abandon the Khmer Rouge but seemed to understand that Pol Pot and his close associates were unacceptable to the West. Martin agreed that there had been a shift in the Chinese position. Beijing did not want to be held responsible for the Khmer Rouge blocking an agreement and they had consequently 'pushed them to attend the JIM'. Martin also said that the Thais were also aware but 'they claimed that Khmer Rouge resistance was still necessary' and Bangkok also did not want to offend China. McLaren said that 'the UK was not a leading player and looked to Paris, given France's historical role in the region'. London was however 'keen to do what we could to help'. Both agreed that it would be necessary to convene an international conference at some point. In the words of McLaren, 'the JIM had brought the parties together for the first time. Once they agreed on the basic elements of a solution, we could consider whether a conference was appropriate and, if so, what sort.' Both Martin and McLaren concurred that the JIM was 'a step in the right direction'. With regard to the elements of a Cambodian settlement, both concurred that a coalition of all four Cambodian factions

---

[97] See also, From Tokyo to FCO, 'Cambodia', 12 July 1988, *FCO 15/5267*.

was preferable to a two-party coalition. However, they had doubts as to whether the Khmer Rouge would accept a prominent role for the Sihanoukist, and while Hun Sen would probably be prepared to share power with Sihanouk this was unlikely to be on 'an equal footing'. As for a two-party coalition, a bilateral agreement between Hun Sen and Sihanouk was viewed as 'unrealistic'. Much as both the French and British (McLaren said that if the UK backed a settlement which included the Khmer Rouge, 'it would be difficult to defend') felt that 'it would be easier ... if Pol Pot and his close associates were excluded', it 'was unrealistic to try to exclude the Khmer Rouge altogether'. Finally, we come to the point that would lead to the next section of this narrative: Sihanouk, having 'been framed by the Khmer Rouge once', would therefore want 'political and military guarantees that he would be in charge if he went back to Phnom Penh', thus 'guarantees were the key'. The major questions hanging over any internal settlement were 'how the Khmer Rouge can be accommodated or excluded and how their longer-term objective of regaining sole control can be circumscribed'.[98] Both Martin and McLaren agreed that Moscow kept Vietnam under control and the Chinese (and Thais) were the ones who could influence the Khmer Rouge by starving them of weapons. It was important for France, the UK, the US, and others to put combined pressure on the Chinese. Martin also expected to see 'further Soviet steps following the Sino-Soviet bilateral meeting in August'. On at least one point, Moscow, Hanoi, and some Western countries had a 'coincidence of interest' – the Soviets 'profess deep concern about the danger that a Vietnamese withdrawal will let Pol Pot and his cronies back in'. The Chinese clearly held the key.[99]

IV

In its annual review of 1988, the British Foreign Office noted that the Cambodian factions were 'in danger of being overtaken by outside events'. China and Moscow had 'bigger fish to fry' and unless the Cambodians agreed to a compromise, the Soviets and the Chinese might strike a deal. The consequence would be 'civil war, and a possible return of Khmer Rouge influence'. That said, in 1988, 'the external

---

[98] 'Cambodia: Annual Review 1988', 20 February 1989, FCO 15/5618.
[99] UK/Soviet Talks on Asia: Moscow, 13–14 September 1988, FCO 15/5265.

players have not yet narrowed their differences sufficiently to impose an agreed settlement package'. British officials were, however, somewhat hopeful that 'the accelerating rapprochement' between and among the external powers 'may induce the Cambodian factions to display greater flexibility'. At the same time, there was also the 'distinct danger that any settlement would, like previous Indochinese agreements of 1954, 1962 and 1973, be contrived to meet the interests of external players, without assuaging the conflict between the local forces'.[100]

Qian Qichen recalled that it was only in the late 1980s that Moscow 'began to show a flexible attitude toward the key issues that had hampered the normalization of Sino-Soviet relations' – the Soviets no longer avoided discussions of Cambodia.[101] However, while Moscow acknowledged that the withdrawal of Vietnamese troops from Cambodia was a key factor, they did not commit to ensuring that the Vietnamese troops would pull out, only that 'it would do what it could to promote the process of solving the issue of Cambodia'. The Chinese reading of the meetings was that Moscow's 'new attitude was more positive than the old one' and that the Soviets intended to first pull out of Afghanistan and then resolve the Cambodia issue as soon as possible. The Soviets began their troop withdrawal from Afghanistan on 15 May 1988, a process which was completed on 15 February 1989. Qian met with his Soviet counterpart, Eduard Shevardnadze, in June 1988 in New York. Shevardnadze suggested that the Geneva agreement regarding Afghanistan could serve as a template for Cambodia. Qian said that 'the withdrawal of the Soviet Union from Afghanistan was a good thing, and therefore welcome. But China was more concerned about Cambodia.'[102]

Moscow subsequently requested a special session on Cambodia, which took place from 27 August to 1 September 1988 in Beijing when the two vice-foreign ministers, Igor Rogachev and Tian Zengpei, reached 'an internal understanding, having found some common ground and similar views' regarding Cambodia. Although 'disputes still persisted ... the meetings indicated the Soviet side was showing flexibility on the issue of Vietnamese troops in Cambodia'.

[100] 'Cambodia: Annual Review 1988', 20 February 1989, FCO 15/5618.
[101] The following account is summarised from Qian Qichen, *Ten Episodes in China's Diplomacy* (New York: HarperCollins Publishers, 2005), pp. 21–23.
[102] Qian Qichen, *Ten Episodes in China's Diplomacy* (New York: HarperCollins Publishers, 2005), p. 38.

Qian met his Soviet counterpart Shevardnadze in Moscow from 1–3 December 1988; the objective of the visit was to lay the groundwork for a meeting of the heads of state of China and the Soviet Union. Following up on the August 1988 meeting, Qian 'pointed out emphatically that the Vietnamese troops must withdraw from Cambodia before the end of June 1989'. Qian emphasised that both Moscow and Beijing 'should be on the same opinion on a time limit for the withdrawal and make it happen'. After that, all external powers should stop supporting any party in the civil war. As for the internal issues of Cambodia, Qian briefly stated that China would support: (1) a four-party coalition government headed by Sihanouk; (2) the military forces of all parties being frozen, reduced, and eventually dissolved; (3) an international peacekeeping force that should be stationed in Cambodia; and (4) the institution of strict international surveillance and an international guarantee. It is evident from the discussion (and in other forums that the Chinese participated in) that China's concern was not the Khmer Rouge but Vietnam's continued presence in Cambodia. Beijing also did not expect or support Heng Samrin heading a future Cambodian government. However, they held that the Khmer Rouge should not be excessively weakened (yet) given the Vietnamese military presence in Cambodia. But the Khmer Rouge should also not be allowed to monopolise power.[103]

Chinese interest in the Khmer Rouge was never ideological but geopolitical linked to the Sino-Soviet dispute. Indeed, Singapore too noted that by the end of August 1988, the Chinese appeared to have decided on their position on Cambodia. For some time, they were uncertain how to respond to international pressures to dissociate themselves from the Khmer Rouge. Just as one should not overestimate Soviet influence over Vietnam, one should also not overestimate Chinese influence over the Khmer Rouge or Vietnam's influence over the PRK, as in each set of relationships they needed each other.[104]

---

[103] 'Cambodia', Internal Department document, 29 July 1988, FCO 15/5271. The Chinese leaders conveyed this to Secretary of State George Shultz in Beijing, 14–15 July 1988; From Peking to FCO, 14 April 1989, 'Cambodia: Chinese Line', FCO 15/5620.

[104] Ang Cheng Guan, *Singapore, ASEAN and the Cambodian Conflict, 1978–1991* (Singapore: NUS Press, 2013), p. 107. Singapore sources described similar conditions to those Qian highlighted by Shevardnadze, except for the withdrawal deadline. For differences between Hanoi and the PRK, see,

In response to Qian, the Soviet side did not want to promise the time limit for the withdrawal of Vietnamese troops, arguing that Moscow 'had no way to give orders to Vietnam'. However, they conveyed a message from the Vietnamese which said they wanted to discuss the timetable of withdrawal directly with the Chinese. Both the Soviets and the Chinese eventually reached agreement at the meeting that the complete withdrawal of Vietnamese troops should be set between June and December 1989. As for the other matters, the Soviets did not have any disagreement with the Chinese except that these matters 'should be accompanied by a repudiation of the past policies of Cambodia [and the] realization of a dialogue between the countries of Indochina and ASEAN. And, after all parties in Cambodia had reached a political settlement, then all countries should immediately stop military aid to the various parties'.

On 2 February 1989, Shevardnadze paid a return visit to China to prepare for the summit meeting, where he met Qian to continue the December 1988 discussion on Cambodia. Qian proposed to publicly announce the agreements reached in December on Cambodia alongside the date of the summit meeting as a 'package agreement', which the Soviets initially agreed. Shortly after, the Soviet side 'suddenly changed its mind and went back on its words'. It refused to publish any joint statement on Cambodia and agreed only to publishing the summit date. The Chinese side stood firm and eventually, on 6 February, both sides simultaneously announced the joint communiqué on Cambodia and the date of Gorbachev's visit to China. Gorbachev visited China from 15 to 18 May 1989 (during the Tiananmen protests), bringing the Sino-Soviet rift to an end.

Soviet–US relations also improved – Washington, which had been mostly disinterested in the Cambodia problem, was willing to discuss the issue with the Moscow at the summit level – culminating in Presidents H. W. Bush and Gorbachev declaring the end of the Cold War in Malta on 3 December 1989, not long after the fall of the Berlin Wall on 10 November 1989. As Vladislav M. Zubok noted,

Kosal Path, *Vietnam's Strategic Thinking during the Third Indochina War* (Madison: University of Wisconsin Press, 2010), p. 200. Hun Sen objected to Vietnam's 'Red Solution', which was for the PRK to reconcile with the Khmer Rouge and establish a new socialist regime in Cambodia acceptable to Vietnam and China.

on 30 October 1986, Gorbachev said that the financial crisis 'has clutched us by the throat' ... By 1987, the Soviet state had no other means to increase its revenues besides taxes and price increases ... After 1988, Gorbachev was in a hurry to end the Cold War because he had a personal need to compensate for his declining prospects at home with breakthroughs in foreign policy. As a result, Gorbachev's diplomacy often failed to win a better deal with the United States and its allies.

It is worth noting that in May 1988, Hanoi announced that it would withdraw 50,000 troops from Cambodia between June and December 1988, to be monitored by international observers. Available evidence suggested that by early December 1988, only about 15,000 Vietnamese troops had been withdrawn. Hanoi had announced a substantial troop withdrawal from mid-December 1988 and invited Western journalists to witness the event. Most observers were sceptical that Hanoi could achieve the 50,000 figures by the end of 1988. Under Soviet pressure, Hanoi declared that it would withdraw all its troops in 1990, and earlier if there was a political settlement. The deadline was revised to September 1989.[105] By late September 1989, the Vietnamese, according to US and Thai sources, had withdrawn most of their troops. Vietnamese troop withdrawal from Cambodia, while welcome, raised the concern that the Khmer Rouge might take power again, thus the imperative to disarm the Khmer Rouge as soon as possible.[106]

---

[105] 'Cambodia: Annual Review 1988', 20 February 1989, FCO 15/5618.
[106] Michael Armacost (US undersecretary of state for political affairs) raised this concern with Qian Qichen in June 1988. When President Bush visited China in February 1989, he too raised US concern about the return of the Khmer Rouge. See Qian Qichen, *Ten Episodes in China's Diplomacy* (New York: HarperCollins Publishers, 2005), pp. 40–41. Lee Kuan Yew also expressed a similar concern. See 'Singapore chief fears for Cambodia', *New York Times*, 25 October 1989.

Epilogue

I

The International Conference on Cambodia was convened at the Kleber Conference Centre in Paris from 30 July to 30 August 1989. It failed to resolve the conflict.[1] Had it succeeded, it would have been an even more memorable year for the French as 1989 was also the 200th anniversary of the French Revolution. That the conference failed was unfortunate but not a surprise (as explained later) although some participants, such as the British, held the view that 'there was ... every reason to hope and expect' the conference 'to succeed' for reasons such as improvement in Sino-Soviet relations, Vietnam's serious economic problems, and the impulse of national reconciliation between the Cambodian faction and Sihanouk, which was 'the key factor ... behind whom all Cambodians and factions could unite'.[2]

We may recall from our discussion in Chapter 5 that the Cambodian conflict could only end if four interconnected elements of the conflict were resolved: (1) mutual threat perceptions of Vietnam and Cambodia, the most intractable of which was over the Khmer Rouge, which happened to be the strongest component of the anti-Vietnam resistance; (2) Sino-Vietnamese relations; (3) mutual threat perceptions of Vietnam and Thailand; and (4) superpower rivalries, particularly between China and the Soviet Union. If we follow the developments up to the eve of the International Conference on Cambodia described earlier, except for (4), and while there were some positive movements in (2) and (3), the first three elements were still not close enough to a

---

[1] For an account and discussion of the conference, see Ang Cheng Guan, *Singapore, ASEAN and the Cambodian Conflict, 1978–1991* (Singapore: NUS Press, 2013), pp. 129–137. For details of the proceedings, see also, FCO 15/5652, FCO 15/5653, FCO 15/5654.

[2] From Paris to FCO, 29 August 1989, 'Lord Brabazon's Statement', FCO 15/5654.

resolution, especially (1). In the case of (1), the Cambodian factions could not reach agreement on two issues: the structure of the quadripartite coalition government (proposed by Sihanouk) and power-sharing, and the role of the Khmer Rouge.[3]

According to the PRK account, the CGDK launched the 1989 military offensive with 'high hopes and determination', but the offensive collapsed due to 'several bad tactical decisions' which led to the loss of key territories and the neutralisation of the bulk of its forces. The Khmer Rouge remained the only force 'cohesive enough to fight as regular units'. The remaining components of the CGDK – the non-communist factions – 'began to fear the Khmer Rouge dominance'.[4]

The Khmer Rouge problem was like an albatross around one's neck and would drag on till 1997, but more of this later. Suffice to say here that with the departure of Vietnamese troops from Cambodia and the end of the Cold War (leading to greater attention to human rights, especially in the West), the focus shifted back to the Khmer Rouge atrocities. Towards the end of the Paris Conference, as recounted by Kishore Mahbubani (Singapore's permanent representative to the Number), Foreign Minister Nguyen Co Thach insisted that the conference declaration should explicitly call for the non-return of the genocidal policies and practices of the Khmer Rouge. Everyone knew that the Vietnamese were never concerned about Pol Pot's record. Thach knew that the Khmer Rouge would never agree to such a reference and the conference would therefore fail, 'a failure which the Vietnamese wanted because they were not ready to relinquish control over

---

[3] See Stephen J. Solarz, 'Cambodia and the International Community', *Foreign Affairs*, Volume 69, Number 2, Spring 1990, pp. 99–115. Hun Sen believed that a quadrilateral government would disadvantage him since the other three factions were against him, and it would also legitimize the Khmer Rouge and give them (one of the four factions) a better chance to get back into power. Hun Sen's call for a continuation of the status quo till after the general elections was unacceptable to the CGDK as it would legitimize 'a regime imposed ... by force of Vietnamese arms'. Hun Sen's control of the administrative apparatus would also ensure the PRK's victory in an election, thus it first had to be dismantled. Hun Sen's analysis of the Khmer Rouge within the CGDK is well summarised in Pov Sok, *Samdech Hun Sen: Supreme Founder and Father of Peace of Cambodia* (Phnom Penh: Ponleu Khmer Printing and Publishing House, 2021), pp. 203–204.

[4] Boraden Nhem, *The Third Indochina Conflict: Cambodia's Total War*, MA thesis, University of Delaware, 2014, pp. 101, 107. For a military history of the 1989 CGDK combined offensive, see pp. 68–100.

Cambodia'. Yet the 'Western officials did not dare to challenge him for fear of being branded defenders of Pol Pot ... In practical terms, from the viewpoint of the ordinary Cambodian, the strong Western consensus against the Khmer Rouge had backfired and ruined any chance of agreement because it prevented Western delegations from exposing Nguyen Co Thach's scuttling of the peace conference.'[5] Indeed, Singapore observed that the US was the 'most nervous delegation' as they were concerned about media criticism back home regarding their apparent support for the Khmer Rouge. US officials were nervous over how the failure of the International Criminal Court (ICC) would be interpreted in Washington. The congress and the media had reacted negatively to the ICC and increasingly viewed support for Sihanouk as support for the Khmer Rouge.[6] On 18 July 1990, Secretary of State James Baker, bowing to Senate pressure, announced that the US would no longer support the CGDK at the Number and that it would only provide aid to Sihanouk and Sann, as well as begin providing humanitarian aid through Hun Sen's State of Cambodia (SOC).

There were several analyses as to why the conference failed. Qian Qichen recalled that 'the dispute over the Khmer Rouge was so sharp that the conference was unable to reach any agreement'. Baker was of the view that the 'internal problems of Cambodia' could never be resolved by 'relying on the four Cambodian factions alone' and therefore 'China, the Soviet Union, the United States, and ASEAN should draft a plan for the settlement of those internal issues in Cambodia'. In a December 1989 conversation between French Foreign Minister Roland Dumas and Baker, Dumas said that 'it had been very apparent at the Paris Conference that the real clue to a settlement was not the parties on the ground but their outside backers'. Dumas was reportedly 'at pains to emphasise that the main lesson of the Paris Cambodia Conference had been that the key to a solution lay with Vietnam and the Soviet Union on the one hand, and China and the United States on the other than with the parties themselves'.[7] While that might have been the only way forwards, the Chinese felt that there must still be

---

[5] Kishore Mahbubani, *Can Asians Think?* (Singapore: Times Book International, 1998), pp. 168–169.
[6] US Policy on Cambodia after the ICC, *Information Note on Kampuchea*, 11 September 1989.
[7] From FCO to Paris, 5 December 1989, 'Secretary of State's Meeting with the French Foreign Minister: Cambodia', *FCO* 15/5632.

some degree of buy-in by the four factions, particularly Sihanouk, 'who might object to the big powers' asking him to be head of state while imposing a prefabricated arrangement on him'.[8]

According to the British analysis, the timing was wrong. It ought to have been convened after the Vietnamese troops had withdrawn from Cambodia, which we may recall only occurred in September 1989. Moscow was either unwilling or unable to 'deliver the Vietnamese' prior to the conference. Beijing remained determined to make Vietnam 'eat crow' for its 1978 invasion 'and to go on using the Khmer Rouge as its military persuader'. Washington was 'reluctant to re-engage its prestige and influence in Indochina'. The French did not conceive or execute the conference well. ASEAN's performance was 'unedifying' – it was not clear what Thailand's policy was (given the mixed messages from the Thai Foreign Ministry and the Thai military), Indonesia was 'obsessed with justifying JIM II', while Singapore and Thailand thought that 'the Paris Conference has replaced JIM'. For the British, it was 'a missed opportunity and everyone stands to lose, some more than others … the best hope is continuing military stalemate leading to a resumption of the Paris Conference and a comprehensive settlement'.[9] Asked in an interview, Lord Brabazon (who represented the UK at the Paris Conference) said that the four internal parties were 'simply unable to come to a settlement and there was nothing we or anyone else really could do to persuade them to do otherwise'.[10]

The US side claimed that they 'had always accepted that a comprehensive settlement at Paris was unlikely', and US Deputy Assistant Secretary of State David Lambertson described the US as 'only a second-tier player' (along with other Western countries); 'the key actors were Vietnam, China and the Soviet Union'. According to Lambertson, US interest was directly related to its treaty commitment to Thailand. The conference had shown a 'broad spectrum of interest in ensuring that the Khmer Rouge did not gain power'. US objectives had accordingly been to 'maximise the influence of the non-Communist resistance: to minimize the Khmer Rouge and to secure Vietnamese withdrawal'.

---

[8] Qian Qichen, *Ten Episodes in China's Diplomacy* (New York: HarperCollins Publishers, 2005), pp. 48–50.
[9] From Paris to FCO, 31 August 1989, 'Paris Conference on Cambodia', *FCO* 15/5654.
[10] *Today Programme*, 30 August 1989: Lord Brabazon, *FCO* 15/5654.

It clearly emerged in Paris that 'the situation was not at present ripe for settlement. Nevertheless, some useful groundwork had been done which would remain valid in future',[11] a view that Qian Qichen shared when he wrote: 'the conference did provide an opportunity for countries relevant to the Cambodia issue and the four sides in Cambodia to sit together for the first time to discuss the issue and lay a solid foundation for its final settlement'.[12] Lord Brabazon, in his 30 August 1989 statement, expressed sentiments more or less on the same lines: 'it's about one of the first times the four parties have all sat round a table together, so that must be at least encouraging, it's not very encouraging but it's better than nothing at all'.[13]

The Australians were also pessimistic regarding the prospects for agreement at the conference. They did not 'go to the conference with any prescription for an internal solution'. Canberra saw that as 'a matter for the Cambodian parties themselves'. Like the US and Singapore, Australia wanted to avoid 'a partial solution' (which India proposed) and would 'continue to press for a comprehensive settlement'. Indeed, many participants were concerned that in the rush to reach an agreement, the conference might settle for a vaguely worded agreement which left substantive issues unresolved. Singapore insisted that there should be a clear agreement that the rule of unanimity must apply to all substantive issues. In his 30 August 1989 press conference, Senator Gareth Evans said:

[W]e spent the first day of this conference establishing that the settlement process was for the time being dead. We spent the last two days writing the obituary. It's been a very sterile process, there's no doubt about that, very frustrating and very depressing. There are however some good things that have come out of it. For the last month the committees have been working, in some cases very effectively, to define and refine the details that will have to go into the final settlement.[14]

---

[11] From Brussels to FCO, 1 September 1989, 'Cambodia: Paris Conference', *FCO 15/5654*.
[12] Qian Qichen, *Ten Episodes in China's Diplomacy* (New York: HarperCollins Publishers, 2005), p. 48.
[13] *Today Programme*, 30 August 1989: Lord Brabazon, FCO 15/5654.
[14] From Canberra to FCO, 20 July 1989, 'Cambodia: International Conference', *FCO 15/5659*; From Paris to Canberra, 31 August 1989, 'Cambodia Conference: Senator Evan's Press Conference', *FCO 15/5659*; Ang Cheng Guan, *Singapore, ASEAN and the Cambodian Conflict, 1978–1991* (Singapore: NUS Press, 2013), pp. 130, 135.

Finally, in a speech delivered on 1 November 1989 to the American Academy of Diplomacy and the School of Advanced International Studies, Johns Hopkins University, Tommy Koh (who represented Singapore at the conference) drew the following conclusion from the ICC, which is worth citing in full:

What lessons can we learn from the ICC about multilateral negotiations? First, it is always helpful, perhaps necessary to prepare carefully before convening an international conference. If France had held preparatory meetings at the level of senior officials, it would either have improved the prospects of the Conference or convinced France that Vietnam was not ready to strike a compromise. Second, in the case of regional conflicts in the Third World, the agreement of the five permanent members of the Security Council is a necessary, but not a sufficient reason for success. The Soviet Union was either unwilling or unable to persuade Vietnam to seek a compromise in Paris. Third, in the case of regional conflicts in the Third World, the key to the solution is often held, not by the great powers alone, but in concert with the regional players. Fourth, although it is preferable to have a single Chairman to two Co-Chairmen preside over a conference or committee, the system of Co-Chairmanship can sometimes work if the Co-Chairmen are carefully chosen and if they are able to work in tandem. Fifth, timing is of the utmost importance. In the case of the Cambodian conflict, the Vietnamese had not yet given up their aspiration for hegemony over Cambodia. Therefore Vietnam and its surrogate, Hun Sen, rejected compromise at the Conference table.[15]

II

On 17 January 1990, Michael Leifer gave a second talk on Cambodia at the Asia Society (which was subsequently published in the June 1990 issue of *Asian Affairs* where he reiterated that unless Sino-Vietnamese relations were repaired, the final phase of the Cambodian conflict would remain incomplete,[16] a view that now declassified archival documents corroborate). We may recall that this was his second update on Cambodia to the Asia Society, eight years after his

---

[15] 'The Paris Conference on Cambodia: An Example of a Multilateral Negotiation', in Tommy Koh, *The Quest for World Order: Perspectives of a Pragmatic Idealist* (Singapore: Times Academic Press, 1998), pp. 87–96.
[16] Michael Leifer, 'The Stakes of Conflict in Cambodia', *Asian Affairs*, Volume 21, Number 2, 1990, pp. 155–161. See also Michael Leifer, 'Cambodian Conflict: The Final Phase', *Conflict Studies*, Number 221, May 1989.

first in 1982 (summarised in Chapter 5). Notably, he did not express confidence that a resolution was in sight. But as he pointed out, as with so many contemporary political issues, the pace of events is such that no sooner have you written a line than you must revise it. Indeed, events and developments were happening at a furious pace during the late 1980s, as described earlier. The Berlin Wall fell on 10 November 1989, heralding the collapse of communism in eastern Europe.

We must now turn our attention to developments in Sino-Vietnam relations. We may recall that in his February 1985 speech marking the 55th anniversary of the founding of the VCP, Le Duan said that friendship between China and Vietnam would have to be restored. However, as late as 1988, Beijing refused to talk directly to the Vietnamese because of the latter's military presence in Cambodia.

In its effort to wean itself from its dependency on the Soviet Union, the Vietnamese simultaneously pursued a two-pronged strategy. First, a 'multi-directional orientation' – reaching out to the West and to the US – which was spearheaded by Nguyen Co Thach. Unfortunately for Thach, Washington, for the second time, was not ready to respond to Hanoi's overture. (The first was when Washington chose normalising relations with China ahead of Vietnam, leading Vietnam to align with the Soviet Union in 1978.) Second, reaching out to China, the remaining pillar of socialism/communism, led by General Secretary Nguyen Van Linh, whose priority was defending the socialist state, especially in the wake of the Tiananmen Incident (June 1989) and the developments in eastern Europe.[17]

We may recall that in December 1988, at a meeting between Qian Qichen and Shevardnadze, the Soviets informed Qian that the Vietnamese wanted to discuss the timetable of withdrawal directly with the Chinese. Vietnam's Foreign Minister Nguyen Co Thach asked twice to visit China in 1988 but was turned down.[18]

The first Sino-Vietnamese meeting at the vice-ministerial level in nine years took place in January 1989 without publicity. It apparently took place in secret. Vice-Foreign Minister Dinh Nho Liem told the Chinese that Hanoi's long-term plan was to settle the Cambodian issue as soon

---

[17] 'Chengdu 1990: Nguyen Co Thach and Vietnam's Normalisation with China', Lewis Stern's Vietnam Blog, http://vietpoliticsblog.blogspot.sg/2012_07_01_archive.html, accessed on 7 October 2013.
[18] Qian Qichen, *Ten Episodes in China's Diplomacy* (New York: HarperCollins Publishers, 2005), pp. 41–42.

as possible, to normalise relations with China, and 'to concentrate its efforts on economic construction', to which Qian Qichen replied: 'if the basic aspects of the Cambodian issue could be resolved, improvement and normalization of the relations between China and Vietnam would be a natural result'.[19]

Hanoi eventually withdrew all its troops from Cambodia in September 1989. If the Vietnamese had not done so, it was unlikely that there would be any progress in Sino-Vietnamese relations, which in turn would mean no progress in resolving the Cambodian conflict.

Not long after Leifer's Asia Society talk, a second round of vice-ministerial talks between China and Vietnam took place from May 1990. The Thais learned about this visit when Foreign Minister Siddhi visited Beijing in March–April 1990. Siddhi apparently got on well with the Chinese, 'who seem to think him (in their terms) sounder than Chatitchai'. He was informed by Chinese Foreign Minister Qian that Dinh Nho Liem would be visiting in May, ostensibly 'to inspect the Vietnamese Embassy'. According to Qian, 'the Chinese side is prepared to meet him should the Vietnamese accept national reconciliation and the unity of the factions then this might form the basis for a solution'. The British assessment was that while Liem's visit was billed as one of inspection, 'as was his first "secret" visit ... in January 1989, the Chinese are clearly prepared to see him', although they have 'so far resisted any suggestion that they should talk directly to the Vietnamese'.[20]

Liem visited China from 1 to 10 May 1990. The visit was described as 'useful'. All aspects of a solution of the Cambodian problem were discussed. Differences remained but there was some progress. The two sides did not agree that Vietnam had withdrawn all its troops. Liem said that Vietnam 'could accept any style of international supervision'. Liem asked the Chinese to stop supplying the resistance, but the Chinese were only prepared to do so after an agreement had been reached. Both sides eventually agreed that after an international agreement, all countries (including China and Vietnam) would stop supplying any military aid. The two sides disagreed on the composition of

---

[19] Qian Qichen, *Ten Episodes in China's Diplomacy* (New York: HarperCollins Publishers, 2005), p. 44.
[20] From British Embassy in Peking to Foreign and Commonwealth Office, London, 'Visit of Thai Foreign Minister', 5 April 1990, FCO 15/6221.

the interim administration (meaning the SNC). Whereas the Chinese stuck to their formula on the involvement of all four factions with no one faction dominating, the Vietnamese proposed that the SNC should be in two halves. If Sihanouk agreed, the Khmer Rouge (but not the Pol Potists) could be included. China and others could not accept the maintenance of power of the Heng Samrin regime, which would have given the regime an unfair electoral advantage. The key issue of the role and power of the SNC thus remained unresolved. Both sides agreed on the need to avoid a civil war. The Vietnamese said that Hun Sen would not sign any international agreement which did not refer to genocide. The Chinese retorted that this point had caused the failure of the earlier negotiations. The Vietnamese eventually agreed not to raise this issue again in international fora. The Chinese finally agreed that Nguyen Co Thach could visit China only 'in the context of normalization' but stated that they were 'not yet at that stage'. Normalisation was still conditional on a comprehensive Cambodian settlement. There would be a third round of talks, but the date had not been fixed.[21]

On 2 September 1990, at the invitation of the Chinese, Nguyen Van Linh, Prime Minister Do Muoi, and Advisor Pham Van Dong flew to Chengdu to meet secretly with the Chinese. By this time, Le Duan, Truong Chinh, and Le Duc Tho (who died in October 1990) had all passed away and a new generation of leaders had replaced them. Van Tien Dung, who led the 1978 invasion and was 'the least inclined to cooperate with China', had been retired. Only Pham Van Dong, who was eighty-four years of age in 1990, remained in an advisory role to a new and younger generation of leaders.

Tran Quang Co, who was then vice-minister of foreign affairs, in his 2003 memoir,[22] recalled that the Chengdu meeting focused mainly on the Cambodia issue and barely discussed the normalisation of relations which the Vietnamese were given to expect. Due to their hastiness to improve their relationship with China, the Vietnamese side accepted all the demands of the Chinese with regard to the establishment and composition of the SNC of Cambodia which were disadvantageous

---

[21] From British Embassy in Peking to Foreign and Commonwealth Office, London, 'Visit of Dinh Nho Liem', 15 May 1990, FCO 15/6221.
[22] *Hoi Ky Tran Quang Co*, https://docs.google.com/file/d/0B0oimFzfxC6leHMtc FU3Skg1WGM/preview?pli=1&resourcekey=0-OMQtCljZgHPDjWIWjnG38g, accessed on 15 December 2022.

to the Vietnamese-backed Phnom Penh regime. The Vietnamese were initially opposed to a quadripartite government headed by Sihanouk, arguing that Sihanouk should work with Hun Sen instead to counter the Khmer Rouge. The Chinese, on the other hand, wanted to protect the Khmer Rouge and insisted on giving Sihanouk one additional vote in the quadripartite power-sharing (the Vietnamese-installed regime led by Hun Sen (6), the Khmer Rouge (2), the KPNLF led by Son Sann (2), FUNCINPEC led by Sihanouk's son Ranaridhh (2) and Sihanouk (1)). The meeting was meant to be a secret, but soon after the Chinese made public the Chengdu agreement, thus embarrassing the Vietnamese and compromising their public negotiating position.[23]

Soon after the Chengdu meeting, General Vo Nguyen Giap visited China from 18 to 26 September 1990, where he attended some Asian Games ceremonies as 'a specially invited honored guest' and met with Vice-Premier Li Peng and other 'old friends'. His meeting with Li Peng 'was mainly devoted to Cambodia'. We still do not know why the Chinese agreed to the visit since 'no breakthroughs' had been announced. The Friendship Gate was reopened for Giap on 18 September and he flew up from Nanning to Beijing the next day. The British assessment was that Giap's visit and the symbolic opening of the Friendship Gate 'clearly shows an improvement in bilateral relations'.[24]

III

At this point, we need to pause and turn our attention back to Thailand – ASEAN's front-line member state most directly threatened by this conflict. We may recall from Chapter 5 the election of a new Thai government in August 1988 and the meeting between the new Thai Prime Minister Chatichai Choonhavan and Hun Sen in January 1989, marking the start of a significant shift in the Thai approach towards the Cambodian conflict.

---

[23] See *Hoi Ky Tran Quang Co*, https://docs.google.com/file/d/0B0oimFzfxC6leH MtcFU3Skg1WGM/preview?pli=1&resourcekey=0-OMQtCljZgHPDjWIWjnG38g, accessed on 15 December 2022. For a Chinese account, see Qian Qichen, *Ten Episodes in China's Diplomacy* (New York: HarperCollins Publishers, 2005), chapter 2.

[24] From British Embassy I Peking to Foreign and Commonwealth Office, London, 'China/Vietnam: Visit of General Giap', 13 October 1990, FCO 15/6221.

On 15 November 1989, Thai Foreign Minister Siddhi announced that the Thai MFA would now accord a lower priority to the Cambodian problem. A review of the international situation and its implications for Thailand reached the conclusion that with most of the Vietnamese troops withdrawn from Cambodia in September 1989, the threat to its security from the Thailand–Cambodia border was no longer a serious concern. Moscow had also become friendlier towards Thailand and less inclined to support ideological expansion. The review further noted the impatience of the West and their strong anti-Khmer Rouge feelings. Thus, the best way forwards was to accept any compromise solution which was acceptable to the four Cambodian factions. The Thai military, which shared similar views with the Thai MFA, would however continue to support the CGDK resistance forces and to facilitate the flow of supplies to the Cambodian resistance, but Bangkok also wanted the flexibility and the options to shift its position on Cambodia should the need arise.[25] The Thais could in fact 'coerce' the CGDK if they wanted to as they controlled their military supplies.

PRK official history revealed that in December 1989, Thai Prime Minister Chatichai secretly sent a military general to meet Hun Sen in Laos. Following that, in January 1990, Chatichai sent his foreign minister and more than seventy officials to Hanoi 'to end the long-running dispute with Vietnam'. In late January 1990, Hun Sen visited Bangkok at the invitation of Chatichai and both sides signed several trade agreements. Chatichai, according to the PRK's interpretation, wanted 'to revive the Thai economy' which was 'lagging behind Singapore'.[26] The PRK gave the Thais much credit for their help in reaching the agreement on the creation of the SNC, which we may recall was eventually agreed upon on 9 September 1990 in Tokyo. In his account of the chronology, Prak Sokhonn (deputy prime minister of Cambodia) noted that the SNC was first mooted by Hun Sen during his second meeting with Sihanouk in 1988 and discussed at the first JIM in July 1988. No agreement was reached then. By March 1990, 'with the support' of General Chavalit Yongchaiyudh, 'the agreement to create the SNC was settled with just a title amendment' and adopted in Tokyo

[25] The Thai Foreign Ministry (MFA) Position on Cambodia, *Information Note on Kampuchea*, December 1989.
[26] Pov Sok, *Samdech Hun Sen: Supreme Founder and Father of Peace of Cambodia* (Phnom Penh: Ponleu Khmer Printing and Publishing House, 2021), pp. 416–417.

'with the support of the host and H. E. Chavalit Yongchaiyudh, also present at the event'. The composition of the SNC was determined in Jakarta and 'the first SNC meeting took place in the Embassy of the Kingdom of Cambodia in Bangkok'.[27]

IV

Between Congressman Stephen Solarz and Australian Minister for Foreign Affairs Gareth Evans, they cobbled together a new initiative to resolve the Cambodian conflict, which Evans announced in the Australian parliament on 24 November 1989. Canberra, in 1983, withdrew its co-sponsorship of the annual ASEAN resolution on Cambodia in the UN General Assembly because it believed that 'the resolution was too one-sidedly critical of Vietnam and took insufficient account of Pol Pot's genocide'.[28]

The core of the Australian proposal was for the United Nations 'to assume responsibility for the administration of Cambodia during the interim period between the establishment of a ceasefire and the emergence of a new government following an internationally supervised election'.[29] This proposal was the seed that eventually led to the creation of UNTAC, which we discuss later. Solarz noted that 'the Cambodian endgame has entered a new and critical stage' and 'it does not seem like an exaggeration to suggest that the Australian proposal constitutes the last best hope for a peaceful resolution of the Cambodian conflict. No less certain is the danger the Khmer Rouge poses for Cambodians if negotiations fail.'[30] Eric Schwartz (assistant secretary of state for population, refugees, and migration) recalled in an obituary on Stephen

---

[27] 'DPM Prak Sokhonn shares historical truth related to Paris Peace Agreement', *AKP Phnom Penh*, 23 October 2021.
[28] Ken Berry, *Cambodia: From Red to Blue: Australia's Initiative for Peace* (Canberra: Allen & Unwin, 1997), p. 6.
[29] Stephen J. Solarz, 'Cambodia and the International Community', *Foreign Affairs*, Volume 69, Number 2, Spring 1990, p. 100; Stephen Solarz interviewed by Charles Stuart Kennedy on 18 November 1996, the Association for Diplomatic Studies and Training, Foreign Affairs Oral History Project, www.adst.org/OH%20TOCs/Solarz,%20Stephen.toc.pdf, accessed on 6 January 2023. See also, Ken Berry, *Cambodia: From Red to Blue – Australia's Initiative for Peace* (Canberra: Allen & Unwin, 1997), pp. 22–23, chapter 2.
[30] See Stephen J. Solarz, 'Cambodia and the International Community', *Foreign Affairs*, Volume 69, Number 2, Spring 1990, pp. 99–115, which succinctly summarised the history of the conflict and delineated the issues.

Solarz's passing in 2010 that 'when the Bush administration was reluctant to promote the idea of UNTAC, Solarz 'sold the idea to the Australian Foreign Minister, who secured its acceptance by the international community'.[31] It is worth recalling that Evans' proposal was similar to Sihanouk's call from way back for Cambodia to be placed under a form of 'UN trusteeship'.

The five permanent members of the UN Security Council met on six occasions to resolve the impasse among the Cambodian factions and to discuss the Australian proposal, the first being in January 1990. A Cambodian Summit was convened in Tokyo from 4–6 June 1990 where the idea of an SNC was discussed.

At their fifth meeting of the five permanent members, in July 1990, they reached agreement on two key areas of UN involvement: (1) transitional arrangements regarding the administration of Cambodia during the pre-election period and (2) military aspects of the settlement. The agreement on the establishment of the SNC was significant and both the Russians and the Chinese reportedly made considerable concessions which made it possible. The SNC was empowered to represent Cambodian sovereignty and delegate all necessary powers to UNTAC. However, the relative degree of power of the SNC and UNTAC had yet to be worked out.[32]

During the sixth meeting, in August 1990, they reached an agreement on the outlines for a comprehensive political settlement for Cambodia. They had adopted a framework document on administrative arrangements, military arrangements, elections, human rights, and internal guarantees. US officials told the ASEAN missions in Washington that 'there was a sense of finality among the Permanent Five this time' and a British official commented that it was the 'last opportunity' for the Cambodian factions. The full agreement of the Cambodian factions was the next essential step before the framework document could be implemented. The five permanent members urged the Cambodian factions to support the framework document in its entirety, as a package. It was non-negotiable. Details needed to be worked out within the

---

[31] 'Passing of Stephen J. Solarz', https://2009-2017.state.gov/j/prm/releases/letters/2010/181272.htm, accessed on 6 January 2023,
[32] The Fifth Meeting on Cambodia of the Five Permanent Members of the UN Security Council, Paris, 16–17 July 1990, *Information Note on Kampuchea*, 28 July 1990.

Epilogue

framework. Richard Solomon recalled that building consensus on the UN plan was much easier than getting the Cambodian factions to 'shift their conflict'.[33]

Indonesian Foreign Minister Ali Alatas was to convene a meeting in Jakarta for the four factions to form the SNC. Both Moscow and Beijing reportedly promised to do their utmost to influence their clients to show flexibility at the coming Jakarta meeting.[34] The Jakarta Meeting on Cambodia was held on 9–10 September 1990. Its success was seen as 'a triumph' for Ali Alatas after the failed series of JIM meetings, as well as the Informal Meeting on Cambodia in February 1990 which Jakarta had again convened in the hope of getting the four factions to reach agreement. The success of the September Jakarta meeting apparently owed much to the secret high-level meeting between the Chinese and Vietnamese in Beijing on 3–4 September mentioned earlier. Although Sihanouk sent a representative instead of attending the Jakarta meeting himself, despite Chinese persuasion, the meeting agreed that Sihanouk should be the chairman of the SNC.

The first meeting of the SNC was held in Bangkok on 17–19 September 1990 but made no headway in reaching a political settlement. The factions could not agree on the PRK's condition that if the Council elected Sihanouk as the chairman, Hun Sen must automatically be appointed the vice-chairman.[35] On 15 October, the United Nations General Assembly (UNGA) unanimously adopted a new ASEAN-sponsored resolution on Cambodia which nominated the SNC for the Cambodian seat at the UN. However, given that the Cambodian factions were not ready and there was no Cambodian delegation at the UN, the 45th UNGA declared the Cambodian seat vacant on 16 October.

In late November 1990, Sihanouk revealed that the Chinese had told him that if nothing was done to stop the war in Cambodia the conflict would go on indefinitely without any winners and losers. In Sihanouk's view, this was a change in Chinese thinking compared

---

[33] Richard H. Solomon, *Exiting Cambodia* (Washington, DC: United States Institute of Peace Press, 2000), p. 72.

[34] The Sixth Meeting of the Five Permanent Members of the UN Security Council on Cambodia, New York, 27–28 August 1990, *Information Note on Kampuchea*, 31 August 1990; 'Cambodia: Jakarta Meetings', FCO 15/6039.

[35] Jakarta Meeting on Cambodia, 9–10 September 1990, *Information Note on Kampuchea*, 15 September 1990.

to three or four years previously, when Deng Xiaoping was still in power and had encouraged the resistance to continue fighting. On 22 November, the Chinese Foreign Ministry spokesperson announced that since the adoption of the Permanent Five plan on Cambodia in September 1990, China had stopped providing military assistance to the Cambodian resistance, including the Khmer Rouge. There were two views. One was that the Khmer Rouge could continue to fight for another seven years even without Chinese support. The Khmer Rouge's objective was to topple the PRK while the Ranariddh-led ANS and the Khmer Rouge would continue to be 'discreet allies on the battlefield' to achieve this goal. Another view held that the senior Khmer Rouge leadership had already agreed on the UN role and therefore Khmer Rouge military pressure was only for the purpose of ensuring the PRK accepted the UN plan.[36] In the third quarter of 1991, the SNC met three times in quick succession: June, July, and August 1991. The issue of chair and vice-chair of the SNC was finally resolved at the SNC meeting in Pattaya on 24–26 June 1991. Sihanouk had forced the pace when at the SNC meeting in Jakarta on 2–4 June, and apparently without consulting the other NSC members he proposed that he be appointed chair and Hun Sen as vice-chair. Hun Sen agreed, while the Khmer Rouge, not surprisingly, opposed this. As Ranariddh explained, Sihanouk's view was that time was running out for the non-communist resistance as their international support was eroding. Australia and Japan were favourable to Hun Sen, and while Ali Alatas was playing a positive role he was under strong domestic pressure. It was therefore necessary to achieve agreement on the establishment of the SNC under his leadership as quickly as possible to take the initiative away from Hun Sen. China supported Sihanouk's decision. That this was finally agreed at Pattaya was evidence that the Chinese must have leaned on the Khmer Rouge. A Chinese diplomat in New York said that 'the Chinese put all their cards in Sihanouk's hands, and trust Sihanouk'.[37]

A Sino-Vietnamese deal had also apparently been struck to resolve their outstanding differences over Cambodia towards the end of June

---

[36] Current Khmer Rouge Strategy, *Information Note on Kampuchea*, 3 December 1990.
[37] An Assessment of the Cambodian Issue after the Pattaya SNC meeting, 24–26 June 1991, *Information Note on Kampuchea*, 27 June 1991.

Epilogue

or thereabouts. The challenge of assessing Sino-Vietnam relations is, as British officials noted, 'the chronic secretiveness of both sides', particularly the Vietnamese side: 'The Vietnamese are extremely economical with information on recent contacts with Peking.'[38] The British believed that 'there may have been greater agreement that is now apparent'.[39] British sources also reveal that the Vietnamese were anxious to improve relations with China, which in a way concurs with Tran Quang Co's description in his memoir of Vietnamese 'hastiness' (recounted earlier).

When asked, the Vietnamese side denied that there were any more contacts with the Chinese after Giap's visit to China in September 1990, but British sources revealed that there indeed were.[40] Perhaps most notable was Vietnamese Deputy Foreign Minister Nguyen Dy Nien's three-day visit in April 1991 to China for talks with Vice-Foreign Minister Xu Dunxin on the Cambodia issue and the normalisation of Sino-Vietnamese relations. The visit was reported to be 'satisfactory' and both sides agreed to continue to consult with each other 'in the near future'.[41] They met again in August 1991 (the fifth set of Sino-Vietnamese vice-foreign minister talks since 1989). Taking place after the resolution of the SNC issue, it was 'the best meeting so far'.[42] The other was Minister of Defence Le Duc Anh's unpublicised visit in August 1991. Anh (who subsequently rose to the position of president of Vietnam in the following year) apparently played a key role in persuading the Chinese to agree to normalise relations with Vietnam. The visit 'remains shrouded in secrecy'.[43] On the other hand, Nguyen Co Thach, who had pursued an equidistant foreign policy between China and the West, was removed from the Politburo in July 1991, apparently to appease the Chinese. Thach had written to US

---

[38] From British Embassy in Hanoi to Foreign and Commonwealth Office, London, 'Sino-Vietnamese Relations', 16 August 1991, FCO 15/6452.
[39] From British Embassy in Peking to Foreign and Commonwealth Office, London, 'China/Vietnam: Visit of General Giap', 13 October 1990, FCO 15/6221.
[40] From British Embassy in Peking to Foreign and Commonwealth Office, London, 'Sino-Vietnamese Contacts', 6 March 1991, FCO 15/6452.
[41] From British Embassy in Peking to Foreign and Commonwealth Office, London, 'Sino-Vietnamese Relations and Cambodia', 14 August 1991, FCO 15/6452.
[42] From British Embassy in Peking to Foreign and Commonwealth Office, London, 'Sino-Vietnamese Relations: Briefing', 14 August 1991, FCO 15/6452.
[43] From British Embassy in Hanoi to Foreign and Commonwealth Office, London, 'Sino-Vietnamese Relations', 16 August 1991, FCO 15/6452.

Secretary of State James Baker suggesting talks between the two sides, but no location, date, or level of talks were decided. However, the MIA Office at Hawaii might have continued pre-talk talks.[44] Vice-Deputy Foreign Minister Nguyen Dy Nien (in August 1991) and Foreign Minister Nguyen Manh Cam (in September 1991) also separately visited China. Cam's visit was the first time in more than a decade that the foreign ministers of both countries had met. Both sides 'agreed to continue to exert active efforts for a final settlement'.[45] On 23 October 1991, the Third Indochina conflict finally came to an end at the reconvened International Conference on Cambodia in Paris.

Both Vietnam and China also finally normalised relations in November 1991 during the visit of Vietnamese General Secretary Do Muoi and Prime Minister Vo Van Kiet to Peking (5–9 November 1991). Many bilateral issues remained unresolved at the point of normalisation. At the very least, agreement was reached on the 'principles which would govern relations' and, most importantly for this study, removed a major 'roadblock' for the resolution of the Cambodian conflict.[46]

V

We now reach the final part of this narrative: the UNTAC phase of the Cambodia story (1992–1993) and its immediate aftermath.[47] It is not

---

[44] From British Embassy in Hanoi to Foreign and Commonwealth Office, London, 'Relations between Vietnam and China and Between Vietnam and USA', 1 July 1991, FCO 15/6452.

[45] Qian Qichen, *Ten Episodes in China's Diplomacy* (New York: HarperCollins Publishers, 2005), p. 52. See also, From British Embassy in Hanoi to Foreign and Commonwealth Office, 'Vietnam–China Relations', 9 September 1991, FCO 15/6452; From British Embassy in Peking to Foreign and Commonwealth Office, 'China–Vietnam Relations', 10 September 1991, FCO 15/6452; From British Embassy in Peking to Foreign and Commonwealth Office, 'Vietnamese Foreign Minister's Visit to China', 16 September 1991, FCO 15/6452.

[46] From British Embassy in Hanoi to Foreign and Commonwealth Office, 'Visit of High Level Vietnamese Delegation to Peking', 1 November 1991, FCO 15/6452; From British Embassy in Peking to Foreign and Commonwealth Office, 'China/Vietnam: Do Muoi and Vo Van Kiet Visit', 12 November 1991, FCO 15/6452; From British Embassy in Hanoi to Foreign and Commonwealth Office, 'Vietnam/China: Visit of High Level Delegation to Peking', 19 November 1991. For Sino-Vietnamese relations after normalization, see Ang Cheng Guan, 'Vietnam–China Relations since the End of the Cold War', *Asian Survey*, Volume 38, Number 12, December 1998, pp. 1122–1141.

[47] See, for example, Julio A. Jeldres, 'The UN and the Cambodian Transition', *Journal of Democracy*, Volume 4, Number 4, October 1993, pp. 104–116;

possible to talk about the Paris Peace Agreement without reference to UNTAC, which was mandated 'to discharge its responsibilities effectively and complete impartiality' in a relatively short time.[48]

The UN sent an advance peacekeeping force – United Nations Advance Mission in Cambodia (UNAMIC) – to the country in November 1991, which was replaced by UNTAC in March 1992. UNAMIC was absorbed by UNTAC in March 1992. The UN custody of Cambodia ended soon after the 23 May 1993 elections, in September 1993.

Keith B. Richburg in the *Washington Post* recalled that 'Cambodia has been widely touted as a success story – a model of global peacekeeping in the post-Cold War world'. The United Nations apparently spent close to $3 billion in its efforts to 'break the cycle of tragedy' in Cambodia. But in 1995, '2½ years after UN-sponsored elections were supposed to have ushered in a new era of democracy and economic recovery, Cambodia appears to be sliding back to its familiar pattern of political assassination and repression', a view shared by Michael Leifer.[49]

Did this change come as such a surprise? Probably not. In the annual reviews of Cambodia in 1987 and 1988 prepared by the Southeast Asia Desk of the Foreign and Commonwealth Office (FCO), it was cautioned that 'we should be under no illusion However that any settlement which may ultimately emerge will be easy to implement. The Cambodian factions will be uneasy bedfellows and will not abide by Western rules for the elections which international observers may be

---

David W. Roberts, *Political Transition in Cambodia 1991–99: Power, Elitism and Democracy* (Richmond: Curzon Press, 2001); Benny Widyono, *Dancing in Shadows: Sihanouk, the Khmer Rouge, and the United Nations in Cambodia* (London: Rowman & Littlefield, 2008); Joel Brinkley, *Cambodia's Curse: The Modern History of a Troubled Land* (New York: Public Affairs, 2011); Yasushi Akashi, 'An Assessment of the United Nations Transitional Authority in Cambodia (UNTAC)', in Pou Sothirak, Geoff Wade, and Mark Hong (eds), *Cambodia: Progress and Challenges since 1991* (Singapore: ISEAS, 2012), chapter 12. For a critical assessment of the Paris Peace Agreement and UNTAC, see David W. Roberts, *Political Transition in Cambodia 1991–99: Power, Elitism and Democracy* (Richmond: Curzon, 2001).

[48] Ambassador Sothirak Pou, Bradley Murg, Charadine Pich, and Courtney Weatherby, *The Paris Peace Agreements: Looking Forward and Moving Forward* (The Stimson Center and Cambodian Institute for Cooperation and Peace, October 2021), p. 25.

[49] Keith B. Richburg, 'Democracy in a free fall as Cambodia appears to slide back to old ways' republished in *The Straits Times*, 12 December 1995; Michael Leifer, 'Cambodia's politics have regressed since the UN's intervention', *The Straits Times*, 23 December 1995.

asked to monitor.'[50] Malaysian Prime Minister Mahathir Mohamad was sceptical that Sihanouk would be able to control the various factions in Cambodia after a settlement.[51] In an interview many years later, in 2000, Laetitia van den Assum (Netherland's Bangkok-based ambassador to Thailand, Burma, Laos, and Cambodia) noted that 'Cambodia does not yet have a tradition of sharing power in the sense it is known in other parts of the world'.[52]

In assessing the role of UNTAC in the brief period leading to the 1993 general elections, it is useful to begin with the fact that left on their own, the four Cambodian factions would continue to fight among themselves. The peace agreement was essentially foisted on them by their respective sponsors in an international environment that had dramatically changed when the conflict began in the late 1970s. Cambodia's domestic politics, on the other hand, had not changed. The Paris Peace Agreement established UNTAC 'to oversee the country through a ceasefire and the creation of a new government through nation-wide elections', in short, 'an international midwife to a brokered peace agreement endorsed by the UN Security Council'.[53] But 'all groups resented the intrusive role of UNTAC, complied reluctantly, and guarded their sovereignty where they could'.[54]

UNTAC was the 'first of the mega-peace keeping operations ... mounted by the UN', with 'all the attendant teething problems', which was to be expected. It was 'always going to be difficult to execute given the complexity, the magnitude and the compressed timeframe'.[55]

---

[50] 'Cambodia: Annual Review 1987', 19 February 1988, *FCO* 15/5237; 'Cambodia: Annual Review 1988', 20 February 1989, *FCO* 15/5618.
[51] From FCO to British High Commission in Kuala Lumpur, 29 September 1988, *FCO* 15/5273.
[52] 'Cambodian reflections from the Dutch ambassador', *Phnom Penh Post*, Number 9/15, 21 July–3 August 2000.
[53] Philippe na Champassak, 'The Experiences of an International Polling Station Officer', in Viberto Selochan and Carlyle Thayer (eds), *Bringing Democracy to Cambodia: Peacekeeping and Elections* (Canberra: Australian Defence Studies Centre, 1996), p. 107.
[54] Kelvin Rowley, 'Second Life, Second Death: The Khmer Rouge after 1978', in Susan E. Cook, *Genocide in Cambodia and Rwanda: New Perspectives* (New Brunswick: Transaction Publishers, 2006), p. 199.
[55] Philippe na Champassak, 'The Experiences of an International Polling Station Officer', in Viberto Selochan and Carlyle Thayer (eds), *Bringing Democracy to Cambodia: Peacekeeping and Elections* (Canberra: Australian Defence Studies Centre, 1996), p. 107.

Compounding the 'unprecedented nature' of the Paris Peace Agreement was the fact that UNTAC was tasked with a 'peace building mission in addition to peace-making and peacekeeping'.[56]

Michael Leifer, writing in 1994, noted that UNTAC was entrusted with the responsibility for ensuring 'a neutral political environment' which would be 'conducive to free and fair elections'. To that end, UNTAC was also charged with exercising 'direct control' of a broad sphere ranging from foreign affairs to national defence, finance, public security, and more. However, these tasks 'proved to be beyond UNTAC's capability partly because of its "conventional peacekeeping mandate in addressing the problem of the Khmer Rouge" and because of its failure to attempt seriously to control the way which the SOC employed its security apparatus against political opponents'.[57] In a 1998 interview, the Pulitzer Prize-winning former correspondent for the *New York Times*, Henry Kamm, pointedly said that UNTAC was 'painted as a great success because the United Nations did a rather clever trick'. Kamm explained: the Paris Agreement under which the UN forces came into Cambodia was supposed to 'pacify' the country and 'hold elections'. All the Cambodian parties 'signed on to a surrender of their military' but everyone refused to give up power, beginning with the Khmer Rouge. Thus, 'an agreement that was supposed to bring peace and to demilitarise Cambodia was never respected, and then the United Nations sort of hid this away and said the purpose was to hold free elections'. Kamm, however, put most of the blame on 'the major powers who bring about UN resolutions and make UN decisions. The major powers raised no objection when this United Nations-sponsored agreement was totally ignored really and not really applied.'[58]

---

[56] Carlyle A. Thayer, 'The UN and Cambodia: A Critical Overview', in Viberto Selochan and Carlyle Thayer (eds), *Bringing Democracy to Cambodia: Peacekeeping and Elections* (Canberra: Australian Defence Studies Centre, 1996), p. 129.

[57] Chin Kin Wah and Leo Suryadinata (eds), *Michael Leifer: Selected Works on Southeast Asia* (Singapore: ISEAS, 2005), p. 233, see chapter 19. SOC (State of Cambodia from 1989–1993 under Hun Sen). See also, John Sanderson, 'The Role of the Military Component', in Viberto Selochan and Carlyle Thayer (eds), *Bringing Democracy to Cambodia: Peacekeeping and Elections* (Canberra: Australian Defence Studies Centre, 1996), chapter 2.

[58] Online NewsHour, 'Conversation on Cambodia' (with Henry Kamm), a *NewsHour with Jim Lehrer* transcript, 29 December 1998.

John Sanderson, who was commander of the military component of UNTAC, recalled that they could not get access to areas held by the Khmer Rouge.[59] It is perhaps worth noting that whereas many analysts and observers were of the view that the Paris Peace Agreements would give the Khmer Rouge the opportunity to regain power, Lee Kuan Yew was convinced that in a free election, the Khmer Rouge would lose and Sihanouk would win.[60] In the event, the Khmer Rouge eventually chose to opt out of the peace process. Both Leifer's and Kamm's assessments of the UNTAC sojourn in Cambodia are generally shared by others, such as Kelvin Rowley in his very sharp and succinct account of the period.[61] Rowley rightly noted that in the short term, the success of UNTAC 'can be judged by the extent to which it implemented the details of the Paris Agreement before it left Cambodia'. In the longer term, however, UNTAC's success 'will be judged less on this than on whether it succeeded in establishing a stable liberal democracy' in the country and this would depend on 'forces in Cambodian politics rather than UNTAC itself'.[62] UNTAC did deliver the general election in a timely manner with minimal disruption. But as Yasushi Akashi (special representative of the secretary-general and chief of mission, UNTAC) said, while what UNTAC achieved was 'quite significant', it was 'yet far from completing that process'.[63]

---

[59] John Sanderson, 'The Role of the Military Component', in Viberto Selochan and Carlyle Thayer (eds), *Bringing Democracy to Cambodia: Peacekeeping and Elections* (Canberra: Australian Defence Studies Centre, 1996), p. 51.
[60] 'Extract from Record of PM's Talks with Lee Kuan Yew, August 1988', FCO 15/5272.
[61] Kelvin Rowley, 'The Making of the Royal Government of Cambodia', in Viberto Selochan and Carlyle Thayer (eds), *Bringing Democracy to Cambodia: Peacekeeping and Elections* (Canberra: Australian Defence Studies Centre, 1996), pp. 1–44.
[62] Kelvin Rowley, 'The Making of the Royal Government of Cambodia', in Viberto Selochan and Carlyle Thayer (eds), *Bringing Democracy to Cambodia: Peacekeeping and Elections* (Canberra: Australian Defence Studies Centre, 1996), p. 2.
[63] Yasushi Akashi quoted in Viberto Selochan and Carlyle Thayer (eds), *Bringing Democracy to Cambodia: Peacekeeping and Elections* (Canberra: Australian Defence Studies Centre, 1996), pp. 113–114. See also, Yasushi Akashi, 'As Assessment of the United Nations Transitory Authority in Cambodia (UNTAC)', in Pou Sothirak, Geoff Wade, and Mark Hong (eds), *Cambodia: Progress and Challenges since 1991* (Singapore: Routledge, 2012), chapter 12; Sou Soubert, 'The 1991 Paris Peace Agreement: A KPNLF Perspective', in Pou Sothirak, Geoff Wade, and Mark Hong (eds), *Cambodia: Progress*

Although FUNCINPEC, led by Ranariddh, won the elections, albeit by a small margin, he was however pressured to share power with Hun Sen, who became second prime minister.

VI

It is perhaps fitting to describe Cambodia–Vietnam relations in the period after the 1993 elections here, considering that the relationship was one of the principal causes of the Third Indochina conflict.[64]

In August 1993, the two co-prime ministers, Hun Sen and Ranariddh, visited Vietnam (as well as Thailand and Laos). The visit also came in the wake of a series of victories by the coalition forces against the Khmer Rouge in north-western Cambodia, who had been killing ethnic Vietnamese there. It was reported that the Vietnamese laid out a lavish welcome and hailed the visit as 'marking the start of a "new era" in the long-turbulent relations between two countries'.

The two principal issues discussed during the visit were that of the ethnic Vietnamese refugees located at the Vietnam–Cambodia border and the border disputes along their land frontier and in the Gulf of Thailand. The fate of the ethnic Vietnamese refugees at the Vietnam–Cambodia border who had fled to Vietnam because of the atrocities of the Khmer Rouge was the urgent issue. It was estimated that the Khmer Rouge had killed some 100 since spring. Vietnam had referred to these killings as 'genocide' and 'racist attacks'. During the visit (23–25 August 1993), the United Nations headquarters in Cambodia reported that two more ethnic Vietnamese were killed. The refugees, who supposedly had Cambodian identity papers and were mainly from the Tonle Sap region where they have lived for generations, were awaiting permission to return to Cambodia. The actual number is controversial. But as new laws on immigration and unemployment have not been drawn up, Phnom Penh was acutely concerned about the political and social ramifications of their return. Phnom Penh further claimed that

---

and Challenges since 1991 (Singapore: Routledge, 2012), chapter 13; Ken Berry, 'The Role and Performance of UNTAC: An Australian Perspective', in Pou Sothirak, Geoff Wade, and Mark Hong (eds), *Cambodia: Progress and Challenges since 1991* (Singapore: Routledge, 2012), chapter 14.

[64] The following reconstruction is taken from Ang Cheng Guan, 'Vietnam–Cambodia relations from the Paris Peace Conference (1991) to membership of ASEAN', *South East Asia Research*, Volume 8, Number 1, March 2000.

200,000 to 500,000 were illegal immigrants. Vietnam, on the other hand, placed the figure at 100,000.

The other issue discussed was the territorial disputes along the Vietnam–Cambodia frontier and in the Gulf of Thailand. On 7 July 1982, the government of the PRK, represented by then Foreign Minister Hun Sen, signed an agreement with Hanoi represented by the late Foreign Minister Nguyen Co Thach, delimiting the sea boundary between the two countries.[65] A year later, on 20 July 1983, both foreign ministers concluded a treaty on the principles for the settlement of their border problems. A joint committee for national border delimitation was subsequently established. On 27 December 1985 in Phnom Penh, Hun Sen and Nguyen Co Thach signed a treaty on national border delimitation, which encompassed both land and sea, between the PRK and Vietnam.[66] The agreements signed by Hun Sen and Thach were, however, not recognised by the Sihanouk-led CGDK, which comprised the KPNLF, FUNCINPEC, and DK, established on 22 June 1982. This was essentially a united front against the PRK, which was seen as being controlled by Vietnam. During the 23–25 August 1993 discussions, the leaders once again agreed to make every effort to resolve the issue through negotiations. The communiqué released at the end of the visit stated that both sides would set up commissions of technical experts to examine their border disputes and the issue of ethnic Vietnamese in Cambodia.[67]

From the time of Nguyen Manh Cam's visit to Phnom Penh in January 1992 to Hun Sen and Ranariddh's visit to Hanoi, the political situation in Cambodia can at best be described to be in a 'transitory state'. Until the general election of May 1993, the sovereignty, independence, and unity of Cambodia were enshrined in the SNC, which was only a temporary entity. When the two-co-premiers travelled to Hanoi for talks, Cambodia was led by an interim coalition – the constitution had yet to be approved and it was not clear then whether Cambodia would have one or two prime ministers. The constitution was only passed on 21 September 1993 and Ranariddh and Hun Sen

[65] *Voice of Democratic Kampuchea*, 13 August 1982, SWB/FE/7105/A3/9.
[66] *Vietnam News Agency*, 28 December 1985, SWB/FE/8143/A3/1.
[67] For details of the visit of Hun Sen and Ranariddh to Hanoi, see *Agence France Presse*, 22, 23, and 25 August 1993; *Reuters North American Wire*, 23 August 1993; *Kyodo News Service*, 24 and 25 August 1993; *The Reuter Library Report*, 23 and 25 August 1993.

became the first and second prime ministers respectively. Sihanouk was also formally reinstated as head of state.[68] It was therefore not unexpected when Ranariddh admitted that the visit to Vietnam 'was not very positive or profitable' and that nothing very substantive was achieved.[69] Subsequent reports confirmed that the interim status prevented decisions on major issues.[70]

Hanoi was clearly very anxious to resolve the two outstanding issues, particularly that of the ethnic Vietnamese refugees. In February 1994, Foreign Minister Nguyen Manh Cam paid his second visit to Phnom Penh for two days of talks. This was also the first high-level meeting since the formation of the new Cambodian government of the post-UNTAC period. Cam met with Norodom Sirivudh, who was then deputy prime minister as well as foreign minister, to discuss the refugee problem. The issue was not resolved. The Phnom Penh government refused to allow the ethnic Vietnamese living in Cambodia to return until the passage of the immigration law, which went before the General Assembly in April.[71] In April, Vietnamese Prime Minister Vo Van Kiet travelled to Phnom Penh to discuss the issue again but apparently the talks were unsuccessful.[72] It was evident from Sihanouk's interview with the *Far Eastern Economic Review* in May that the deep-seated suspicion of Vietnamese intentions towards Cambodia persisted.[73] The draft immigration bill was due to be debated by the Cambodian National Assembly in August. The Vietnamese were unhappy with the bill and proposed the formation of an expert group to study and discuss the issue.[74] Nevertheless, in the same month the National Assembly passed the immigration law which did not guarantee citizenship and left vague what was to be done about the ethnic Vietnamese refugees still stranded at the border. Hanoi then asked the Phnom Penh government to postpone implementing the law until after the forthcoming visit to Vietnam of first Prime Minister Ranariddh.[75]

---

[68] For details, see *Phnom Penh AKP*, 22 September 1993, *FBIS-EAS-93–183*.
[69] *The Reuter Library Report*, 27 August 1993.
[70] *Reuters World Service*, 15 February 1994.
[71] *Reuters World Service*, 15 February 1994; *Associated Press*, 18 February 1994.
[72] *Associated Press*, 2 April 1994.
[73] 'The centre cannot hold: Sihanouk fears for the future of his country', *Far Eastern Economic Review*, 19 May 1994, p. 20.
[74] *Reuters World Service*, 26 August 1994; *Associated Press*, 10 September 1994.
[75] *Agence France Presse*, 15 January 1995.

In the view of the Vietnamese, the law if implemented could 'adversely affect the long-standing friendship between the two countries'. By January 1995, the immigration law was still not enforced.

Prince Norodom Ranariddh paid a working visit to Vietnam from 15 to 17 January 1995 to resolve the two issues of the ethnic Vietnamese in Cambodia and the disputed land and sea borders. The issue of navigation rights along the Mekong River also further strained relations between the two countries. The Vietnamese authorities had begun to prevent cargoes bound for Phnom Penh from proceeding along the Mekong River beyond Hanoi. The Vietnamese charged that the ships were transporting banned goods, for example used vehicles. Ranariddh believed that the Vietnamese action was a reaction to Cambodia's immigration laws. A related issue was Vietnam's plan to build a bridge on its side of the border, which Cambodia felt was too low to allow the transit of large ships.[76] Ranariddh was accompanied by a delegation of forty that included ministers from: foreign, interior, defence, forestry, fisheries, public works, education, agriculture, and commerce. According to Ranariddh, there were many issues to discuss, but the main purpose was to improve relations, which was very necessary.[77] The discussions reaped some modest achievements. Agreements were concluded on cultural and scientific exchanges, educational cooperation, agriculture, and foreign affairs. Ranariddh assured Vietnam that Phnom Penh would not carry out any mass expulsions of foreigners. Vietnam's Prime Minister Vo Van Kiet in turn expressed his understanding regarding Cambodia's immigration bill. The ethnic Vietnamese issue remained unresolved, but both sides agreed to form a group of experts to jointly study the implementation of the immigration laws and its ramifications. Regarding the border issue, it was agreed that existing borders would be respected until the problem could be discussed in detail by a joint commission. Soon after the visit, the Cambodian government announced that it was ready to let approximately 4,000 ethnic Vietnamese who fled to Vietnam almost two years previously to return to Cambodia. Those who had Cambodian identity papers (issued before 1970) could return as early as February 1995.[78]

In August 1995, Vietnamese President Le Duc Anh paid a two-day visit to Cambodia. The most senior Vietnamese leader to visit

[76] *Kyodo News Service*, 9 January 1998.
[77] *Agence France Presse*, 15 January 1995. [78] *ITAR-TASS*, 23 January 1995.

Cambodia since premier Vo Van Kiet's in April 1994, Anh was the general who oversaw Vietnam's military operation in Cambodia in 1978. The visit was largely symbolic, but symbolism has always had an important place in Cambodia (as in Vietnam). Anh laid wreathes at the Independence Monument and the Cambodia–Vietnam Friendship Monument, which pays homage to those who died during the invasion of December 1979. He also pledged 1,000 tons of rice for the Cambodians, who were facing food shortages.[79] Both sides agreed to discuss their border differences gradually and to leave the borders as they were for the time being. It was also proposed that foreign ministerial talks take place in September to tackle the other issues, such as the height of the bridge to be built on the lower course of the Mekong River.[80]

At the end of the visit, Foreign Minister Ung Huot announced the formation of a Vietnam–Cambodia Inter-Governmental Commission, which would meet for the first time on 9 September 1995. The commission would investigate the border issue, the bridge issue, commercial access along the Mekong, purchase of electric power from Vietnam, tourism ventures, Vietnamese immigration, and settlement in Cambodia, among other things. Ung Huot reiterated that there would be no mass expulsion of illegal foreigners despite domestic pressure to do so. He also made it known that there would be a meeting in October to try to resolve the issue of 3,600 ethnic Vietnamese who fled Cambodia in 1993 after a series of massacres and were currently trapped on the border.[81] Only after Anh's visit did Sihanouk finally make his long-delayed trip to Hanoi from 14 to 16 December 1995 – his first since 1975.

Looking back, 1995 was one of the better years in the development of Vietnam–Cambodia relations since October 1991. It may be worth noting that it was Le Duc Anh who visited Cambodia before Sihanouk visited Vietnam. The subtext here is particularly significant when we note that these are two countries where hierarchy, size, power, and rituals are all important. Although no substantial agreements were reached in the year and outstanding issues remained hanging in the air, the seeds for eventual resolution were at least planted. Unfortunately, the growing differences between CPP and FUNCINPEC in the

---

[79] *Deutsche Press-Agentur*, 9 August 1995.
[80] *Kyodo News Service*, 8 August 1995.   [81] *U.P.I.*, 9 August 1995.

following year (which culminated in the coup of July 1997) derailed the process.

The unresolved border demarcation between the two countries had always been a potential for conflict and a convenient issue which anti-Vietnamese elements exploited. In January 1996, Vietnamese armed soldiers and farmers were alleged to have illegally entered Cambodian territory, including the provinces of Svay Rieng, Kompong Cham, and Prey Veng, to build houses and cultivate farmland. The violations were said to have begun on 27 December 1995 in Svay Rieng, which Vietnam denied. Both Ung Huot and Co-Interior Minister Sar Kheng met Tran Huy Chuong, Vietnam's ambassador to Cambodia, and all were committed to a peaceful solution to their border dispute. In January 1996, Sar Kheng paid a working visit to Hanoi for talks. On 24 January, a Cambodian newspaper printed an article that essentially argued that the Khmer Empire had shrunk to a 'barely visible dot on the world map'. It cited a statement by Sihanouk in 1992 that Cambodia had lost ten to forty kilometres of territory to Vietnam. The writer then posed the question where the borderline now lies and whether 'Cambodian land will become Vietnamese land and Cambodians will be turned into one of Vietnam's minority groups'.[82]

Not all Cambodians shared the same view. In February, the chief of police in Cambodia's Kandal province, which had a twenty-nine-kilometre common border with Vietnam's An Giang province, was reported to have said that there was no border problem with Vietnam and that the latter actually provided water to Cambodia for farming. As for the areas where the border was unclear, the authorities in both provinces considered them as 'white zones' that were off limits to either side. He also made the point that more contacts between local authorities at district, communal, and provincial levels could solve and avert problems.[83]

Ranariddh, who demonstrated a penchant for evoking the Vietnamese threat, was reported to have warned of the possible use of force if talks failed to resolve the border dispute. Hanoi retorted that if his remark were true, it would not be in the interests of friendly ties and likely to damage relations.[84] It is significant to note that Second

---

[82] *IBRU Boundary and Security Bulletin*, Spring 1996, p. 37.
[83] *IBRU Boundary and Security Bulletin*, Spring 1996, p. 38.
[84] *Reuters North American Wire*, 16 March 1996.

Prime Minister and Chairman of the Council of Ministers Hun Sen did not share Ranariddh's sentiment. At a meeting of the Council of Ministers to discuss the Cambodia–Vietnam boundary issue on 7 February, peace, friendship, and cooperation were stressed.[85] As Co-Minister of Interior Sar Kheng said, the border dispute was tied to domestic politics.

In March, VCP leader Do Muoi and Ranariddh would have had the opportunity to discuss the border issue when they both attended the 6th Party Congress of the Lao People's Revolutionary Party in Vientiane.[86] Soon after, in April, Vo Van Kiet led a sixteen-member delegation, which included the foreign minister and the deputy ministers of interior, commerce, transport, and planning and investment, to Phnom Penh for a day of talks in an effort to resolve the border dispute. According to the communiqué issued at the end of the visit, the two sides agreed to settle the border issue without resorting to the use of force. It was also decided that local authorities should address border issues first, and if they failed, the issues could then be referred to provincial authorities and finally to the related ministries.[87] They also agreed to hold a working group meeting at the expert level as soon as possible, possibly in the last week of April. Regarding the ethnic Vietnamese residing in Cambodia, both sides agreed to convene urgently a third meeting of the working group at expert level. It was also proposed that a consular agreement be signed as soon as possible. Both sides also affirmed their determination to strengthen bilateral relations by taking concrete measures to boost cooperation in finance, transportation and communication, agriculture, forestry, education, and security. Finally, Vietnam also welcomed Cambodia's intention to join ASEAN and expressed willingness to help Cambodia integrate.[88]

On 17 May 1996, it was reported that more ethnic Vietnamese were being killed. Gunmen apparently attacked a floating village on the edge of Tonle Sap and killed seventeen people, of which fourteen were Vietnamese. Hanoi lodged a formal protest. The border experts from both countries met for the first time in Ho Chi Minh City from 20 to 23 May. We do not have the details except that the negotiations

---

[85] *IBRU Boundary and Security Bulletin*, Spring 1996, p. 38.
[86] *Xinhua News Agency*, 18 March 1996.
[87] *Associated Press*, 8 April 1996; *Agence France Presse*, 10 April 1996; *Xinhua News Agency*, 10 April 1996.
[88] *Xinhua News Agency*, 11 April 1996.

proceeded in what was described as a 'friendly and frank' manner and that the next meeting would be in held in Phnom Penh. The rivalry between the two co-premiers and their parties intensified as the next election drew closer. The ethnic Vietnamese always had to bear the consequences whenever the political struggles in Phnom Penh intensified. During the 1993 United Nation-sponsored election, one of the key themes of FUNCINPEC's campaign was that voting for the CPP would mean keeping Cambodia beholden to the hated Vietnamese and further impoverishing the country. The Khmer Rouge (and at the time FUNCINPEC as well) continued to propagate the image of Hun Sen and the CPP as the 'Vietnamese-installed regime' long after the 1989 Vietnamese withdrawal from Cambodia. In 1996–1997, Ranariddh was again courting the staunchly anti-Vietnamese Khmer Rouge. For example, in early June 1997, an unidentified attacker bombed a memorial for the Vietnamese war dead in Sihanoukville. Two days after, Ranariddh added fuel to fire when he remarked that the Cambodia–Vietnam Friendship Monument in central Phnom Penh had been standing there for too long and that if he were to win next year's election, he would have it removed.

Meanwhile, the second Vietnam–Cambodia Inter-Governmental Cooperation Commission convened in Phnom Penh from 26 to 28 February 1997 and was attended by Vietnam's Foreign Minister Nguyen Manh Cam. The commission announced that an agreement on trade, road and water transportation, and information cooperation would be signed soon, and that discussion on other matters would continue.[89] The critical issues were, however, still not resolved.

Turning to the China factor in Vietnam–Cambodia relations, Cambodia–China relations had also been improving since the withdrawal of Vietnamese forces in 1989. China was becoming increasingly a major player in Cambodia. In April 1996, General Zhang Wannian, chief of the PLA General Staff Department, visited Cambodia. China granted $1 million in non-lethal aid to Cambodia and was considering providing training assistance to the Cambodian coalition government.[90] According to a December 1997 report in the *Far Eastern Economic Review*, China was the second-largest Asian aid donor to Cambodia, next to Japan. Many of the most prominent investors

---

[89] *Voice of Vietnam External Service*, 1 March 1977, SWB/FE/2857/B/1.
[90] *Phnom Penh Post*, 23 August–5 September 1996, FBIS-EAS-96–167.

in Phnom Penh were from mainland China. The Chinese has also been providing military assistance to Hun Sen in his fight against the Khmer Rouge.[91] According to one source, it was Zhang who conveyed Beijing's invitation to Hun Sen to visit China, and Beijing was apparently miffed by Ranariddh's contacts with Taipei, which included discussions on a possible direct air link between Phnom Penh and Taipei and the opening of a consular office in Phnom Penh.[92] Beijing could have decided that in view of Sihanouk's age and poor health, it was prudent to cultivate Hun Sen.

Both CPP and FUNCINPEC were also courting Beijing. In mid-June 1996, Loy Simchheang, secretary-general of FUNCINPEC, met then Prime Minister Li Peng in Beijing.[93] During Vietnam's 8th Party Congress, on 1 July 1996 in Hanoi, Wen Jiabao (acting leader of the CCP Central Committee delegation, alternate member of the Politburo and secretary of the CCP Central Committee secretariat) held separate talks with Chea Sim (chairman of the CPP and chairman of Cambodia's National Assembly) and Chhim Seakleng (leader of FUNCINPEC delegation).[94] About a fortnight later, on 12 July 1996, it was announced that Hun Sen had been invited to visit China from 18 to 22 July 1996. There was no elaboration as to purpose of the visit except that it was part of a friendship programme between the two countries. According to Hun Sen, the trip to China had been planned much earlier.[95]

It is worth noting that the Chinese disclosed the visit shortly after Sihanouk left Beijing for Cambodia. When the news was announced, Hun Sen and Ranariddh were in Tokyo attending a 'consultative group' meeting on financial aid to Cambodia for 1996 and 1997.[96] In China, Hun Sen met Chinese President Jiang Zemin and Premier

---

[91] 'Dancing with the Dragon', *Far Eastern Economic Review*, 11 December 1997, pp. 26–27. According to Sophie Richardson, although Beijing 'remained the only actor not to have publicly condemned the KR [Khmer Rouge], ... this was not to be confused with endorsement'. See Sophie Richardson, *China, Cambodia, and the Five Principles of Peaceful Coexistence* (New York: Columbia University Press, 2010), p. 146.
[92] *Phnom Penh Post in English*, 19 December 1997–1 January 1998, FBIS-EAS-97-363.
[93] *Reaksmei Kampuchea*, 10–11 July 1996, FBIS-EAS-96-137.
[94] China Radio International, 2 July 1996, SWB/FE/2656/B/3.
[95] *Reaksmei Kampuchea*, 20 July 1996, FBIS-EAS-96-141.
[96] *Reaksmei Kampuchea*, 14 July 1996, FBIS-EAS-96-137.

Li Peng and toured Zhuhai, which is one of China's special economic zones in Guangdong Province, as well as Shenzhen.[97] Coincidentally, a senior Vietnamese military delegation led by Chief of General Staff Pham Van Tra was also in Beijing during this time.[98] There is, however, no report of any meeting between the Vietnamese and Cambodians.

VII

The coalition government led by two prime ministers did not last. The rivalry between the two co-premiers culminating in the ouster of first Prime Minister Ranariddh was common knowledge. As Cambodian parliamentarian Ahmad Yahya commented in a December 1996 interview, 'the coalition exists only on paper, only in theory. It just doesn't work.'[99] As the saying goes, 'two tigers cannot share one mountain', and the very public uneasy alliance, not unexpectedly, broke down in July 1997, resulting in the defeat of Ranariddh. According to Son Soubert (second vice-president of the National Assembly, 1993–1998), the July crisis was 'a grave consequence' of the failure of UNTAC to help create a national army in the transition period and the failure to achieve national reconciliation through a democratic process.[100]

We may recall that the principal condition demanded by Beijing for normalisation of relations between China and Vietnam was Vietnamese withdrawal from Cambodia. It is reasonable to assume that the Chinese remained sensitive to any new Vietnamese interference or involvement in Cambodian affairs. There was no evidence that Hanoi was involved in the 1997 political crisis. Sino-Vietnam relations had been improving gradually since 1991 and did not appear to have been affected by the crisis.[101] Both Vietnam and China were not unhappy with Hun Sen and were comfortable with each other's current relations with Cambodia.

[97] For Hun Sen's visit to China, see *SWB/FE/2668/B/3*; *SWB/FE/2669/G/1*; *SWB/FE/2670/G/1*; *SWB/FE/2673/G/3*.
[98] See *SWB/FE/2670/G/1*.
[99] 'Row over prince shakes Khmer coalition', *The Straits Times*, 17 December 1996.
[100] Son Soubert, 'The 1991 Paris Peace Agreement: A KPNLF Perspective', in Pou Sothirak, Geoff Wade, and Mark Hong (eds), *Cambodia: Progress and Challenges since 1991* (Singapore: Routledge, 2012), chapter 13. Son Soubert is the son of Son Sann, one of the three leaders of the CGDK.
[101] See Ang Cheng Guan, 'Vietnam–China Relations since the End of the Cold War', *Asian Survey*, Volume 38, Number 12, December 1998, pp. 1122–1141.

Epilogue

As a result of the coup/political crisis, depending on one's point of view,[102] Cambodia's seat at the United Nations was suspended. The details of Cambodian domestic politics need not delay us too much here.[103] What is perhaps relevant to note is that had it not been for the 1997 coup and ensuing political crisis, Cambodia would have been admitted into ASEAN on 23 July 1997 during the 30th ASEAN ministerial meeting (also the 30th anniversary of the founding of ASEAN) in Kuala Lumpur. Because of the political uncertainty in Cambodia, the decision was taken at the ASEAN foreign ministers special meeting on 10 July to postpone indefinitely its admission. Apparently, it took 'more than a little persuasion' to secure both Malaysia's and Vietnam's agreement to convene the special meeting of the foreign ministers. The 'critical swing' factor was Indonesia. For the first time in its history, ASEAN expressed disapproval of a violent change of government in a neighbouring country.[104] That said, the ASEAN member states were no longer willing to get involved in Cambodian domestic politics. Bilahari Kausikan, who was Singapore's permanent secretary to the Number in 1997, recalled Prince Ranariddh asking to meet him in New York soon after the coup. When they met, Ranariddh greeted him, saying, 'Bilahari, the struggle begins again'. 'What he said is seared in my memory. I could hardly believe my ears. I told him as politely as possible, that he had been given his chance and this time the struggle, if there was to be one, was his struggle, not Singapore's struggle or ASEAN's struggle', he recalled.[105]

A general election was subsequently held a year later in July 1998, and in early December a new coalition government was formed with Hun Sen as the sole prime minister, which came as no surprise. As Henry Kamm noted, 'the election merely ratified a totally irregular state

---

[102] See Huw Watkin's interview of Australian ambassador to Cambodia, Tony Kevin, 'Was there a coup in Cambodia?', *Quadrant*, Volume 41, Number 12, December 1997,

[103] See Ang Cheng Guan, 'Vietnam–Cambodia Relations from the Paris Peace Conference (1991) to Membership of ASEAN', *South East Asia Research*, Volume 8, Number 1, March 2000. See also Michael Vickery, *Kicking the Vietnam Syndrome in Cambodia: Collected Writings 1975–2010*, chapters 5 and 6, http://michaelvickery.org/vickery2010kicking.pdf, accessed on 25 January 2023.

[104] 'Postponement of Cambodia's Entry into ASEAN', *Information Note on Cambodia*, 11 July 1997.

[105] Bilahari Kausikan, *Singapore Is Still Not an Island: More Views on Singapore's Foreign Policy* (Singapore: Straits Times Press, 2023), pp. 131–132.

of affairs that existed before ... he [Hun Sen] lost the UN-sponsored elections in 1993, but bludgeoned his way into power, into a share of power ... It was Hun Sen and his machines, which has run Cambodia since then [1993]'.[106] Cambodia regained its seat in the Number and reapplied for admission into ASEAN. It eventually became the tenth member of ASEAN on 30 April 1999.[107]

In recent years, due to the erosion of democratic and human rights provisions that were spelled out in the Paris Peace Agreement, there has been a reassessment of the legacy of the 1991 agreement. Hun Sen embarked on rewriting the history of those years. He also insisted that the agreement had now been superseded by the 1993 constitution, and in 2020 his government ended the national holiday commemorating the signing of the 1991 Paris Peace Agreement. The PRK version of history is that it was only in 1998 that Cambodia achieved 'prevailing peace under the government's win-win policy initiated by Hun Sen'.[108] On the other hand, those who are opposed to Hun Sen and his CPP continue to hold the terms of the Paris Peace Agreement 'as a benchmark against which current political developments are to be measured, so as to hold the government accountable', as well as a supportive 'legal tool' to justify the involvement of the international community in Cambodian domestic politics. As the prominent opposition personality, Sam Rainsy said: 'It is about control of history and of the future.'[109]

---

[106] Online NewsHour, 'Conversation on Cambodia' (with Henry Kamm), a *NewsHour with Jim Lehrer* transcript, 29 December 1998.

[107] The admission was somewhat controversial and involved Vietnamese machinations. See Ang Cheng Guan, 'Vietnam–Cambodia Relations from the Paris Peace Conference (1991) to Membership of ASEAN', *South East Asia Research*, Volume 8, Number 1, March 2000.

[108] Torn Vibol, 'Path of peace: govt commemorates 32nd anniversary of Paris Agreements', *Khmer Times*, 23 October 2023. See also, Pov Sok, *Samdech Hun Sen: Supreme Founder and Father of Peace of Cambodia* (Phnom Penh: Ponleu Khmer Printing and Publishing House, 2021), p. 216.

[109] 'Paris Peace Accords' legacy in Cambodia is mixed and politically contentious as 30th anniversary nears', 3 September 2021, www.voacambodia.com/a/paris-peace-accords-legacy-in-cambodia-is-mixed-and-politically-contentious-as-30th-anniversary-nears/6211020.html, accessed on 31 January 2023; 'Time to accept Cambodia as it is', *Khmer Times*, 23 January 2023; Astrid Noren-Nilsson, 'The end of the beginning for the Cambodian People's Party', *East Asia Forum*, 27 January 2023.

List of Characters/Dramatis Personae

Australia

Gareth John Evans	Australian Minister for Foreign Affairs (1988–1996)
John Murray Sanderson	Commander of the Military Component of UNTAC (1993)
Noel St. Clair Deschamps	Australian Ambassador to Cambodia (1962–1969) Australian Ambassador to Chile (1969–1973)
Wilfred Graham Burchett	Australian journalist (1940–1978)
William George Hayden (Bill Hayden)	Australian Minister for Foreign Affairs and Trade (1983–1988)

Bulgaria

Stanko Todorov Georgiev	Bulgarian Prime Minister (1971–1981) Bulgarian Chairperson of the National Assembly (1981–1990)

Cambodia

Ahmad Yahya	Cambodian Secretary of State for Social Affairs, Veterans, and Youth Rehabilitation (2000s)
Bunheang Ung	Survivor of the Khmer Rouge's Killing Fields (1952–2014)
Chea Sim	President of the National Assembly of Cambodia (1981–1993, 1993–1998) Cambodian People's Party President (1991–2015)

Chhim Seakleng	Governor of Phnom Penh (1993–1998) Cambodian Minister of Rural Development (1998–2001) Member of Parliament (1998–2008)
Haing S. Ngor	Survivor of the Khmer Rouge's Killing Fields (1940–1996) Cambodian-born American actor
Heng Samrin	Head of State of the People's Republic of Kampuchea (1979–1989) General Secretary of Kampuchean People's Revolutionary Party (1981–1989) President of the National Assembly of Cambodia (2006–2023)
Hun Manet	Son of Hun Sen Cambodian Prime Minister (since August 2023)
Hun Sen	Cambodian Minister of Foreign Affairs (1979–1986) Deputy Prime Minister of the People's Republic of Kampuchea (1981–1985) Cambodian Second Prime Minister (1993–1998) Cambodian Prime Minister (1985–1993, 1998–2023)
Ieng Sary	Deputy Prime Minister of Democratic Kampuchea (1976–1979) Cambodian Minister of Foreign Affairs (1976–1979)
Julio A. Jeldres	Senior Private Secretary to Sihanouk (1981–1991)
Khieu Ponnary	First Wife of Pol Pot (1956–1979)
Khieu Samphan	Chairman of the State Presidium of Democratic Kampuchea (1976–1979)
Lon Nol	Cambodian Minister of National Defence (1959–1966, 1968–1971) Cambodian Prime Minister of the Khmer Republic (1969–1971) President of the Khmer Republic (1972–1975)

List of Characters/Dramatis Personae

Loy Simchheang Secretary-General of FUNCINPEC (1990s)
Norodom Ranariddh Second son of Norodom Sihanouk
  Cambodian First Prime Minister
  (1993–1997)
  President of the National Assembly
  (1998–2006)
  President of FUNCINPEC (1992–2006,
  2015–2021)
Norodom Sihanouk Cambodian Prime Minister (1955–1960)
  Cambodian Head of State (1960–1970)
  President of Cambodia (1982–1988)
  Crown Prince/King of Cambodia
  (1941–1955, 1993–2004)
Norodom Sirivudh Half Brother of Norodom Sihanouk
  Crown Prince
  Cambodian Minister of Foreign
  Affairs and International Cooperation
  (1993–1994)
  Cambodian Deputy Prime Minister
  (2004–2006)
  Cambodian Minister of Interior
  (2004–2006)
Nuon Chea Deputy Secretary of the Communist
  Party of Kampuchea (1960–1981)
  Acting Prime Minister of Democratic
  Kampuchea (September 1976–October
  1976)
  President of the Standing Committee of
  the Kampuchean People's Representative
  Assembly (1976–1979)
Pol Pot (Saloth Sar) Prime Minister of Democratic
  Kampuchea (1976–1979)
  General Secretary of the Communist
  Party of Kampuchea (1963–1981)
Sam Rainsy Cambodian Minister of Economy and
  Finance (1993–1994)
  Member of the National Assembly
  (1993–1995, 1998–2005, 2008–2011,
  2014–2015)

Sar Kheng	Vice-President of the Cambodian People's Party (since 2015) Cambodian Interior Minister (1992–2023)
Sieu Heng	Leader of the Khmer People's Revolutionary Party (1950s)
Sok Thuok (Vorn Vet)	Deputy Prime Minister of the Economy of Democratic Kampuchea (1975–1978)
Son Ngoc Minh (Achar Mean)	Co-founder of the Kampuchean People's Revolutionary Party (1951)
Son Sann	Cambodian Prime Minister (1967–1968)
Son Sen	Cambodian Minister of National Defence (1976–1979) Deputy Prime Minister of Democratic Kampuchea (1976–1979)
Son Soubert	Second Vice-President of National Assembly (1993–1998)
Suk Sutsakhan	Commander-in-Chief of the Khmer People's National Liberation Front (1980s)
Tea Banh	Cambodian Deputy Prime Minister (2004–2023) Cambodian Minister of National Defence (1987–2023)
Tou Samouth (Achar Sok)	Co-founder of the Kampuchean People's Revolutionary Party (1951) General Secretary of the Kampuchean People's Revolutionary Party (1951–1960)
Ung Huot	Cambodian Prime Minister (1997–1998) Cambodian Minister of Foreign Affairs and International Cooperation (1994–1998)
Youk Chhang	Survivor of the Khmer Rouge's Killing Fields Executive Director of the Documentation Centre of Cambodia (since 1995)

List of Characters/Dramatis Personae

France

Claude Martin	Director for Asia and the Pacific, Quai d'Orsay (1980s)
Etienne Manac'h	French Ambassador to China (1969–1975)
François Marie Adrien Maurice Mitterrand	President of France (1981–1995)
Roland Dumas	French Minister of Foreign Affairs (1988–1993)

India

Kunwar Natwar Singh	Indian Minister of External Affairs (2004–2005) Indian Deputy Foreign Minister (1980s)

Indonesia

Ali Alatas	Indonesian Minister of Foreign Affairs (1988–1999)
Leonardus Benjamin Moerdani	8th Commander of the Republic of Indonesia Military Forces (1983–1988) Commander of Operational Command for the Restoration of Security and Order (1983–1988) 17th Minister of Defence and Security (1988–1993)
Mochtar Kusumaatmadja	Indonesian Minister of Foreign Affairs (1978–1988)
Suharto	President of Indonesia (1968–1998)

Japan

Yasushi Akashi	Special Representative of the Secretary-General and Chief of Mission to the United Nations Transitional Authority in Cambodia (1992–1993)

Laos

Souphanouvong	President of Laos (1975–1986)

Malaysia

Hussein bin Dato' Onn	Malaysian Prime Minister (1976–1981)
Mahathir bin Mohamad	Malaysian Deputy Prime Minister (1976–1981) Malaysian Prime Minister (1981–2003, 2018–2020)
Muhammad Ghazali Shafie	Malaysian Minister of Home Affairs (1973–1981)
Tengku Ahmad Rithauddeen Ismail	Malaysian Minister of Foreign Affairs (1984–1986)
Tun Haji Abdul Razak bin Dato' Hussein	Malaysian Prime Minister (1970–1976)

Netherlands

Laetitia van den Assum	Netherland's Bangkok-based Ambassador to Thailand, Burma, Laos, and Cambodia (1995–2000)

People's Republic of China

Deng Xiaoping	Chairman of the Central Advisory Commission (1981–1989)
Deng Yingchao	Wife of Zhou Enlai Chairman of the Chinese People's Political Consultative Conference (1983–1988) Second Secretary of the Central Commission for Discipline Inspection (1978–1982)
Geng Biao	Head of Chinese Communist Party's Central Foreign Communication Department (1970s)

List of Characters/Dramatis Personae

Han Hsu	Chinese Deputy Chief Liaison to the United States (1973–1979)
	Chinese Vice-Minister of Foreign Affairs (1982–1985)
	Chinese Ambassador to the United States (1985–1989)
Hu Yaobang	General Secretary of the Chinese Communist Party (1982–1987)
Hua Guofeng	Premier of the People's Republic of China (1976–1980)
Huang Hua	Chinese Minister of Foreign Affairs (1976–1982)
Jiang Zemin	President of the People's Republic of China (1993–2003)
Kang Sheng	Director of the Central Social Affairs Department (1939–1945)
	Vice Chairperson of the Chinese People's Political Consultative Conference (1959–1964)
	Vice-Chairman of the Standing Committee of the National People's Congress (1965–1975)
	Vice-Chairman of the Chinese Communist Party (1959–1975)
Li Peng	Premier of the People's Republic of China (1988–1998)
Li Xiannian	Vice-Premier of the Chinese Communist Party (1954–1980)
Mao Zedong	Chairman of the People's Republic of China (1954–1959)
Qian Qichen	Chinese Minister of Foreign Affairs (1988–1998)
Tian Zengpei	Chinese Vice-Minister of Foreign Affairs (1988–1998)
Wang Bingnan	Secretary-General of the Chinese Delegation to the Geneva Conference (1954)
Wang Dongxing	Vice-Chairman of the Chinese Communist Party (1988–1998)

Wen Jiabao	Director of the General Office of the Chinese Communist Party (1986–1993) Vice-Premier of the People's Republic of China (1998–2003) Premier of the People's Republic of China (2003–2013)
Wu Xueqian	Chinese Minister of Foreign Affairs (1982–1988)
Xu Shiyou	Commander of the Nanjing Military Region (1954–1974) Commander of the Guangzhou Military Region (during the Sino-Vietnamese War in 1979)
Zhang Wannian	Chief of the General Staff Department of the People's Liberation Army (1992–1995)
Zhou Enlai	Chinese Minister of Foreign Affairs (1949–1958) Premier of the People's Republic of China (1954–1976)

Romania

Nicolae Ceausescu	President of Romania (1974–1989)

Singapore

Goh Keng Swee	Singaporean Minister for Interior and Defence (1965–1967) Singaporean Minister for Defence (1970–1979)
Kishore Mahbubani	Singaporean Permanent Representative to the United Nations (1998–2004)
Lee Hsien Loong	Singaporean Prime Minister (since 2004)
Lee Kuan Yew	Singaporean Prime Minister (1959–1990)
Ng Eng Hen	Singaporean Minister for Defence (since 2011)
S. R. Nathan	Singaporean Permanent Secretary of the Ministry of Foreign Affairs (1979–1982)

List of Characters/Dramatis Personae 183

S. Rajaratnam Singaporean Minister for Foreign Affairs
(1965–1980)
Tommy Koh Thong Bee Singaporean Representative at
the Paris Conference on Cambodia
(1989)

Union of Soviet Socialist Republics

Eduard Ambrosisdze Shevardnadze Soviet Minister of Foreign Affairs (1974–1989)
Igor Rogachev Soviet Vice-Minister of Foreign Affairs (1980s)
Ivan Vasilyevich Arkhipov Soviet Deputy Chairman of the Council of Ministers (1980–1986)
Konstantin Ustinovich Chernenko Chairman of the Presidium of the Supreme Soviet (1984–1985)
Leonid Ilyich Brezhnev Chairman of the Presidium of the Supreme Soviet (1960–1964, 1964–1982)
Mikhail Sergeyevich Gorbachev General Secretary of the Communist Party of the Soviet Union (1985–1991) President of the Soviet Union (1990–1991)
Nikita Sergeyevich Khrushchev Premier of the Soviet Union (1958–1964)
Vyacheslav Mikhaylovich Molotov Minister of Foreign Affairs (1939–1949, 1953–1956)
Yuri Vladimirovich Andropov Chairman of the Presidium of the Supreme Soviet (1983–1984)

Thailand

Chaovalit Yongchaiyuth Commander-in-Chief of the Royal Thai Army (1986–1990)
Supreme Commander of the Armed Forces (1987–1990)
Chatichai Choonhavan Thai Prime Minister (1988–1991)
Kavi Chongkittavorn Reporter for *The Nation* newspaper (since 1984)

184 List of Characters/Dramatis Personae

Kraisak Choonhavan	Son of Chatichai Choonhavan Adviser to the Prime Minister (1988–1991)
Kriangsak Chamanan	Thai Prime Minister (1977–1980)
Kukrit Pramoj	Thai Prime Minister (1975–1976)
Prayut Chan-o-cha	Thai Prime Minister (2014–2023)
Prem Tinsulanonda	Commanding General of the Second Army Area (1974–1977) Thai Prime Minister (1980–1988) President of the Privy Council (1988–2019)
Siddhi Savetsila	Thai Minister of Foreign Affairs (1980–1990)
Thanat Khoman	Thai Minister of Foreign Affairs (1959–1971) Thai Deputy Prime Minister (1981–1983)

United Kingdom

Derek Tonkin	Diplomat of the United Kingdom based in Phnom Penh (1961–1963)
Donald Hawley	High Commissioner of the United Kingdom to Malaysia (1977–1981)
Edward Richard George Heath	Prime Minister of the United Kingdom (1970–1974)
Elizabeth II	Queen of the United Kingdom and other Commonwealth realms (1952–2022)
Ivon Anthony Moore-Brabazon	Represented the United Kingdom at the Paris Conference on Cambodia (1989)
James Eric Sydney Cable	Member of the British Delegation to the Geneva Conference on Indochina (1954)
John Dunn Hennings	High Commissioner of the United Kingdom to Singapore (1978–1982)
Malcolm MacDonald	President of Great Britain China Centre (1970s)
Robert Anthony Eden	Secretary of State for Foreign Affairs of the United Kingdom (1935–1938, 1940–1945, 1951–1955)

List of Characters/Dramatis Personae 185

Robin John Taylor McLaren Ambassador of the United Kingdom to China (1991–1994)
Roy Harris Jenkins President of the European Commission (1977–1981)

United States of America

Alexander Meigs Haig Jr. United States Secretary of State (1981–1982)
Cyrus Roberts Vance Sr. United States Secretary of State (1977–1980)
David Floyd Lambertson United States Deputy Assistant Secretary of State (1987–1990)
Emory Coblentz Swank United States Ambassador to Cambodia (1970–1973)
 Head of Cleveland Council of World Affairs (1977–1987)
Eric Paul Schwartz United States Assistant Secretary of State for Population, Refugees, and Migration (2009–2011)
George H. W. Bush President of the United States (1989–1993)
George Schulz United States Secretary of State (1982–1989)
George Stanley McGovern United States Senator (1963–1981)
Gerald Ford President of the United States (1974–1977)
Henry Alfred Kissinger United States National Security Adviser (1969–1975)
 United States Secretary of State (1973–1977)
Henry Kamm Pulitzer Prize-winning journalist for the *New York Times* (1973–1996)
James Addison Baker III United States Secretary of State (1989–1992)
James Earl Carter Jr. United States (1977–1981)
John Dimitri Negroponte United States Deputy Assistant Secretary of State for East Asian and Pacific Bureau (1980–1981)

John Foster Dulles	United States Secretary of State (1953–1959)
John H. Holdridge	United States National Intelligence Officer for East Asia/Pacific (1978–1981)
Keith B. Richburg	United States Journalist for the *Washington Post* (1986–2013)
Morton Isaac Abramowitz	United States Ambassador to Thailand (1978–1981)
Murray Zinoman	United States Political Counselor at the United States Embassy in Kuala Lumpur (1980s)
Patricia Mary Byrne	United States Ambassador to Burma (1979–1983)
Richard Charles Albert Holbrooke	United States Assistant Secretary of State for East Asian and Pacific Affairs (1977–1981)
Richard Harvey Solomon	United States Assistant Secretary of State for East Asian and Pacific Affairs (1989–1992)
Richard Milhous Nixon	President of the United States (1969–1974)
Robert B. Oakley (Bob Oakley)	United States Deputy Assistant Secretary of State for East Asia and Pacific Affairs (1977–1979)
Robert Shaplen	United States journalist for the *New Yorker* (1962–1978)
Ronald Wilson Reagan	President of the United States (1981–1989)
Stephen Joshua Solarz	United States Congressman (1969–1993)
Theodore George Osius III	United States Ambassador to Vietnam (2014–2017)
Walter Bedell Smith	United States Under Secretary of State (1953–1954)
Walter Frederick Mondale	United States Vice-President (1977–1981)
William Jefferson Clinton (Bill Clinton)	President of the United States (1993–2001)
Zbigniew Kazimierz Brzeziński	United States National Security Adviser (1977–1981)

List of Characters/Dramatis Personae

Vietnam

Bui Tin	Vice-Chief Editor of the *People's Daily* (Nhan Dan) (1970s)
Dinh Nho Liem	Held various appointments in the Ministry of Foreign Affairs, including Minister of Foreign Affairs
Do Muoi	Chairman of the Council of Ministers of Vietnam (1988–1991) General Secretary of the Communist Party of Vietnam (1991–1997)
Duong Danh Dy	First Secretary of the Vietnamese Embassy in China (appointed 1979)
Ho Chi Minh	President of the Democratic Republic of Vietnam (1945–1969)
Hoang Tung	Editor-in-Chief of *Nhan Dan* newspaper (1954–1984(?))
Hoang Van Hoan	Vietnamese Ambassador to China (1950–1957)
Hoang Van Loi	Vietnamese Deputy Foreign Minister (1960s)
Le Duan	First Secretary of the Vietnamese Communist Party (1960–1986)
Le Duc Anh	4th Chief of the General Staff (1986–1987) Vietnamese Minister of Defence (1987–1991) President of Vietnam (1992–1997)
Le Duc Tho	Member of the Politburo of the Communist Party of Vietnam (1955–1986) Advisor to the Party Central Committee (1986–1990)
Le Thanh Nghi	Vietnamese Deputy Prime Minister (1960–1981) Vice-President of Vietnam (1982–1987)
Ngo Dinh Diem	President of South Vietnam (1955–1963)
Nguyen Co Thach	Vietnamese Minister of Foreign Affairs (1980–1991)

	Vietnamese Deputy Prime Minister (1987–1991)
Nguyen Dy Nien	Vietnamese Deputy Minister of Foreign Affairs (1987–2000)
Nguyen Duy Trinh	Vietnamese Minister of Foreign Affairs (1965–1980)
Nguyen Huu Tho	Vice-President of Vietnam (1976–1992)
Nguyen Manh Cam	Vietnamese Minister of Foreign Affairs (1991–2000)
Nguyen Ngoc Truong	Vietnamese Ambassador to Mexico, Peru, and Panama (1996–1999) Vietnamese Ambassador to Sweden and Finland (2002–2006)
Nguyen Van Linh	General Secretary of the Communist Party of Vietnam (1986–1991)
Pham Hung	Head of the Central Office for South Vietnam (1967–1975)
Pham Van Dong	Head of the North Vietnamese Delegation to the Geneva Conference on IndoChina (1954) North Vietnamese Prime Minister (1955–1976) Vietnamese Prime Minister (1976–1987)
Pham Van Tra	Chief of General Staff (1995–1997)
Phan Hien	Vietnamese Vice-Minister of Foreign Affairs (1970s)
Tran Huy Chuong	Vietnamese Ambassador to Cambodia (1990s)
Tran Quang Co	Vietnamese Vice-Minister of Foreign Affairs (1986–1997)
Tran Van Tra	Chairman of the Military Affairs Committee of the Central Office for South Vietnam (1964–1976) Vietnamese Vice-Minister of Defence (1978–1982)
Truong Chinh	Chairman of the National Assembly of Vietnam (1960–1981) Member of the Politburo of the Communist Party of Vietnam (1951–1986)

List of Characters/Dramatis Personae

Van Tien Dung	Chief of Staff of the People's Army of Vietnam (1954–1974) Commander-in-Chief of the People's Army of Vietnam (1974–1980)
Vo Dong Giang	Vietnamese Minister of Foreign Affairs (1983–1987)
Vo Nguyen Giap	Commander-in-Chief of the People's Army of Vietnam (1946–1975) Vietnamese Deputy Prime Minister (1955–1991)
Vo Van Kiet	Vietnamese Prime Minister (1991–1997)

Bibliography

Books and Book Chapters

Allison, Graham and Robert D. Blackwill with Ali Wyne. *Lee Kuan Yew: The Grand Master's Insights on China, the United States, and the World* (Cambridge: The MIT Press, 2012).

Ang, Cheng Guan. *Ending the Vietnam War: The Vietnamese Communists' Perspective* (London: RoutledgeCurzon, 2004).

Ang, Cheng Guan. *Lee Kuan Yew's Strategic Thought* (London: Routledge, 2013).

Ang, Cheng Guan. *Singapore, ASEAN and the Cambodian Conflict, 1978–1991* (Singapore: National University of Singapore Press, 2013).

Ang, Cheng Guan. *Southeast Asia after the Cold War: A Contemporary History* (Singapore: National University of Singapore Press, 2019).

Ang, Cheng Guan. *The Vietnam War from the Other Side: The Vietnamese Communists' Perspective* (London: RoutledgeCurzon, 2002).

Barnett, Anthony. 'Interview with Le Duc Tho', in Anthony Barnett and John Pilger (eds.), *Aftermath: The Struggle of Cambodia and Vietnam* (London: New Statesman, 1982).

Becker, Elizabeth. *When the War Was Over: Cambodia and the Khmer Rouge Revolution* (New York: Public Affairs, 1986).

Berry, Ken. *Cambodia: From Red to Blue: Australia's Initiative for Peace* (Canberra: Allen & Unwin, 1997).

Berry, Ken. 'The Role and Performance of UNTAC: An Australian Perspective', in Pou Sothirak, Geoff Wade and Mark Hong (eds.), *Cambodia: Progress and Challenges since 1991* (Singapore: Routledge, 2012).

Brinkley, J. *Cambodia's Curse: The Modern History of a Troubled Land* (New York: Public Affairs, 2011).

Broinowski, Richard. *The Vote for Cambodia: Australia's Diplomatic Intervention* (Canberra: Australia Institute of International Affairs, 2021).

Bruce, David K. E. and Priscilla Mary Roberts. *Window on the Forbidden City: The Beijing Diaries of David Bruce, 1973–1974*. Centre of Asian Studies Occasional Papers and Monographs, no. 145 (Hong Kong: Centre of Asian Studies, University of Hong Kong, 2001).

Bibliography

Bui, Tin. *Following Ho Chi Minh: Memoirs of a North Vietnamese Colonel* (London: Hurst & Company, 1995).
Burchett, Wilfred. *The China Cambodia Vietnam Triangle* (Chicago: Vanguard Books; London: Zed Press, 1981).
Byron, J. and R. Pack. *The Claws of the Dragon* (New York: Simon & Schuster, 1992).
Cable, James. *The Geneva Conference of 1954 on IndoChina* (London: Macmillan, 1986).
Calkins, Laura M. *China and the First Vietnam War 1947–54* (London: Routledge, 2013).
Champassak, Philippe na. 'The Experiences of an International Polling Station Officer', in Selochan, Viberto and Carlyle Thayer (eds.), *Bringing Democracy to Cambodia: Peacekeeping and Elections* (Canberra: Australian Defence Studies Centre, 1996).
Chanda, Nayan. *Brother Enemy: The War after the War: A History of Indochina since the Fall of Saigon* (New York: Colliers Books, 1986).
Chandler, David P. *The Tragedy of Cambodian History: Politics, War and Revolution since 1945* (New Haven: Yale University Press, 1991).
Chandler, David P. *Brother Number One: A Political Biography of Pol Pot* (Boulder: Westview Press, 1992).
Chandler, David P. *A History of Cambodia* (Boulder: Westview Press, 1992).
Chandler, David P. *Facing the Cambodian Past: Selected Essays 1971–1994* (Sydney: Allen & Unwin, 1996).
Chang, Pao-min. *Beijing, Hanoi, and the Overseas Chinese* (Berkeley: University of California, Center for Chinese Studies, 1982).
Chanoff, David and Doan Van Toai. *Portrait of the Enemy: The Other Side of the War in Vietnam* (London: I.B. Tauris, 1987).
Chhay, Sophal. *Hun Sen: War & Peace in Cambodia and Southeast Asia* (Phnom Penh: publisher unknown, 2020).
Chin, Kin Wah, and Leo Suryadinata (compiled). *Michael Leifer: Selected Works on Southeast Asia* (Singapore: ISEAS, 2005).
Chinvanno, Anuson. (interviewed and edited), Thai Diplomacy: In Conversation with Tej Bunnag, 2022, Thai Diplomacy: in conversation with Tej Bunnag – ศูนย์ศึกษาการต่างประเทศ (mfa.go.th).
Clymer, Kenton. *Troubled Relations: The United States and Cambodia since 1870* (DeKalb: Northern Illinois University Press, 2007).
Conboy, Kenneth. *The Cambodian Wars: Clashing Armies and CIA Covert Operations* (Kansas: University of Kansas Press, 2013).
Deth, Sok Udom, *A History of Cambodia-Thailand Diplomatic Relations 1950–2020* (Glienicke: Galda Verlag, 2020).

Do, Khue Dieu, '"Victory of the Aggregate Strength of the Era": Le Duan, Vietnam and the Three Revolutionary Tidal Waves' in Marc Opper and Matthew Galway (eds.), *Experiments with Marxism-Leninism in Cold War Southeast Asia* (Canberra: Australia National University Press, 2022).

Duiker, William J. *Vietnam since the Fall of Saigon* (Ohio: Ohio University Center for International Studies, 1985).

Duiker, William J. 'Vietnam Moves toward Pragmatism' in *Current History*, April 1987, pp. 148–151.

Elliot, David W. P. *Changing Worlds: Vietnam's Transition from Cold War to Globalization* (New York: Oxford University Press, 2012).

Elliot, David W. P. *The Third Indochina Conflict* (Colorado: Westview Press, 1981; London: Routledge, 2019).

Engelbert, Thomas, and Christopher E. Goscha. *Falling out of Touch: A Study on Vietnamese Communist Policy towards and Emerging Cambodian Communist Movement, 1930–1975* (Victoria: Monash Asia Institute, 1995).

Evans, Grant, and Kelvin Rowley. *Red Brotherhood at War* (London: Verso, 1984).

Faligot, R. *Chinese Spies from Chairman Mao to Xi Jinping* (Melbourne: Scribe Press, 2019).

Gaiduk, Ilya. *The Soviet Union and the Vietnam War* (Chicago: Ivan R. Dee, 1966).

Galway, Matthew. *The Emergence of Global Maoism: China's Red Evangelism and the Cambodian Communist Movement* (Ithaca: Cornell University Press, 2022).

Goemans, H. E. *War and Punishment: The Causes of War Termination and the First World War* (New Jersey: Princeton University Press, 2000).

Gunn, Geoffrey C., and Jefferson Lee. *Cambodia Watching Down Under* (Institute of Asian Studies, Chulalongkorn University, IAS Monograph, Number 047, 1991).

Hansen, Anne Ruth, and Judy Ledgerwood (eds.), *At the Edge of the Forest: Essays on Cambodia, History and Narrative in Honor of David Chandler* (Ithaca: Southeast Asia Program, Cornell University, 2008).

Hayton, Bill. *Vietnam: Rising Dragon* (New Haven: Yale University Press, 2010).

Heder, Steve. *Cambodian Communism and the Vietnamese Model, Volume 1: Imitation and Independence 1930–1975* (Bangkok: White Lotus Press, 2004).

Hoan, Hoang Van, *A Drop in the Ocean* (Beijing: Foreign Languages Press, 1988).

Holdridge, John H. *Crossing the Divide: An Insider's Account of the Normalization of US-China Relations* (Lanham: Rowman & Littlefield, 1997).
Hurst, Steven. *The Carter Administration and Vietnam* (London: Macmillan Press, 1996).
Hussain, Rajmah. *Malaysia at the United Nations: A Study of Foreign Policy Priorities, 1957–1987* (Kuala Lumpur: University of Malaya Press, 2010).
Jeldres, Julio A. *Norodom Sihanouk & Zhou Enlai: An Extraordinary Friendship on the Fringes of the Cold War* (Phnom Penh: Sieuk Rith Institute, 2021).
Jeldres, Julio A. (translated), *Shadow over Angkor, Volume One: Memoirs of His Majesty King Norodom Sihanouk* (Phnom Penh: Monument Books, 2005).
Jeshurun, Chandran. *Malaysia: Fifty Years of Diplomacy 1957–2007* (Kuala Lumpur: The Other Press, 2007).
Kalb, Marvin, and Deborah Kalb. *Haunting Legacy: Vietnam and the American Presidency from Ford to Obama* (Washington, DC: Brookings Institution Press, 2011).
Kiernan, Ben. *How Pol Pot Came to Power* (London: Version, 1985).
Kiernan, Ben. 'Wild Chickens, Farm Chickens, and Cormorants: Kampuchea's Eastern Zone under Pol Pot' in David P. Chandler and Ben Kiernan (eds.), *Revolution and Its Aftermath in Kampuchea: Eight Essays* (Monograph Series No. 25, New Haven: Yale University Southeast Asia Studies, 1983).
Kiernan, Ben, and Chanthou Boua (eds.), *Peasants and Politics in Kampuchea 1942–1981* (London: Zed Press, 1982).
Kissinger, Henry. *On China* (New York: The Penguin Press, 2011).
Klintworth, Gary. *Vietnam's Intervention in Cambodia in International Law* (Canberra: Australian Government Publishing Service, 1989).
Koh, Tommy. *The Quest for World Order: Perspectives of a Pragmatic Idealist* (Singapore: Times Academic Press, 1998).
Lee, Kuan Yew. *From Third World to First: The Singapore Story: 1965–2000* (Singapore: Times Editions, 2000).
Li, Xiaobing. *The Dragon in the Jungle: The Chinese Army in the Vietnam War* (New York: Oxford University Press, 2020).
Li, Xiaobing. *Lich Su Quan Doi Nhan Dan, Tap II* (Hanoi: Nha Xuat Ban Quan Doi Nhan Dan, 1988).
Liu, Xiaohong, *Chinese Ambassadors: The Rise of Diplomatic Professionalism since 1949* (Seattle: University of Washington Press, 2001).
Mahbubani, Kishore. *Can Asians Think?* (Singapore: Times Book International, 1998).

Mark, Chi-Kwan. *China and the World since 1945: An International History* (London: Routledge, 2012).
Mehta, Harish C., and Mehta, Julie B. *Strongman: The Extraordinary Life of Hun Sen, From Pagoda Boy to Prime Minister of Cambodia* (Singapore: Marshall Cavendish, 2013).
Mentrey-Monchau, Cecile. *American-Vietnamese Relations in the Wake of the War* (Jefferson: McFarland, 2006).
Mertha, Andrew. *Brothers in Arms: Chinese Aid to the Khmer Rouge, 1975-1979* (Ithaca: Cornell University Press, 2014).
Morey, Roy D. *The United Nations at Work in Asia: An Envoy's Account of Development in China, Vietnam, Thailand and the South Pacific* (Jefferson: McFarland & Company, 2014).
Morris, Stephen J. *Why Vietnam Invaded Cambodia: Political Culture and the Causes of War* (Stanford: Stanford University Press, 1999).
Muhammad Ghazali, Shafie. *Malaysia: International Relations: Selected Speeches* (Kuala Lumpur: Creative Enterprise Sendiran Berhad, 1982).
Nathan, S. R. *An Unexpected Journey: Path to the Presidency* (Singapore: Editions Didier Millet, 2011).
Nem, Sowath. *Civil War Termination and the Source of Total Peace in Cambodia* (Phnom Penh: Ponleu Khmer Printing House, 2012).
Ngo, Federick J. 'Revision for Rights? Nation-Building Through Post-War Cambodian Social Studies Textbooks, 1979–2009' in James H. Williams (ed.), *(Re) Constructing Memory: School Textbooks and the Imagination of the Nation* (Rotterdam: Sense Publisher, 2014).
Ngor, H. S., and Warner, R. *Surviving the Killing Fields* (London: Pan Books, 1989).
Nguyen, Lien-Hang T. *Hanoi's War: An International History of the War for Peace in Vietnam* (Chapel Hill: University of North Carolina Press, 2012).
Nguyen-vo, Thu-huong. *Khmer-Viet Relations and the Third Indochina Conflict* (Jefferson: McFarland & Company, 1992).
O'Dowd, Edward C. *Chinese Military Strategy in the Third Indochina War: The Last Maoist War* (London: Routledge, 2007).
Osius, Ted. *Nothing Is Impossible: America's Reconciliation with Vietnam* (New Brunswick: Rutgers University Press, 2022).
Painter, David S. *The Cold War: An International History* (London: Routledge, 1999).
Path, Kosal. *Vietnam's Strategic Thinking during the Third Indochina War* (Wisconsin: The University of Wisconsin Press, 2020).
Poonkham, Jittipat. *A Genealogy of Bamboo Diplomacy: The Politics of Thai Détente with Russia and China* (Canberra: ANU Press, 2022).

Bibliography 195

Pov, Sok. *Samdech Hun Sen: Supreme Founder and Father of Peace of Cambodia* (Phnom Penh: Ponleu Khmer Printing and Publishing House, 2021).
Qian, Qichen. *Ten Episodes in China's Diplomacy* (New York: HarperCollins Publishers, 2005).
Richardson, S. *China, Cambodia, and the Five Principles of Peaceful Coexistence* (New York: Columbia University Press, 2010).
Roberts, David W. *Political Transition in Cambodia 1991–99: Power, Elitism and Democracy* (Richmond: Curzon Press, 2001).
Roberts, Priscilla. (ed.), *Behind the Bamboo Curtain: China, Vietnam and the World beyond Asia* (Washington, DC: Woodrow Wilson Center Press, 2006).
Ronayne, P. *Never Again? The United States and the Prevention and Punishment of Genocide since the Holocaust* (Boulder: Rowman & Littlefield Publishers, Inc., 2001).
Rowley, Kelvin. 'Second Life, Second Death: The Khmer Rouge After 1978' in Susan E. Cook (ed.), *Genocide in Cambodia and Rwanda: New Perspectives* (New Brunswick: Transaction Publishers, 2006), p. 199.
Rowley, Kelvin. 'The Making of the Royal Government of Cambodia' in Viberto Selochan and Carlyle Thayer (eds.), *Bringing Democracy to Cambodia: Peacekeeping and Elections* (Canberra: Australian Defence Studies Centre, 1996).
Salisbury, Harrison E. *To Peking and Beyond: A Report on the New Asia* (New York: Quadrangle, 1973).
Samphan, Kieu. *Cambodia's Recent History and the Reasons behind the Decisions I Made* (Phnom Penh: Ponleu Khmer Printing and Publishing House, 2004).
Samrin, Heng. *The People's Struggle Cambodia Reborn* (Singapore: Editions Didier Millet, 2018).
Sanderson, John. 'The Role of the Military Component' in Viberto Selochan and Carlyle Thayer (eds.), *Bringing Democracy to Cambodia: Peacekeeping and Elections* (Canberra: Australian Defence Studies Centre, 1996).
Savavanamuthu, J. *Malaysia's Foreign Policy: The First Fifty Years: Alignment, Neutralism, Islamism* (Singapore: ISEAS, 2010).
Schmidt, Helmut. *Men and Powers: A Political Retrospective* (New York: Random House, 1989).
Selochan, Viberto, and Carlyle Thayer (eds.), *Bringing Democracy to Cambodia: Peacekeeping and Elections* (Canberra: Australian Defence Studies Centre, 1996).
Shaplen, R. *Bitter Victory: A Veteran Correspondent's Dramatic Account of His Return to Vietnam and Cambodia Ten Years after the End of the War* (New York: Harper & Row, Publishers, 1986).

Shinde, B. E. *Mao Zedong and the Communist Policies 1927–1978* (New Delhi: Sangam Books, 1993).
Shiraishi, Takashi, and Motoo Furuta (eds.), *Indochina in the 1940s and 1950s* (Ithaca: SEAP, Cornell University, 1992).
Short, Philip. *Pol Pot: Anatomy of a Nightmare* (New York: Henry Holt and Company, 2004).
Sihanouk, Norodom. *War and Hope: The Case for Cambodia* (New York: Pantheon Books, 1980).
Smith, R. B. *An International History of the Vietnam War, Volume 1: Revolution and Containment 1955–1961* (London: Macmillan, 1983).
Smith, R. B. *An International History of the Vietnam War, Volume III: The Making of a Limited War, 1965–66* (London: Macmillan, 1991).
Solomon, Richard H. (ed.), *Asian Security in the 1980s: Problems and Policies for a Time of Transition* (Cambridge: Oelgeschlager, Gunn & Hain, Publishers, Inc., 1979).
Solomon, Richard H. *Exiting Indochina: US Leadership of the Cambodia Settlement & Normalization with Vietnam* (Washington, DC: United States Institute of Peace Press, 2000).
Sophal, Chhay. *Hun Sen: War & Peace in Cambodia and Southeast Asia* (Phnom Penh: Misael Trane, 2020).
Sothirak, Pou, Geoff Wade, and Mark Hong (eds.), *Cambodia: Progress and Challenges since 1991* (Singapore: ISEAS, 2012).
Sothirak, Pou, Bradley Murg, Charadine Pich, and Courtney Weatherby. *The Paris Peace Agreements: Looking Forward and Moving Forward* (Washington, DC: The Stimson Center and Cambodian Institute for Cooperation and Peace, October 2021).
Soubert, Sou. 'The 1991 Paris Peace Agreement: A KPNLF Perspective' in Pou Sothirak, Geoff Wade, and Mark Hong (eds.), *Cambodia: Progress and Challenges since 1991* (Singapore: Routledge, 2012).
Stuart-Fox, Martin, *A History of Laos* (Cambridge: Cambridge University Press, 1997).
Stuart-Fox, Martin, and Bunhaeng Ung, *The Murderous Revolution: Bunhaeng Ung's Life with Death in Pol Pot's Kampuchea* (Bangkok: The Tamarind Press, 1986).
Tarling, Nicholas. *Regionalism in Southeast Asia: To foster the political will* (London: Routledge, 2006).
Thayer, Carlyle A. (ed.), *Bringing Democracy to Cambodia: Peacekeeping and Elections* (Canberra: Australian Defence Studies Centre, 1996).
Thayer, Carlyle A. 'The UN and Cambodia: A Critical Overview' in Viberto Selochan and Carlyle Thayer (eds.), *Bringing Democracy to Cambodia: Peacekeeping and Elections* (Canberra: Australian Defence Studies Centre, 1996).

Torigian, Joseph. *Prestige, Manipulation, and Coercion: Elite Power Struggles in the Soviet Union and China after Stalin and Mao* (New Haven: Yale University Press, 2022).
Truong, Nhu Tang, *Journal of a VietCong* (London: Jonathan Cape, 1986), pp. 101, 219.
Vance, Cyrus. *Hard Choices: Critical Years in America's Foreign Policy* (New York: Simon & Schuster, 1983).
Vogel, Ezra F. *Deng Xiaoping and the Transformation of China* (Cambridge: The Belknap Press of Harvard University Press, 2011).
Vu, Tuong, *Vietnam's Communist Revolution: The Power and Limits of Ideology* (Cambridge: Cambridge University Press, 2017).
Wade, Mark Hong (ed.), *Cambodia: Progress and Challenges since 1991* (Singapore: Routledge, 2012).
Wanandi, Jusuf. *Shades of Grey: A Political Memoir of Modern Indonesia 1965–1998* (Singapore: Equinox Publishing, 2012).
Westad, O. A., and S. Quinn-Judge. (eds.), *The Third Indochina War: Conflict between China, Vietnam and Cambodia, 1972–79* (London: Routledge, 2006).
Wheeler, Nicholas J. *Saving Strangers: Humanitarian Intervention in International Society* (Oxford: Oxford University Press, 2002).
Wijers, Gea D. M. 'Framing Cambodian Affairs: French and American Scholarship, Media and Geopolitics' in Albert Tzeng, William L. Richter, and Ekaterina Koldunova (eds.), *Framing Asian Studies: Geopolitics and Institutions* (Singapore: ISEAS, 2018).
Yara, Suos, Sok Siphana, and Kimly Ngoun (eds.), *Hun Sen's Thought and Vision for Cambodia* (New York: Universal Peace Federation Publication, 2022).
Zhai, Qiang. *China and the Vietnam Wars, 1950–1975* (Chapel Hill: The University of North Carolina Press, 2000).
Zhang, Shu Guang. *Beijing's Economic Statecraft during the Cold War, 1949–1991* (Washington, DC: Woodrow Wilson Center Press, 2014).
Zhang, Xiaoming. *Deng Xiaoping's Long War: The Military Conflict between China and Vietnam, 1979–1991* (Chapel Hill: The University of North Carolina Press, 2015).

Articles, PhD theses and Working Papers

Alex, Willemyns. 'Cambodia and China: Rewriting (and Repeating) History'. *The Diplomat*, 15 January 2018.
Ang, Cheng Guan. 'Vietnam-China Relations since the End of the Cold War' in *Asian Survey*, Volume 38, No. 12, December 1998, pp. 1122–1141.

Ang, Cheng Guan. 'Vietnam-Cambodia relations from the Paris Peace Conference (1991) to membership of ASEAN' in *South East Asia Research*, Volume 8, Number 1, March 2000, pp. 55–78.

Aryanta, Nugraha. *Indonesia's Foreign Policy in the Making of Regional International Society in Southeast Asia*, Unpublished PhD thesis, Flinders University, 2022.

Asselin, Pierre, 'Choosing Peace: Hanoi and the Geneva Agreement on Vietnam, 1954–1955' in *Journal of Cold War Studies*, Volume 9, Number 2, Spring 2007, pp. 95–126.

Banerjee, Jyotirmoy, 'Indonesia, Malaysia and the Indochina Crisis: Between Scylla and Charybdis' in *China Report*, Volume 17, 1981, p. 41 http://chr.sagepub.com/content/17/1/41.citation

Becker, Elizabeth. 'The Progress of Peace in Cambodia' in *Current History*, April 1989.

Benzaquen-Gautier, Stephanie, 'The Relational Archive of the Khmer Republic (1970–1975): Revisiting the "coup" and the "civil war" in Cambodia through Written Sources' in *South East Asia Research*, pp. 450–468, 5 November 2011, https://doi.org/10.1080/09678 28X.2021.1989987, accessed on 8 November 2022.

Busyzynski, Leszek. 'New Aspirations and Old Constraints in Thailand's Foreign Policy' in *Asian Survey*, Volume XXIX, Number 11, November 1989, pp. 1057–1072.

Buszynski, Leszek. 'Soviet Foreign Policy and Southeast Asia: Prospects for the Gorbachev Era' in *Asian Survey*, Volume 26, Number 5, May 1986, pp. 591–609.

Chanda, Nayan, 'Vietnam's Invasion of Cambodia, Revisited' in *The Diplomat*, 1 December 2018.

Chandler, David P. *Introduction 'My' Cambodia 1960–1962*, www.levandehistoria.se/sites/default/files/material_file/skriftserie-8-beneath-a-beautiful-piece-of-cloth.pdf, accessed on 21 September 2022.

Chandler, David P. 'Revising the Past in Democratic Kampuchea: When was the Birthday of the Party?' in *Pacific Affairs*, Volume 56, Number 2, Summer 1983, pp. 288–300.

Chang, Pao-min, 'The Sino-Vietnamese Dispute over the Ethnic Chinese' in *China Quarterly*, Number 90, June 1982, pp. 195–230.

Chee, Stephen. 'Southeast Asia in 1988: Portents for the Future' in *Southeast Asian Affairs 1989* (Singapore: ISEAS, 1989), pp. 3–36.

Ciociari, John D. 'China and the Pol Pot Regime' in *Cold War History*, Volume 14, Number 2, 2014, pp. 215–235.

Connolly, Chris A. 'Kissinger, China, Congress, and the Lost Chance for Peace in Cambodia' in *Journal of American-East Asian Relations*, Volume 17, Number 3, 2009/2010, pp. 205–229.

Deth, Sok Udom, *The People's Republic of Kampuchea 1979–1989: A Draconian Savior?*, Master of Arts thesis, Center for International Studies, Ohio University, June 2009.
Eisenman, Joshua. 'China's Vietnam War Revisited: A Domestic Politics Perspective' in *Journal of Contemporary China*, Volume 28, Number 119, 2019, pp. 729–745.
Elliot, David W. P. 'Vietnam in Asia: Strategy and Diplomacy in a New Context' in *International Journal*, Volume 38, Number 2, Spring 1983, pp. 287–315.
Frings, K. Viviane. 'Rewriting Cambodian History to "adapt" It to a New Political Context: The Kampuchean People's Revolutionary Party's Historiography (1979–1991)' in *Modern Asian Studies*, Volume 31, Number 4, 1997, pp. 807–846.
Gordon, Bernard K. 'The Third Indochina Conflict', in *Foreign Affairs* (Fall 1986), pp. 66–85.
Grossheim, Martin. 'How the Vietnamese began to Remember a Forgotten War', 7 September 2021, www.wilsoncenter.org/blog-post/how-vietnamese-began-remember-forgotten-war?fbclid=IwAR1WY6_b6nKqBXA-Cwc2p1df5Q5MR5orjG9jt72gxIcj9l_ggOrb0g2QsYc, accessed on 12 April 2022.
Grossheim, Martin. 'Remembering a Forgotten War: The Vietnamese State, War Veterans and the Commemoration of the Sino-Vietnamese War (1979–89)' in *Journal of Southeast Asian Studies*, Volume 53, Number 3, 2022, pp. 459–487.
Heder, Stephen. 'Origins of the Conflict' in *Southeast Asia Chronicle*, Number 64, September/October 1978, pp. 3–18.
Heder, Stephen. *'Reflections on Cambodian Political History: Backgrounder to Recent Developments'*, Strategic and Defence Studies Centre, Canberra, Working Paper No. 239, September 1991.
Heng, Kimkong. 'Cambodia-Vietnam Relations: Key Issues and the Way Forward' in *Perspective*, Number 36, 12 April 2022.
Heng, Kimkong. 'January 7 in Cambodia: One Date, Two Narratives' in *The Diplomat*, 16 January 2019.
Hoang, Minh Vu, 'The Third Indochina War and the Making of Present-Day Southeast Asia, 1975–1995', Unpublished PhD dissertation, Cornell University, December 2020. https://ecommons.cornell.edu/handle/1813/103452, accessed on 14 April 2022.
Hoang, Tung, D. B. Ngu, and Kathleen Gough, 'A Hanoi Interview' in *Contemporary Marxism*, Number 12/13, Southeast Asia, Spring 1986.
Hoi Ky Tran Quang Co, accessed online on 15 December 2022.
Horn, Robert C. 'Southeast Asian Perceptions of US Foreign Policy' in *Asian Survey*, Volume 25, Number 6, June 1985, pp. 678–691.

Hunt, Luke. 'The Truth about War and Peace in Cambodia' in *The Diplomat*, 5 January 2019; Courtney Weatherbee and William M. Wise, 'Why the Paris Peace Agreements Deserve a Place in Cambodia's National Calendar' in *The Diplomat*, 31 January 2022.
Huw, Watkin's interview of Australian ambassador to Cambodia, Tony Kevin, 'Was there a coup in Cambodia?' in *Quadrant*, 41. 12, December 1997,
Jeldres, Julio A. 'Cambodia Relations with Vietnam: Historical Mistrust and Vulnerability' in *Journal of Greater Mekong Studies*, Volume 2, Number 1, February 2020, pp. 63–74.
Jeldres, Julio A. 'The UN and the Cambodian Transition' in *Journal of Democracy*, Volume 4, Number 4, October 1993, pp. 104–116.
Kiernan, Ben. 'Cambodia's Twisted Path to Justice', *The History Place*, www.historyplace.com/pointsofview/kiernan.htm, accessed on 9 November 2022.
Kiernan, Ben (guest editor), 'Thematic Issue: Conflict and Change in Cambodia' in *Critical Asian Studies*, Volume 34, Number 4, December 2002, pp. 483–495.
Kolko, Gabriel. 'Avoiding Misconceptions about Indochina' in *Journal of Contemporary Asia*, Volume 9, Number 1, 1979, pp. 116–118.
Lai-to, Lee, 'Deng Xiaoping's ASEAN Tour: A Perspective on Sino-Southeast Asian Relations' in *Contemporary Southeast Asia*, Volume 3, Number 1, June 1981, pp. 58–75.
Lau Teik, Soon, 'Shifting Alignments in Regional Politics' in *Southeast Asian Affairs 1986* (Singapore: ISEAS, 1986), pp. 3–11.
Le Hong, Hiep. 'Performance-based Legitimacy: The Case of the Communist Party of Vietnam and Doi Moi' in *Contemporary Southeast Asia*, Volume 34, Number 2, 2012, pp. 145–172.
Lee Hsien Loong at the IISS Shangri-La Dialogue 2019, The View from Singapore and Southeast Asia. www.pmo.gov.sg/Newsroom/PM-Lee-Hsien-Loong-at-the-IISS-Shangri-La-Dialogue-2019, accessed on 5 April 2022.
Leifer, Michael. 'Cambodia's Politics Have Regressed since the UN's Intervention' in *The Straits Times*, 23 December 1995.
Leifer, Michael. 'Cambodian Conflict – After the Final Phase' in *Conflict Studies*, Number 221, May 1989, pp. 1–29.
Leifer, Michael. 'The Stakes of Conflict in Cambodia' in *Asian Affairs*, Volume 21, Number 2, 1990, pp. 155–161.
Leifer, Michael. 'The Third Indochina Conflict' in *Asian Affairs*, Volume XIV, Part II, June 1983, pp. 125–131.
Luthi, Lorenz M. 'Beyond Betrayal: Beijing, Moscow and the Paris Negotiations, 1971–1973' in *Journal of Cold War Studies*, Volume 11, Number 1, Winter 2009, pp. 57–107.

Mahbubani, K. 'Cambodia: Myths and Realities' in *Problems of Communism*, July–August 1984.
Mahbubani, K. 'The Kampuchean Problem: A Southeast Asian Perspective' in *Foreign Affairs*, Volume 62, Number 2, Winter 1983–1984, pp. 407–425.
Martini, E. 'Review of *Vietnam at War*, by M. Bradley' in *Journal of Vietnamese Studies*, Volume 5, Number 1, 2010, pp. 218–221. https://doi.org/10.1525/vs.2010.5.1.218
McHale, Shawn. 'Ethnicity, Violence, and Khmer-Vietnamese Relations: The Significance of the Lower Mekong Delta, 1757–1954' in *The Journal of Asian Studies*, Volume 72, Number 2, May 2013, pp. 367–390.
Ming, Nguyen Quang, 'The Bitter Legacy of the 1979 China-Vietnam War' in *The Diplomat*, 23 February 2017.
Morris, Stephen J. *The Soviet-Chinese-Vietnamese Triangle in the 1970s: The View from Moscow*, Working Paper 25, Cold War International History Project, April 1999.
Mosyakov, Dmitry. 'The Khmer Rouge and the Vietnamese Communists: A History of Their Relations as Told in the Soviet Archives', https://gsp.yale.edu/node/297, accessed on 10 May 2022.
Mudrick, Jeff. 'Cambodia's Impossible Dream: Koh Tral', *The Diplomat*, 17 June 2014.
Nair, K. K. *ASEAN-Indochina Relations since 1975: The Politics of Accommodation*, Canberra Papers on Strategy and Defence, Number 30, 1984 (Canberra: ANU, 1984).
Noren-Nilsson, Astrid. 'The End of the Beginning for the Cambodian People's Party' in *East Asia Forum*, 27 January 2023.
Nugraha, Aryanta. *Indonesia's Foreign Policy in the Making of Regional International Society in Southeast Asia*, Unpublished PhD thesis, Flinders University, 2022.
Online NewsHour. 'Conversation on Cambodia' (with Henry Kamm), a NewsHour with Jim Lehrer Transcript, 29 December 1998.
Parameswaran, Prashanth, 'Hun Manet Introductory Visit Highlights Singapore-Cambodian Relations' in *The Diplomat*, 17 June 2019.
Path, Kosal. 'The Sino-Vietnamese Dispute over Territorial Claims, 1974–1978: Vietnamese Nationalism and Its Consequences' in *International Journal of Asian Studies*, Volume 8, Number 2, 2011, pp. 189–220.
Path, Kosal. *Sino-Vietnamese Relations, 1950–1978: From Cooperation to Conflict*, Unpublished PhD dissertation, University of Southern California, December 2008.
Path, Kosal, and Boraden Nhem, 'Vietnam's Military and Political Challenges in Cambodia, and the Early Rise of Cambodia's Strongman, Hun Sen, 1977–79' in *TRaNS: Trans-Regional and -National Studies of*

Southeast Asia, www.cambridge.org/core/journals/trans-trans-regional-and-national-studies-of-southeast-asia/article/abs/vietnams-military-and-political-challenges-in-cambodia-and-the-early-rise-of-cambodias-strongman-hun-sen-197779/C0B8E412FF295B7C38569FCE7F993A69, (published online on 26 July 2021), accessed on 22 August 2022.

Ping, Lee Poh, 'The Indochinese Situation and the Big Powers in Southeast Asia: The Malaysian View' in *Asian Survey*, Volume 22, Number 6, June 1982, pp. 516–523.

Porter, Gareth. 'Hanoi's Strategic Perspective and the Sino-Vietnamese Conflict' in *Pacific Affairs*, Volume 57, Number 1, Spring 1984, pp. 7–25.

Pribbenow, Merle L., II. 'A Tale of Five Generals: Vietnam's invasion of Cambodia' in *The Journal of Military History*, Volume 70, Number 2, April 2006, pp. 459–486.

Richburg, Keith B. 'Democracy in a Free Fall as Cambodia Appears to Slide Back to Old Ways' republished in *The Straits Times*, 12 December 1995.

Shui, Yun, 'An Account of Chinese Diplomats Accompanying the Government of Democratic Kampuchea's Move to the Cardamom Mountains' in *Critical Asian Studies*, Volume 34, Number 4, 2002, pp. 497–519, DOI: 10.1080/146727102762043710

Smith, Ralph. Vietnam's Fourth Party Congress in *The World Today*, Volume 33, Number 5, May 1977, pp. 195–202.

Smith, Roger M. 'Prince Norodom Sihanouk of Cambodia' in *Asian Survey*, Volume 7, Number 6, June 1967, pp. 353–362.

Solarz, Stephen J. 'Cambodia and the International Community' in *Foreign Affairs*, Volume 69, Number 2, Spring 1990, pp. 99–115.

Thayer, Carlyle, 'The Soviet Union and Indochina', Paper presented at the IV World Congress for Soviet and East European Studies, Harrogate, England, 21–26 July 1990.

Thayer, Carlyle. 'Vietnam's Sixth Party Congress: An Overview' in *Contemporary Southeast Asia*, Volume 9, Number 1, June 1987, pp. 12–22.

Thun, Theara, '"Invasion" or "Liberation"? Contested Commemoration in Cambodia and within ASEAN' in *TRaNS*, (2021).

Turley, William S., and Jeffrey Race, 'The Third Indochina War' in *Foreign Policy*, Number 38, Spring 1980.

'US Policy on Cambodia after the ICC', *Information Note on Kampuchea*, 11 September 1989.

Vachon, Michelle. 'King Norodom Sihanouk and Cambodia in the Cold War', https://cambodianess.com/article/king-norodom-sihanouk-and-cambodia-caught-in-the-cold-war, accessed on 7 December 2022.

Vickery, Michael. 'Cambodia (Kampuchea): History, Tragedy, and Uncertain Future' in *Bulletin of Concerned Asian Scholars*, Volume 21, 1989, pp. 2–4.

Vickery, Michael. *Kicking the Vietnam Syndrome in Cambodia: Collected Writings 1975–2010*, http://michaelvickery.org/vickery2010kicking.pdf, accessed on 25 January 2023.
Vincent, Travis. 'Why Won't Vietnam Teach the History of the Sino-Vietnamese War?' in *The Diplomat*, 9 February 2022.
Walt, Stephen M. 'Why Wars are Easy to Start and Hard to End', https://foreignpolicy.com/2022/08/29/war-military-quagmire-russia-ukraine/, accessed on 8 November 2022.
Wang, Chenyi. 'The Chinese Communist Party's Relationship with the Khmer Rouge in the 1970s: An Ideological Victory and a Strategic Failure', Working Paper 88, Cold War International History Project, 13 December 2018.
Wang, Chenyi. *Mao's Legacy and the Sino-Vietnamese War*, Unpublished PhD thesis, 2017, School of Humanities, Nanyang Technological University.
Westad, Odd Arne et al. (ed.), *77 Conversations between Chinese and Foreign Leaders of the Wars in IndoChina, 1964–1977*, Working Paper Number 22, Cold War International History Project, May 1998, Washington, DC.
Widyono, Benny. *Dancing in Shadows: Sihanouk, The Khmer Rouge, and the United Nations in Cambodia* (London: Rowman & Littlefield, 2008).
Willemyns, Alex. 'Cambodia and China: Rewriting (and Repeating) History'. *The Diplomat*, 15 January 2018.
Yin, Qingfei, and Kosal Path, 'Remembering and Forgetting the Last War: Discursive memory of the Sino-Vietnamese War in China and Vietnam' in *TRaNS: Trans-Regional and -National Studies of Southeast Asia*, Volume 9, Number 1, May 2021, pp. 11–29.
Zhai, Qiang, 'China and the Cambodian Conflict, 1970–1975' in *Searching for the Truth*, Second Quarterly Issue, Special English Edition, July 2003.
Zhai, Qiang, 'China and the Geneva Conference of 1954' in *The China Quarterly*, Number 129, March 1992.

Documents

Black Paper: Facts and Evidences of the Acts of Aggression and Annexation of Vietnam against Kampuchea (Department of Press and Information of the Ministry of Democratic Kampuchea, September 1978).
British Foreign Office General Political Correspondence (FCO 371), (UK: The National Archives).
The Chinese Rulers' Cries against Kampuchea (Ministry of Foreign Affairs, Peoples Republic of Kampuchea, April 1984).

Cold War International History Project (CWIHP) Bulletin, (US: Wilson Center).
Declassified Documents Reference System (DDRS).
Foreign Affairs Malaysia, (Kuala Lumpur: Ministry of Foreign Affairs).
Goh, Linda (ed.), *Wealth of East Asian Nations: Speeches and Writings by Goh Keng Swee* (Singapore: Federal Publication, 1995).
Malaysia: International Relations, Selected Speeches by M. Ghazali Shafie (Kuala Lumpur: Creative Enterprise Sendiran Berhad, 1982).
National Archives of Australia series. A1838, A12930.
Senior ASEAN Statesmen (Oral History Centre, National Archives of Singapore, National Heritage Board, 1998).
Singapore Ministry of Foreign Affairs documents.
The Association for Diplomatic Studies and Training, Foreign Affairs Oral History Project.
United Nations, General Assembly and Security Council Documents.
United States, Department of State, Foreign Relation of the United States (FRUS).
Vietnamese Foreign Ministry White Book on Relations with China, October 1979.
Vietnam-Cambodia Conflict, Report prepared at the request of the Subcommittee of Asian and Pacific Affairs Committee of International Relations by the Congressional Research Service, Library of Congress (Washington, DC: US Government Printing Office, 1978).

News Sources

Peking Review (subsequently Beijing Review).
Searching for the Truth.
Summary of World Broadcasts (Far East) (Caversham: BBC Monitoring Service).
United States Foreign Broadcast Information Service (East Asia).
Vietnam Courier.

Index

16-Camps Campaign, 113

Abramowitz, Morton, 105
Ahmad, Zakaria Haji, 97
Alatas, Ali, 131, 155
Ali, Mushahid, 84
American POWs, in Indochina, 58
anti-colonial Cambodian guerilla
  forces, 20
anti-Soviet alliance, formation of, 49
anti-Vietnamese alliance, 49
anti-Vietnamese Khmer resistance, 96
Arkhipov, Ivan, 117
ASEAN, 68, 91, 96, 100, 110, 134, 145
  concept of Zone of Peace, Freedom
    and Neutrality (ZOPFAN), 91
  development of, 120
  expansion of, 10
  foreign ministers special meeting, 173
  initiative to end Cambodia war, 131
  Malaysia's position in, 97
  member states, 103
  participation in JIM process, 132
  reaction to the Chinese invasion
    of Vietnam, 83
  resolution on Cambodia in the UN
    General Assembly, 153
  strategy of isolating and pressurising
    Vietnam, 104
  views on Vietnam's invasion of
    Cambodia, 25
ASEAN Summit, 34th (2019), 5
Asian Affairs, 147
Asselin, Pierre, 36
Assum, Laetitia van den, 160

Baker, James, 144, 158
Berlin Wall, fall of
  (10 November 1989), 140, 148
Berry, Ken, 119

Bingnan, Wang, 36
Bonavia, David, 117
Brabazon, Lord, 145
Brevie Line, 43
Brzeziński, Zbigniew, 56, 61, 62, 93
Bui Tin, 46, 64
Bunhaeng Ung, 66
Burchett, Wilfred, 46
Bush, H. W., 140

Calkins, Laura, 39
Cambodia
  admission into ASEAN, 10
  Chinese aid to, 170
  Chinese leadership preference for
    a 'red Cambodia', 34
  civil war in, 113
  'consultative group' meeting on
    financial aid to, 171
  economic reforms in, 126
  ethnic Vietnamese living in, 22
  French colonisation of, 92
  immigration laws, 166
  international peacekeeping force
    in, 139
  Jakarta meeting on, 155
  Khmer Rouge control of, 22
  killing of ethnic Vietnamese
    in, 163, 169
  Liberation Day ('Victory Day'), 7, 8
  membership of ASEAN, 173
  military coup of July 1997, 10
  Permanent Five plan on Cambodia
    (1990), 156
  Pol Pot political influence over, 24
  relations with
    China, 49
    Soviet Union, 49
  restoration of self-determination
    for, 105

205

Cambodia (cont.)
struggle for independence, 18
US bombing of eastern, 28
Vietnam invasion of, 2, 18, 20, 61, 66, 69, 83
Vietnamese communist cells in, 22
Cambodian Communist movement, 20, 23
Cambodian liberation front, 66
Cambodian National Assembly, 165
Cambodian People's Party (CPP), 4, 8, 20, 26, 167, 171
Cambodian refugees, crossing into Thailand, 93
Cambodian revolution, 27
Cambodian Summit (1990), 154
Cambodian–Vietnam Friendship Monument, 167, 170
Cambodia–Vietnam relations, in the period after the 1993 elections, 163
Carter, Jimmy, 95
Ceausescu, Nicolae, 119
Central Office for South Vietnam (COSVN), 28
Chamanan, Kriangsak, 77
Chanda, Nayan, 72, 73
Chandler, David, 20, 23, 112
Chanthavy, Leap, 2
Chau Doc, massacre at (30 April 1977), 46
Chea Sim, 8, 171
Chee, Stephen, 129
Chen Jian, 20
Chhim Seakleng, 171
China
  5th National People's Congress, 70
  attack on Vietnam, 6, 15
  Central Military Commission (CMC), 75
  clash with Soviet troops near Zhenbao Island, 71
  decision to attack Vietnam, 74
  diplomatic relations with North Vietnam, 35
  elite power struggles in, 73
  fears of Soviet Vietnamese collusion, 57
  fight against Soviet 'strategic encirclement', 76
  global antihegemonic strategy serving broader interests, 72
  Instructions on the Issue of Sino-Vietnamese border defence (1978), 75
  modernisation plans, 74
  National Security Council (NSC), 33
  non-lethal aid to Cambodia, 170
  People's Liberation Army (PLA), 170
  preconditions to punish Vietnam, 76
  preference for 'red Cambodia', 34
  rapprochement with US, 55, 72
  relation with
    America, 33
    Vietnam, 35
  rift with Soviet Union, 39
  role in Third Indochina War, 6
  special economic zone, 172
  support for the Khmer Rouge, 8
  talks with Vietnam on the border issue, 69
  Tiananmen Incident (June 1989), 89, 140
Chinese Communist Party (CCP), 27, 112, 171
Chinese People's Relief Administration, 39
Chinese Politburo, 72
Chongkittavorn, Kavi, 120
Choonhavan, Chatichai, 132, 151
Choonhavan, Kraisak, 133
Clinton, Bill, 55
Clymer, Kenton, 56
Coalition Government of Democratic Kampuchea (CGDK), 109, 112, 113, 114, 123, 127, 128, 136, 143, 152, 164
'Eight-point Plan' of 17 March 1986, 125
PAVN 16-Camps Campaign against, 113
coalition of patriotic forces, creation of, 130
Cold War, 29, 118
  end of, 79, 140, 143
Communist Party of Kampuchea (CPK), 18, 20, 47
Communist Party of the Soviet Union, 28

Index

Conboy, Kenneth, 66
Congress of the Khmer Resistance
  (1950), 19
Council for Mutual Economic
  Assistance (COMECON), 53, 60
  Vietnam's joining of, 62, 69, 72
Cuba of Asia, 77
Cultural Revolution, 27

Democratic Kampuchea (DK), 50,
  106, 108
  ASEAN's recognition of, 102
  Coalition Government of
    Democratic Kampuchea
    (CGDK), 104, 105
  relation with the US, 56
Deng Xiaoping, 34, 49, 72, 73, 86,
  101, 103, 117, 119, 156
  anti-Soviet attitude, 78
  hatred toward the Vietnamese, 52, 78
  meeting with Lee Kuan Yew, 79
  Sino-Vietnamese relations under, 81
  visit to Thailand, Malaysia, US, and
    Singapore, 76
  visit to the United States, 79
Deng Yingchao, 27
Dinh Nho Liem, 148, 149
Do Muoi, 150, 158
Doyle, Kevin, 6
Dulles, John Foster, 36, 38
Dumas, Roland, 144
Duong Danh Dy, 7

Ear, Sophar, 4
East Timor, 99
economic decline, in Vietnam, 135
Economist, The, 125
Eden, Anthony, 37
Engelbert, Thomas, 32
ethnic Vietnamese refugees, 165
ethnic violence, 19
European Commission, 86
European Community, 84
European holocaust, 56
Evans, Gareth, 146, 153

Financial Times, 59
First Indochina War, 20, 35
  Battle of Dien Bien Phu (7 May
    1954), 35

Fonteyne, Jean-Pierre L., 67, 68
food shortages, in Cambodia, 167
Ford, Gerald, 54
Foreign and Commonwealth Office
  (FCO), 159
fraternal socialist countries, 91
French Communist Party
  Congress, 115
French Indochina, 19
French Revolution, 142
French Socialist Party, 127

Gaiduk, Ilya, 40
Gang of Four, 27, 52, 81
General Staff's Combat Readiness Plan
  for Cambodia, 65
Geneva Conference (1954), 18, 20, 29,
  36, 37, 53
  representation of Khmer Issarak and
    Pathet Lao at, 21
Geng Biao, 74
genocide, 56
  against ethnic Vietnamese in
    Cambodia, 163
  committed by the Khmer Rouge, 64
  conducted by the Pol Pot regime, 2
Glasnost, 89
globalist socialist revolutionary
  movement, 81
Goemans, H. E., 123
Goh Keng Swee, 95, 110
Gorbachev, Mikhail, 88, 117, 118
  declaration of end of Cold War
    (3 December 1989), 140
  foreign policy speech, 120
  legacy in Southeast Asia, 121
  on path to bring 'democracy and
    liberal spirit' to Vietnam, 120
  relation with Ronald Reagan, 121
  rise to power, 118
  statement on the Cambodia
    issue, 120
  visit to China, 140
  Vladivostok speech, 119, 121, 124
Gordon, Bernard, 92
guerilla warfare, 56, 64, 113
Gulf of Thailand, 163

Haig, Alexander, 106
Han Hsu, 56

Hawley, Donald, 84
Hayden, Bill, 125
Heath, Edward, 87, 88, 102
Heder, Stephen, 23, 43
Heder, Steve, 29
Heng Samrin, 66, 68, 101, 122, 123, 125
Hennings, John Dunn, 98
Ho Chi Minh City, 36, 47
Hoang Minh Vu, 81
Hoang Tung, 63, 81
Hoang Van Hoan, 36, 37
Hoang Van Loi, 45
Holbrooke, Richard, 55, 58, 93
Holdridge, John, 62
House Select Committee on Missing Persons in Southeast Asia, 58
Hu Yaobang, 112
Hua Guofeng, 70, 74
Huang Hua, 61, 93, 102
human rights, 56, 67
Hun Manet, 5
Hun Sen, 3, 4, 8, 18, 20, 26, 45, 48, 67, 113, 124, 125, 128, 129, 136, 150, 151, 152, 163, 164, 171, 173
  proposal for the creation of a 'high-level national unification council', 129
  State of Cambodia (SOC), 144
Hurst, Steven, 58

Independence Monument, 167
Indochina crisis (March 1979), 96, 111
  prospect of political settlement, 111
Indochina Federation, 24, 60, 71
  refugee problem, 55
  Vietnam's plan to re-establish, 25
  Vietnam-led economic regionalism in, 116
Indochinese Communist Party (ICP), 19
  induction of Pol Pot into, 23
  Second Congress (1951) of, 19
Indochinese Summit Conference (24–25 April), 30
International Conference on Cambodia in Paris (30 July–30 August 1989), 129, 142–143, 144, 158

International Conference on Kampuchea (1981), 106
international peacekeeping force, 139
intra-Kampuchean discussion, 131
Isarn Liberation Party (Thailand), 92

Jakarta Informal Meetings (JIMs), 99, 129, 130, 131, 132, 136
JIM II, 132, 135
Jakarta Meeting on Cambodia (1990), 155
Jakarta–Kuala Lumpur initiative, 96
Jeldres, Julio A., 44, 108, 126
Jenkins, Roy, 86
Jeshurun, Chandran, 96
Jiang Zemin, 171

Kamm, Henry, 161, 173
Kampuchea. See Cambodia
Kampuchean (Khmer) People's Revolutionary Party (KPRP)
  2nd Party Congress (1960) of, 25
  3rd Congress (1963) of, 26
  formation of, 20, 26
  founding members of, 23
  recruitment and training of guerrilla fighters, 20
Kampuchean patriotic forces, 104
Kampuchean People's Revolutionary Army, 113
Kampuchean United Front for National Salvation (KUFNS), 49, 76
Kang Sheng, 27, 30
Kausikan, Bilahari, 173
Khieu Samphan, 44, 103
Khmer Communist Party. See Communist Party of Kampuchea (CPK)
Khmer Communist Party Central Committee, 45
Khmer Empire, 168
Khmer Issarak, 19, 21, 37
  representation at Geneva Conference (1954), 21
  retreatment into North Vietnam, 21, 25
Khmer People's National Liberation Front (KPNLF), 104, 106, 113, 114, 128, 164

Index

Khmer Rouge, 2, 35, 102, 104, 106, 108, 109, 114, 124, 130, 133, 139, 143, 161
  antipathy to the Vietnamese, 19
  anti-Vietnamese propaganda under, 66
  associated with Tou Samouth, 23
  attack on Tay Ninh province of Vietnam, 48
  attacks on Vietnam, 19
  attitude towards the Vietnamese, 44
  Black Book (1978), 24, 29, 31
  capture of Phnom Penh, 42, 90
  Chinese military aid and assistance to, 50, 102
  concerns over US support for, 144
  control of Cambodia, 22
  defectors, 45
  diplomatic relation with Thailand, 92
  end of military cooperation with Vietnamese communists, 32
  genocide committed by, 64
  growth of, 55
  guerilla warfare, 64
  leadership, 31
  objective to topple the PRK, 156
  Paris wing, 23
  pro-Hanoi faction of, 26
  training from Chinese military personnel training, 47
  victories by the coalition forces against, 163
  Vietnamese views of, 24
  Western consensus against, 144
Kiernan, Ben, 114
Kimkong Heng, 4
Kissinger, Henry, 32, 33, 55, 58, 62, 86, 100
Koh, Tommy, 147
Kolko, Gabriel, 43
Kuantan Declaration, 96
Kusumaatmadja, Mochtar, 98, 122

Lambertson, David, 145
Le Duan, 21, 24, 27, 32, 40, 81, 88, 115, 120, 148
  fourteen-point action plan, 21
  meeting with the Chinese leadership in Beijing, 48

Le Duc Anh, 157, 166, 167
Le Duc Tho, 32, 40, 55, 115
Lee Hsien Loong, 1, 2, 3, 4, 5
  meeting with Hun Sen, 5
Lee Kuan Yew, 84, 86, 98, 99, 101, 103, 104, 120, 122, 134, 162
  meeting with Deng Xiaoping, 79
Lee Lai, 76, 77
Lee Poh Ping, 97, 100
Leifer, Michael, 111, 147, 159, 161
Li Peng, 151, 171, 172
Li Xiannian, 75
liberal democracy, 162
Liberation Day (7 January), 3
Lon Nol, 21
  ouster of Sihanouk by, 29

MacDonald, Malcolm, 87
Mahbubani, Kishore, 143
Malayan Communist Party (MCP), 78
Malaysia
  establishment of diplomatic relations with, 78
  proposal of 'proximity talks' (April 1985), 123
Manac'h, Etienne, 34
Mao Zedong, 41, 70
  Five Principles (of peaceful coexistence), 50
  meeting with Pol Pot, 50
Martin, Claude, 135
McGovern, George, 56
McHale, Shawn, 19, 20
McLaren, Robin, 136
Mekong River, issue of navigation rights along, 166
Mertha, Andrew, 50
military stalemate, 111
Moerdani, Benny, General, 96, 98
Mohammed, Mahathir, 85, 160
Mondale, Walter, 87, 101
Morey, Roy D., 93

Nadze, Serad, 113
Nam Bo Regional Committee, 22
Nathan, S. R., 83, 85, 90, 95, 110
National Liberation Front (NLF), 28
national liberation movements, in colonized countries, 81
national unification, 70

National United Front for an
  Independent, Neutral, Peaceful
  and Cooperative Cambodia
  (FUNCINPEC), 104, 113, 163,
  164, 167, 171
National United Front for National
  Salvation (KUFNS), 72
Negroponte, John, 105
New York Times, The, 38, 161
Ngo Dinh Diem, 38
Nguyen, Christelle, 8
Nguyen Co Thach, 46, 51, 58, 62, 73,
  89, 97, 115, 122, 135, 136,
  143, 144, 148, 157, 164
Nguyen Duy Trinh, 63
  visit to ASEAN countries, 91
Nguyen Dy Nien, 157, 158
Nguyen Manh Cam, 158, 164, 165, 170
Nguyen Ngoc Truong, 7
Nguyen Van Linh, 89, 150
Nixon, Richard, 50
  visit to Beijing, 55
Nuon Chea, 29

Oakley, Bob, 62
Onn, Hussein, 95, 96
Osius, Ted, 54
overseas Chinese, 70

Paracel Islands, China and Vietnam
  clash over, 40
Paris Peace Agreement (1973), 32, 57
  Article 21 of, 57
Paris Peace Agreement (1991), 9, 10,
  16, 123, 134, 162, 174
Partai Komunis Indonesia (Community
  Party of Indonesia), 98
Path, Kosal, 116, 126
Pathet Lao, 21, 34, 37
peace keeping operations (PKOs), 160
People's Army of Vietnam (PAVN), 65
  16-Camps Campaign against
  CGDK, 113
People's Republic of China (PRC).
  See China
People's Republic of Kampuchea
  (PRK), 4, 18, 113, 164
  establishment of, 66
  Kampuchean People's Revolutionary
  Army, 113

political reconstitution of the
  government in, 111
Vietnam invasion of, 71
Perestroika, 89
Permanent Five plan on Cambodia
  (1990), 156
Permanent Mission to the United
  Nations, 115
Pham Hung, 28
Pham Van Dong, 21, 38, 44, 57, 63,
  83, 91, 101, 120, 150
Pham Van Tra, 172
Phan Hien, 91
Ping-Pong diplomacy, 116
Pol Pot, 18, 20, 22, 35, 50, 101,
  124, 143
  anti-Vietnamese policy, 52
  attempt to assassinate, 44
  Beijing's support of, 27
  breaking off diplomatic relations
  with Vietnam, 67
  detestation against Vietnam's 'big
  brother attitude', 52
  fight against the Vietnamese
  aggressors, 112
  genocide committed by, 2, 153
  induction into Indochinese
  Communist Party (ICP), 22
  interviews given by, 60
  meeting with Mao Zedong, 50
  mutiny to overthrow regime
  of, 59
  on right to represent Cambodia at
  the UN, 56
  policy of opposing any Vietnamese
  invasion of Cambodia, 24
  proclaiming the 'Victory of January
  6, 1978', 49
  return to power, 130
  trips to North Vietnam and
  China, 26
  US support for, 105
  view of the 1954 Geneva
  Conference, 23
  visit to China, 47
  visit to Hanoi (11–14 June 1975), 43
political settlement, principles of, 132
Poonkham, Jittipat, 78, 133
Pramoj, Kukrit, 77
Prayut Chan-o-cha, 1

Index

Provisional Revolutionary Government
   of South Vietnam (PRGSVN),
   28, 41
public security, 161
Putra, Wisma, 98

Qian Qichen, 118, 119, 138, 139, 144,
   146, 148, 149
Qiang Zhai, 51, 73

racist attacks, against ethnic
   Vietnamese in Cambodia, 163
Rajaratnam, S., 110, 130, 134
Ranariddh, Norodom, 8, 10, 166, 171,
   172, 173
Razak, Tun, 78
Reagan, Ronald, 106, 121
regional conflicts, in the Third
   World, 147
regional hegemony, problem of, 61
Richburg, Keith B., 159
ripeness theory, 111
Rithauddeen, Tengku, 96
Rogachev, Igor, 138
Rowley, Kelvin, 162
Royal Cambodian Armed Forces
   (RCAF), 45
Royal Government of the National
   Union of Kampuchea
   (GRUNK), 29
Royal Society for Asian Affairs, 111

Saigon, fall of (1975), 35, 46, 57, 77, 95
   Sino-Vietnamese relation before, 35
Saloth Sar. *See* Pol Pot
Samrin, Heng, 2
Sanderson, John, 162
Sar Kheng, 168
Savetsila, Siddhi, 94, 133, 134,
   149, 152
Schulz, George, 112
Schwartz, Eric, 153
Second Indochina War.
   See Vietnam War
Shafie, Ghazali, 84
Shangri-La Dialogue, 2
Shaplen, Robert, 115, 116, 124
Shen Zhihua, 20
Shevardnadze, Eduard, 121, 138,
   139, 148

Sieu Heng, 19
Sihanouk, Norodom, 18, 27, 33, 44,
   101, 103, 105, 108, 126, 127,
   131, 151, 155, 171
   Coalition Government of
      Democratic Kampuchea
      (CGDK), 164
   FUNCINPEC Party, 104
   international profile of, 30
   interview with the *Far Eastern
      Economic Review*, 165
   meeting with François
      Mitterrand, 127
   meeting with Hun Sen, 128,
      129, 131
   ouster by Lon Nol, 29
   popularity among Cambodian
      peasantry, 105
   power over the Cambodian
      communists, 22
   resentment against ASEAN's
      recognition of Democratic
      Kampuchea, 102
   resignation as president of the
      CGDK, 136
   royal crusade, 20
   success in gaining independence of
      Cambodia, 20
   Zhou's support for, 34
Simchheang, Loy, 171
Singapore, 79, 98
   relations with Cambodia and
      Vietnam, 5
Singh, Natwar, 122
Sino-French Agreements of 1887 and
   1895, 71
Sino-Soviet border conflict (1969), 87
Sino-Soviet relations, 117, 119, 142
   normalization of, 119, 138
Sino-Thai relationship, 84, 132
Sino-US relations, Ping-Pong
   diplomacy, 116
Sino-Vietnamese Friendship
   Association, 41
Sino-Vietnamese relations, 48, 53,
   123, 148
   deterioration of, 69, 70
   dispute related to Paracel and
      Spratly islands, 71
   normalisation of, 157

Sino-Vietnamese relations (cont.)
  on flow of refugees, 71
  onborder and ethnic Chinese
    issues, 71
  political implications of, 70
  suspension of Chinese aid to
    Vietnam, 69
Sino-Vietnamese War (1979), 7, 12,
  16, 69, 79
  ASEAN countries reaction to, 83
  causes of, 75
  Chinese attack on 17 February
    1979, 81
  Chinese logistic preparation for, 72
  Chinese withdrawal from
    Vietnam, 85
  failure of Chinese punitive action on
    Vietnam, 86
  Soviet military aid to Vietnam
    during, 82
  Soviet support to Vietnam during, 86
  US policy on, 83
  US–China collusion against
    Vietnam, 81
  Vietnam leadership's failure to
    anticipate the Chinese attack, 81
Sirivudh, Norodom, 165
Smith, Ralph, 13, 26
Sok Udom Deth, 68
Sokhonn, Prak, 152
Solarz, Stephen, 126, 153
Solomon, Richard H., 118
Son Ngoc Minh (Achar Mean), 19
Son Sann, 103, 104, 105, 108, 114, 130
Son Sen, 112
Sophal, Diep, 11
Soubert, Son, 172
sovereignty, principle of, 95
Soviet bloc, 54
Soviet Union, 39, 49, 53, 58, 63, 89,
  98, 119, 120
  airlifting of arms to Vietnam, 72
  callfor joint support for Vietnam, 72
  clash with Chinese troops near
    Zhenbao Island in Northeast
    China, 71
  elite power struggles in, 73
  financial crisis, 141
  first military base in Southeast
    Asia, 85

foreign policy, 118
naval and air bases in Vietnam, 122
rift with China, 39, 71
Treaty of Friendship and
  Cooperation with Vietnam,
  60, 63
troop withdrawal
  from Afghanistan, 138
Soviet–US relations, 121, 140
Suharto, President, 96, 131
superpower rivalries, 142
Supreme National Council of
  Cambodia (SNC), 129, 150,
  152, 154, 164
Sutsakhan, Suk, 114
Svay Rieng, 168
Swank, Emory, 111

Tan Bah Bah, 5
territorial buffer, between Thailand
  and Vietnam, 92
Terzani, Tiziano, 59
Thai Nation Party, 132
Thai Nguyen, 82
Thai–Cambodian relations, 77
Thailand
  anti-Khmer Rouge feelings, 152
  communist insurgency movement, 92
  concerns over China's stand toward
    the Khmer Rouge, 133
  establishment of diplomatic relations
    with China, 77, 91
  Khmer Rouge diplomatic relation
    with, 92
  status as an aspiring regional
    economic power, 133
  threat from Vietnamese occupation
    of Cambodia to, 93
Thayer, Carlyle, 6
Third Indochina War, 94, 118, 119
  origins of, 11, 18
Third World, 65
'three revolutionary tidal waves'
  idcology, 81
Tian Zengpei, 138
Tiananmen Incident (June 1989), 89,
  140, 148
Tinsulanonda, Prem, 1, 94, 107
Todorov, Stanko, 112
Tonkin, Derek, 107

Index

Torigian, Joseph, 73
Tou Samouth, 19, 23
  death of, 26
  Khmer Rouge regime associated
    with, 23
Tran Huy Chuong, 168
Tran Quang Co, 150, 157
Tran Van Tra, 31, 32
transitory state, 164
Treaty of Friendship and Cooperation
    (1977), 47, 60, 72, 75
Truong Chinh, 120
Tuong Vu, 81

UN General Assembly (UNGA),
    155, 165
UN Security Council, 56, 147, 160
  discussion on political settlement for
    Cambodia, 154–157
  Permanent Five members of, 154
UN Transitional Authority to
    Cambodia (UNTAC), 159
Ung Huot, 167, 168
United Issarak Front, 19
United Nations (UN), 108, 144
  responsibility for the administration
    of Cambodia, 153
  trusteeship, 154
United Nations Advance Mission in
    Cambodia (UNAMIC), 159
United Nations Development
    Programme (UNDP), 93
United Nations Transitional Authority
    in Cambodia (UNTAC), 10,
    153, 154, 160
  failure to achieve national
    reconciliation through a
    democratic process, 172
  military component of, 162
United States (US)
  backing for Lon Nol regime, 34
  Carter administration, 55, 57,
    79, 107
  negotiations with Vietnam, 58
  concerns over Chinese action against
    Vietnam, 80
  Deng Xiaoping visit to, 79
  diplomatic role in Cambodia after
    the Vietnam War, 34
  economic aid to Vietnam, 75

213

establishment of diplomatic relations
    with China, 55
  Ford administration, 55, 57
  intervention in First Indochina
    War, 36
  military disengagement from
    Indochina, 33
  policies and actions in Cambodia
    during the Vietnam War, 55
  rapprochement with China, 55, 72
  Reagan administration, 106
  relation with Soviet Union, 80, 140
  State Department, 22, 56, 58
USSR. *See* Soviet Union

Van Tien Dung, 150
Vance, Cyrus, 58
vanguard internationalism, 81
Viet Minh, 19
Vietnam
  8th Party Congress, 171
  An Giang province, 168
  anti-China propaganda, 51
  as Cuba of the East, 80
  border war strategy from defensive
    to offensive, 48
  Chinese attack on, 6
  clash with China over Paracel
    Islands, 40
  closeness to Soviet Union, 51
  communist cells in Cambodia, 22
  establishment of diplomatic relations
    with the Philippines, 91
  forgotten Cambodian war, 6
  General Staff's Combat Readiness
    Plan for Cambodia, 65
  goal to dominate Kampuchea and
    Laos, 61
  independence of, 116
  Indochina Federation plan, 60
  invasion of
    Cambodia, 2, 48, 61, 69
    Kampuchea, 25, 71
  joining of COMECON, 62
  Khmer Rouge attacks on, 19
  liberation of Cambodia, 4
  military operation in Cambodia, 167
  Ministry of Foreign Affairs, 3
  Moscow's suspension of industrial
    projects for, 53

Vietnam (cont.)
  naval facilities in Cam Ranh Bay, 121
  neo-colonialist attitude towards both Cambodia and Laos, 25
  non-European capital investments in, 69
  occupation of Phnom Penh, 66
  plan to 'free' Sihanouk, 66
  plan to re-establish the Indochina Federation, 25
  reduction of Chinese economic assistance to, 51
  removal of the Khmer Rouge, 4
  reunification of, 69, 90
  Russian influence in, 122
  sense of insecurity, 63
  Soviet military aid to, 72
  stand on Sino-Soviet dispute, 71
  struggle for independence, 18
  supportfor Heng Samrin regime in Kampuchea, 101
  talks with China on the border issue, 61, 69
  treatment of Chinese residing in, 51, 69, 75
  Treaty of Friendship with Laos, 47
  Soviet Union, 63
  Treaty of Friendship with Soviet Union, 60, 72
  unified communist movement led by, 24
  views on Khmer Rouge regime, 24
  war of resistance against the French, 35
  withdrawal of troops from Cambodia, 105, 117, 119, 138, 141
Vietnam War, 13, 20, 40
  end of, 54
  Washington's escalation of, 56
Vietnam–Cambodia Inter-Governmental Commission, 167
Vietnam–Cambodia relations
  development of, 167
  influence of China in, 170
Vietnam–Cambodia war, 2, 4, 10, 18, 20, 43, 61, 63, 66, 69, 76, 80, 83
Vietnam–Cambodia–China relations, 120

Vietnamese 'blitzkrieg', 49, 64
Vietnamese Communist Party, 22, 38, 88, 115, 120, 148
Vietnamese communists, 23, 32, 40
  disagreements with the Soviets, 53
  reunification of north and south Vietnam (30 April 1975), 22
  reunification plan, 22
  role in First Indochina War, 35
  victory over the French at Dien Bien Phu, 36
Vietnamese People's Army (VPA), 49, 65
  fight with Khmer Rouge, 66
  General Staff's Combat Readiness Plan for Cambodia, 65
  The Order of Battle, 65
Vietnamese Politburo, 35, 48, 171
Vietnamese Worker's Party
  4th Party Congress of, 52, 69
  Central Committee, 61, 69, 72
Vietnamese–Khmer relations, 19
Viraphol, Sarasin, 93
Vo Dong Giang, 83
Vo Nguyen Giap, 37, 151
Vo Van Kiet, 158, 165, 166
Vogel, Ezra, 86

Walt, Stephen, 110
Wanandi, Jusuf, 90, 95, 99
Wang Chenyi, 73
Wang Dongxing, 74
Warsaw Military Alliance, 60, 72
Washington Post, 159
Wen Jiabao, 171
Wheeler, Nicholas, 67
white zones, 168
WikiLeaks, 56, 93
workers' movement, in capitalist countries, 81
Wu Xueqian, 115

Xu Dunxin, 157
Xu Shiyou, 74

Yahya, Ahmad, 172
Yang Kuisong, 71
Yasushi Akashi, 162
Yongchaiyudh, Chavalit, 133, 152, 153

Zhang Jie, 6
Zhang Wannian, 170
Zhou Enlai, 21, 27, 28, 30, 33, 37, 38,
    55, 73, 100

Zinoman, Murray, 97
Zone of Peace, Freedom and
    Neutrality (ZOPFAN), 91
Zubok, Vladislav M., 140

Milton Keynes UK
Ingram Content Group UK Ltd.
UKHW021944041124
450744UK00008B/205